BUTTER

After you've read this galley, we'd love to hear what you think.
Please contact us by e-mail at marketing@algonquin.com.

BUTTER

A RICH
HISTORY

. . .

ELAINE
KHOSROVA

ALGONQUIN BOOKS

OF CHAPEL HILL

2 0 1 6

Published by
Algonquin Books of Chapel Hill
Post Office Box 2225
Chapel Hill, North Carolina 27515-2225

a division of
Workman Publishing
225 Varick Street
New York, New York 10014

"Butter" by Elizabeth Alexander. From Body of Life, published by
Tia Chucha Press. Copyright 1996 Elizabeth Alexander.

Library of Congress Cataloging-in-Publication Data

[TK]

This book is dedicated to my parents,
Clare, who first buttered my bread,
and Eugene,
who taught me to savor it.

BUTTER
Elizabeth Alexander

My mother loves butter more than I do,
more than anyone. She pulls chunks off
the stick and eats it plain, explaining
cream spun around into butter! Growing up
we ate turkey cutlets sauteed in lemon
and butter, butter and cheese on green noodles,
butter melting in small pools in the hearts
of Yorkshire puddings, butter better
than gravy staining white rice yellow,
butter glazing corn in slipping squares,
butter the lava in white volcanoes
of hominy grits, butter softening
in a white bowl to be creamed with white
sugar, butter disappearing into
whipped sweet potatoes, with pineapple,
butter melted and curdy to pour
over pancakes, butter licked off the plate
with warm maple syrup. When I picture
the good old days I am grinning greasy
with my brother, having watched the tiger
chase his tail and turn to butter. We are
Mumbo and Jumbo's children despite
historical revision, despite
our parent's efforts, glowing from the inside
out, one hundred megawatts of butter.

CONTENTS

...

PART TWO

The Recipes

BAKED

Best-Ever Crumb Cake • Brioche • Buttermilk Scones •
Classic Pound Cake • Croissants • Flaky Pastry Dough,
Two Ways • German Pancake • Kouign Amann • Pâte
Brisée Pastry • Pâte Sablée Pastry • Puff Pastry •
Pull-Apart Biscuits • Shortbread, Unplugged •
Tarte Tatin • Yellow Buttermilk Cake

COOKED

Beurre Blanc • Hollandaise • Béarnaise • Béchamel •
Velouté • Beurre Manié • Beurre Monté • Butterscotch
Candies • Butterscotch Pudding • Easy Buttercream
Frosting • Silky European Buttercream • Lemon
Curd • Po Cha

MAKING YOUR OWN BUTTER

Sweet Cream Butter • Cultured Butter • Ghee •
Niter Kibbeh • Clarified Butter • Browned Butter •
Compound Butter • Cold Smoked Butter

. . . .

NORBU MARCHES UP THE STEEP SLOPE, TRYING TO catch up to his mother. The three-year-old carries a small bowl and a look of determination. His blue plastic boots slip often on the dewy turf, but he steadies himself and keeps on, his little body leaning into the tall rise of earth. The boy is headed toward a flat ridge about two hundred yards above where a small herd of yak are gathered. This is a familiar hike for Norbu; every morning he makes the ascent to claim his breakfast—a bowl of warm yak milk that his mother will dispense from the animals.

By the time the boy reaches the ridge, his father, Kado, and mother, Choney, have just begun their daily two-person operation of plein air milking. Norbu knows to stand by as this familiar negotiation of man and beast unfolds. He climbs a wobbly side of the small bamboo-fenced corral surrounding a group of restless calves. Inside, his father ropes one of the young animals by the neck and leads it out a makeshift gate, pushing back other calves that crowd near the opening.

They're hungry for the milk of the mother yaks lingering outside the fence.

But Choney takes the first share of milk. With a wooden pail hung from a rope around her neck, she aims to collect about six gallons of raw, whole milk to fill her churn for butter making this afternoon. Here in Bhutan, yak butter is a virtual currency here in Bhutan, the gold of nomadic highland yak herders like Kado and Choney who sell or trade it for rice, tea, barley, and other bare necessities. As the number of these high-altitude herders dwindles in Bhutan, the appearance of yak butter—often bundled in thick green leaves and tied with bits of string—is increasingly rare in the towns and cities. Norbu's parents can sell theirs for twice the price of cow's butter made in the valleys. Locals place a premium on handmade yak butter not just because it's traditional but because it's considered healthier and better tasting, especially in their *su ja* (black tea whisked with butter and salt). Having loyal customers in the lowlands, Choney's butter is often sold even before she's churned it.

But before this precious butter can be made, let alone change hands far below in the valley, the female yak (locally called *dri* [pronounced "dree"])—must first be induced to give their milk to the cause. That is the work this early morning, like countless mornings before. Mother dri don't readily cooperate with milking, even when it's a routine maneuver as it is for this herd. Maternal instinct dictates that they withhold the milk in their udder for a calf. So to start the "let down" of milk this morning, Choney and Kado use an ancient dairy ploy: One at a time, Kado brings a calf out of the corral, prompting its mother to slowly sidle up alongside her babe. (Domesticating these massive animals is all about shepherding their offspring; yaks will never desert their young.) Kado allows the calf to suckle for a minute, which triggers the release of milk. Then he quickly pulls the young animal off the teat with his rope as Choney steps in; she briefly strokes the flank of the dri—a kind of preemptive milking signal—and then kneels beside the udders. She wears a full-length Bhutanese *kira*, essentially a wrap skirt with a red fleece jacket and red wool cap; it's August, but the temperature hasn't yet edged above 40°F. As Choney sits on her heels, balancing the pail in her lap, she begins milking by first wiping the dri's teats with a wet rag. She wraps her fingers around two teats and alternately pulls and squeezes in a fast, steady rhythm. Dual streams of milk swish into the pail.

The calf, meanwhile, strains against the rope to be with its mother, hungry for more milk. But its mom is indifferent now; she stands placidly as if being milked by Choney is somehow hypnotic. Beneath her thick horns, she gazes east at the horizon. Under a cobalt sky the rounded arcs of land covered in whiskery grass repeat endlessly, endlessly; for the yak, it represents a limitless buffet.

When Choney has mostly emptied the mother's udders, she slowly backs away, then Kado releases the calf, letting it lunge toward the mother for its remaining meal. Besides getting the morning leftovers of milk, the young yak are free to trail their mothers all day long, suckling at will, in the open pastures. It's only at night that the calves are separated in the corral, ensuring that the herders get first dibs at the day's early tide of milk. By contrast, most modern dairy farmers in the West would collect every ounce of their cow's milk; calves are typically fed with man-made rations until they can graze. But nomadic dairymen in Bhutan split the milk capital since buying rations is cost prohibitive and impractical. It's a delicate dairy time-share but one that has sustained preindustrial men and their livestock for millennia.

Norbu is whining for his bowlful of milk. As Choney pours the milk from her small wooden pail into a larger plastic barrel, the boy thrusts out his little bowl to intercede in the transfer. *"Na ong . . . na,"* he says ("Milk, yes . . . milk"). His mom fills the bowl halfway. Norbu holds it to his lips and drains it instantly, going back for a refill and then another.

Finally satisfied, he drops his bowl and dashes to a pile of small rocks. As he tosses them about, his parents continue their quiet work. Hardly a word is exchanged between them. Having descended from countless generations of herding families in these high mountains, both Choney and Kado handle the mighty animals reflexively, whose nature is more familiar to them than the ways of their own twenty-something contemporaries seven thousand feet below in Thimpu, the rapidly modernizing capital of the country.

When the milking is done, Choney's large plastic barrel is nearly full. With one shout of *"Jogay!"* ("Let's go"), Kado sends the yak down the ridge, in the direction of lower pastures. The animals file past the family's two-room stone shelter in a small notch, then over the mountain stream that runs beside it. In one long black shaggy procession, the beasts move over the neighboring slope. Meanwhile, Kado and Choney carry the barrel of milk to the stream and partly submerge it in a cool deep pool. The softly tumbling cold water will eventually chill the milk slightly, making it easier to churn. As Norbu and his parents disappear behind the door of their home, the last dark shapes of the yak vanish over a mountain rim. So ends the first act of Bhutanese butter making—appropriating the animal milk.

Its choreography might appear to be the start of a butter story particular to this time and place, a remote mountainside so unlike other dairy vales elsewhere in the world. But, in fact, the steps are both universal and timeless. Choney and Kado's milking routine not only replays centuries of dairy practice in Bhutan, but it also allows a rare glimpse at the origins of butter. Long before early people settled into dairy farming, they were nomadic hunters who came to realize that it was better to keep certain animals than to kill them. Yak, as well as horses, sheep, and goats, were among the first beasts trained to submit to milking by a new class of shepherds and herders. In practice, these people worked no differently than Choney and Kado. The method for milking a beast in the pasture was identical. And once milk was at hand, stored in various primitive vessels, butter making became a serendipitous accident waiting to happen. Very likely, the first-ever churning was the result of milk's early rough ride on the back of a pack animal, inside a skin sack, where it rocked and bounced its way to butterhood. Every churning since then—no matter how refined the technology—has essentially been a reenactment of that first lucky happenstance, the birth of butter.

Choney turns her milk into butter using one of the earliest

models invented for getting the job done—a plunger churn. It goes by many different names around the world, but the design is standard: a tall, slim wooden bucket covered with a tight doughnut-shaped lid, its center hole just wide enough to fit the handle of a long wooden staff—called the plunger. The bottom end of the plunger is fitted with a crosspiece of wood. The milk or cream is churned into butter by rhythmically pumping this crosspiece up and down. That's it. Assuming the temperature of the liquid is right, grains of butter will eventually start to materialize.

Choney's three-foot-tall churn—a wedding present from her family—is positioned under a small skylight, the only source of daylight, apart from the front door, in an otherwise windowless stonewalled room. The family's two-room home feels like a bunker. And in many ways it is, built by hand to withstand the snow and icy thaw in winter that completely engulfs this treeless mountaintop. There is no furniture. Since they move seasonally, Choney and Kado own only what can be carried on the backs of their yak. A fire pit burns on one side of the room. The family sleeps on the floor, atop thick ruglike blankets that Choney has woven from yak hair. During the day the blankets are stacked neatly in a corner. Wooden shelves on two sides of the room are lined with a few large bowls and pots, plus several tall baskets. On this day, two of the baskets are nearly filled with rounds and wedges of yak butter and semihard cheese. Soon Kado will make the daylong trek down to the city to trade these dairy goods for cash.

As Choney transfers the chilled raw whole yak milk into the churn, Kado prepares butter tea for two men who have

**EARLY-MORNING MILKING IN THE
MOUNTAINS OF BHUTAN. (ELAINE KHOSROVA)**

come to visit—a farmer from the lowlands and a young man who heads the nomadic community in this region. Kado lifts a pot of salted tea off the fire and adds a lump of butter. He rubs the handle of a bamboo whisk back and forth between his palms to spin the ball end inside the tea. The mixture becomes frothy, the opaque color of butterscotch; he serves it in small teacups. Butter tea can be a pungent, oily drink if the butter is rancid, but Kado's version is sublime, with just a hint of salt and a silken butteriness.

Having fastened the lid of the churn to the base with rags and twine, Choney's butter making begins. She stands gripping the plunger, one hand on top of the other, and moves it smoothly up and down like a piston. A thick slushing sound accompanies each rise and fall of the plunger as it plows through gallons of milk in the churn. The technique is simple, but the task is laborious. It's like creating a storm in a bucket, a tempest strong enough to forge solid butter from milky liquid. There's no timer, no clock, just the changing sound of the churn to announce when the butter has started to form. Just before the milk surrenders its fat, the churning becomes muffled, softer, as air meets milk. Then when the butter finally comes, the noise is louder, more percussive. Such acoustics have guided butter makers around the world and throughout history. It's a very old tune, yet one that reliably signals when waves of milk have yielded rafts of butter.

BUTTER

PART
ONE

.....

THE
Story

. . . .

Grass, Cud, Cream

BEGINNING THE BUTTER TRIP

. . . .

The Epping butter is most highly esteemed in London
and its neighbourhood; great part of it is made from
cows which feed during the summer months in Epping
Forest, where the leaves and shrubby plants are understood greatly to contribute to its superior flavour.

—JOSIAH TWAMLEY,
*Essays on the Management
of Dairy*, 1816

I LIVE BETWEEN TWO SMALL DAIRY FARMS IN UPSTATE
New York. At both ends of the dirt road that fronts my
house, cows amble up and down the slanted pastures most of
the year, chewing on the landscape. I often marvel at how
their bodies transform the raw weeds and green of the field
into snow-white milk. The fact that their milk is laden with
the supple fat that men conjure into golden butter seems all the
more incredible. There's a Rumpelstiltskin-like magic to these
dairy conversions. Even if modern science can explain the
processes in cold detail, I find them no less dazzling. In fact, as

I discovered writing this book, knowing all the intricate workings of animal nature and human endeavor that turn plant life
into butter only added to my fascination.

And yet butter is uniformly taken for granted. It is common, after all. The girl next door, lovely but overlooked. Even
for me, a food professional with more than two decades of experience as a pastry chef, test kitchen editor, and food writer,
butter had long lived in the culinary shadows. My work paid
and trained me to seek out the exotic, the celebrity foods, the
Next Big Thing. Not a simple yellow stick that's in everyone's fridge. Although I cooked and baked often with butter
and always had it on the table, I hardly gave this dairy staple
much thought. It wasn't until several years ago, when I was
assigned an editorial project to taste, describe, and rate about
two dozen different brands from creameries around the world,
that I did a double take on butter. On the tasting table were
bricks of butter from as far away as New Zealand, Italy, the
Czech Republic, Ireland, and France, plus domestic brands
from Vermont, Wisconsin, California, and places in between.
At the time, the task seemed like a redundant one. Butter is so
elemental, I thought, how different from one another could
they really be?

But as I examined and tasted each sample, I was surprised
that no two were alike. I found nuances in color, consistency,
milkiness, salt content, sweetness, acidity, freshness, even
nutty and herbal notes. Some glistened; others were matte.
Some butters slumped as they sat at room temperature, others stood firm. Several had a fresh, lactic taste while a few
were cultured and more tangy. One was made from the milk

of goats, another from water buffalo. Cataloging this global collection, with their odd labels and unfamiliar names, I began to sense that these sticks and bricks represented both the universal and the particular of this thing we call butter (which has at least fifty-seven aliases around the world; see appendix B). All the products were essentially made the same way—from churning milk fat—yet each sample was distinguishable from another. It was as if every butter brand was a kind of message in a bottle, relaying a distinct sense of place.

It turns out that my impression wasn't just a romantic one. Every detail of a particular butter's character is indeed formed from the unique commingling of three living variables: man, plant, and beast. They work as a kind of relay team, beginning with the plant forage (or ration) that feeds the dairy animal, which in turn gives milk to the farmer, who then supplies the butter maker with cream, which is then churned into butter (and buttermilk). In combination, all of these individual players and conditions account for both the subtle and substantial butter differences I detected on the tasting table that day. As this trio of live factors varies from one place and time to another, fresh butter can express locality in a very pure, direct way. (Other dairy products, like yogurt and cheese, can make a similar claim, but these fermented products generally require more time and biological intervention to produce. Butter, on the other hand, can be borne almost immediately.)

Before dairy industrialization began in Europe and North America in the late nineteenth century, the local *terroir* of a butter was much in evidence; every farmhouse was in essence a tiny artisan creamery, dispensing its version of the stuff (for better or worse). But by the twentieth century—the era when men and machines would completely displace generations of farmwives and dairymaids in the production of butter—the new milk co-ops and automated creameries ushered in conformity, consistency, and a new standard of freshness. As this industrial dairy model grew, butter from the factory churn came to reflect the technology of megaproducers rather than the terroir of local farms and small-scale makers. National brands emerged, which meant you could buy butter in, say, Michigan that tasted identical to one on the shelf in Maryland. (We've come to take this convenient uniformity for granted too, but it's a very recent phenomenon in the long arc of dairy history.)

Now, in the twenty-first century, technology has been thrown in reverse. A "slow butter" revivalism is emerging, especially where the demand for local products and the lure of artisan food is high. The ranks of these new outliers on the butter-making scene include mostly entrepreneurial low-tech dairy folk looking to sustain their farms and way of life. But there's also a sizable troupe of chefs, avid foodists, and staunch do-it-yourselfers—all batch-churning their own microbutters for an enthusiastic niche of eaters.

Lauding this movement is not to suggest that there's anything wrong with industrial butter production. Indeed, as detailed in chapter 6, the advent of dairy factories in the late nineteenth century greatly raised butter standards across the board and gave it a new threshold of freshness. But whenever a traditional food is rediscovered by artisans, we stand to gain interesting choices, perchance even more delicious, creative, and/or healthful ones. (Consider the modern bread revolution, for example, or the neochocolate scene.) Politically there can be benefits as well, when we get to vote our values by buying less processed, more locally crafted foods that short cut the farm-to-fork journey.

Butter allows another kind of trip too. For the inquisitive eater who savors more than just the taste of things, butter's story is a ticket to appreciating the mighty role a simple food can play in the course of human events. One of the oldest of man-made edibles, butter's history is our history. In part, the purpose of this book is to show how the life and times of butter have been deeply entwined with much that has gone on far from the kitchen and creamery. Beginning with early butter practices devised for the religious, spiritual, and medicinal needs of communities, to its impact on empire building and technology of the Industrial Revolution, and later to butter's twentieth-century battle with margarine makers and fat-free zealots, this is a food, unlike any other, whose history reveals our ambitions as much as our appetite.

The contemporary butter world, in all its multicultural wonder, is no less remarkable. In the course of doing research for this book, I traveled on three continents and across the United States, each stop adding another strong thread to the weave of butter's modern narrative. Of course, I also gleaned many facts about butter from books, articles, and online sources, but for the full sensorial experience of butter and the people and regions it comes from, I had to dust off my passport. To see the making of butter from water buffalo milk in Punjab, India, and taste it fresh from the churn was nothing like watching and sampling sheep butter making in California and cow's butter in Brittany and industrial butter making in Wisconsin.

Front-line food study like this is called field research, but to me it was more like butter hunting. Capturing firsthand details helped me construct a time capsule of butter life as it exists now, as well as record some of the ancient methods that are rapidly disappearing in many remote areas, where new generations have eschewed their parents' subsistence chores and occupations. Working the butter beat also led me to some interesting encounters on the fringes of dairydom. I met with a former Buddhist nun to learn about the intricacies of Tibetan butter carving, and with various scientists to understand udders, soil, and fat metabolism. I spent a week in a large fridge with the artist who sculpts the Iowa State Fair butter cow each year, and I met with a New Jersey man to see his vast personal collection of vintage butter making equipment and ephemera. I've toured the Butter Museum in Cork, Ireland, the Maison du Beurre in Brittany, and gazed up at the infamous Butter Tower in Rouen, France. And in bakeries, restaurants, and culinary schools, I've watched chefs work their magic with butter.

Still, the most essential players in the story of butter aren't the people or institutions that I've met or who appear at various points in its timeline. That honor goes to the animals that first make the milk that begets butter. The true provenance of butter isn't just cultural; it's also anatomical.

THE JERSEY COW IS A FAVORITE BREED AMONG
BUTTER AND CHEESE MAKERS. (SHUTTERSTOCK)

WE OWE THE PLEASURE of every buttery morsel to a legion of four-legged farmstead moms. Because these udder-equipped mothers start to make milk as soon as their newborns arrive and for many months after, we have become the beneficiaries of a seemingly perpetual lactic supply. From this daily cascade of animal milk, butter makers extract the richest portion—cream—to churn into the solids we call butter. (It's possible to churn whole, nonhomogenized milk into butter too, but the process takes much longer and is trickier to manage.)

Considering what causes maternity and milk in the first place, one might argue that butter actually begins with sex, usually with the tryst of a bull and cow that makes a baby calf. And more than a century ago that would have been true. But since the invention of artificial insemination for livestock, this carnal connection to butter is no longer a given. Either by philosophical choice or by necessity, only small dairies (including goat and sheep operations) rely on animal attraction to trigger pregnancy and thereby lactation. Otherwise, many dairy gals never even see a bull (or buck or ram)—let alone cavort with one.

Although maternity flips the switch of milk production in many species all across the world, none make it so abundantly as the kinds of livestock that have become synonymous with dairy farming. Cows especially, but producers also count on the milk from sheep, goats, yak, buffalo, and camels. All of these animals belong to a mixed race of champion milk makers known as ruminants, who share some distinct anatomical features: a three- or four-sectioned stomach and a mouth equipped with an upper "dental pad" instead of teeth. It's these unique body parts—which serve to harvest and ferment plants—that make the lactating ruminant a virtual processing plant on legs, able to turn whole fields of green into butterfat-laden milk. Ruminant milk varies as much as the mothers that produce it. A ewe, for example, will give milk with twice the fat content of cow's milk; goat's milk has fat molecules that are smaller and more digestible, but it lacks carotene so goat butter is white; milk from a yak has less milk sugar (lactose) and more protein than cow's milk; camel's milk is similar to goat's milk in composition, but it can have up to three times as much vitamin C; and the milk of water buffalo has 100 percent more fat than cow's milk.

Cheese makers have long used the idiosyncrasies in different animal milks to their advantage—think of all the choices in the cheese aisle between cow, goat, sheep, and water buffalo products. But for most butter makers, cow's milk is still sine qua non. Delicious butters made from other ruminant milks can be found around the world (one of my favorites was from a water buffalo in India)—but the practical fact is that cows are the most generous, manageable, and affordable source of butterfat, especially in these modern times. The average yield of milk from a cow in the fourteenth century was between 140 to 170 gallons per season; the twenty-first-century Holstein cow now gives an average of 2,574 gallons per lactation. Medieval milk yield records were so low partly because calves got their fair share and because the cows were hand-milked in the field by dairymaids, not by machine. But the greater reason is that cattle were valued primarily for their labor in the fields and only incidentally as a source of milk. They were neither fed nor bred for high milk production, as they have been over the past two centuries. Generations of modern cows have been subject to efficient mechanical or robotic milking equipment, extended lactating periods, and synthetic hormones to increase their milk output.

Abundance, however, is no guarantee of quality. Butter makers continually monitor their cream supply for flaws, knowing full well that it's a capricious commodity. Like milk, it expresses the history of ever-changing conditions, both internal and external to the animal, and each batch of churned cream translates this history to the butter it becomes, affecting the butter's color, density, richness, tanginess, sweetness, and flavor nuances.

Professional butter makers will read, sniff, and measure these subtle variations and adapt their methods accordingly (as described in chapter 8), but the cream's inherent chemical and physical nuances, or lack thereof, can make the difference between a ho-hum butter and a remarkable one. To some extent, when you taste a great butter, you're savoring the sensitive workings of a hidden ecosystem operating inside every milk-making ruminant. This internal apparatus is the precursor to all that happens in the creamery. Like most things in nature, it's ingenious and intricate. In essence, to give butterfat, a ruminating mother plays host to a long procession of digestive ploys whereby anatomy meets botany in order to rearrange chemistry.

THE CREAM-RICH MILK THAT a pastured cow deposits twice a day in the milking parlor begins in the grassy sward beyond her barn home, where she'll typically dine on different kinds of cultivated grasses and legumes, as well as on some wild flowers. If her belly is feeling a little off that day, she might also nibble on certain herbs or shrubs if they're available; cows will self-medicate if given the remedial plant choice in the pasture. While grazing, if a cow spies a clump of grass—or if she's lucky, a tasty patch of clover—she uses her tongue to lasso a bunch of it. She tears the greens free by pinching them between her bottom teeth and a thick upper gum area—the dental pad referred to earlier. (If she could smile broadly, you'd see that she has no top front teeth, just a dark leathery band.) Inside her mouth, the grass gets moistened with saliva and then swallowed—but only temporarily.

This wet grassy mixture stored in the rumen, the first compartment of her stomach, will eventually return to her mouth. But first she'll continue dining on the pasture for about an hour, lopping off and swallowing vegetation. If the grass is soft and high, she can take in a hefty eighty to ninety pounds of fresh plant matter in that time.

Then our gal will find a nice place to settle down, often reclining near others in the herd and almost always listing toward her left side. (For some unknown reason, cows are more comfy this way.) Here she'll leisurely regurgitate all the food she has just collected. Cows rather enjoy this recycled course, which is commonly referred to as chewing their cud. She'll repeatedly bring up a wad of saliva-soaked grass, called a bolus, from her rumen back into her mouth. This soggy plant matter is then chewed from side to side (not up and down as we do) by the lateral action of molars, which slowly breaks down leaves, stems, and other field food into smaller, more digestible pieces.

This macerating (or ruminating) phase takes a while. There's no such thing as fast food in the life of a pastured cow. Chewing cud requires many hours and much saliva (cows produce between ten and forty gallons of saliva every day), especially if the plant food is wild and has been growing for several months. The plant matter gets sheared and smeared, much like the texture of pulled pork. As a result, all the nutrients freed from behind the fibrous skin of plants become prepped for digestion.

If she's completely pasture fed, a cow will generally spend about eight hours a day foraging, eight hours ruminating, and

the balance resting. (Her rumen can hold, on average, a whopping fifty gallons of partially digested food.) If she's given dry
rations from the farmer—as is typical in winter or at high-
density industrial dairies—her feeding time can be cut in half.

MACERATION IS A MECHANICAL precursor for the
wonder to come, the answer to this biological riddle: How
does a ruminant mom transform her lean veggie diet of plants,
which generally has a mere 3 percent fat, into milk that gives
cream with an unctuous 40 percent or more fat—the raw material for butter? I voiced this puzzler to Dr. Dan Schaefer,
an animal science expert at the University of Wisconsin, the
afternoon I sat in his office on campus, surrounded by walls
the color of milk. He paused for some time before responding.
Not often asked to explain such graduate-level phenomena to
a lay enthusiast, the professor was clearly making some mental edits.

The answer to my question, I eventually parsed from
the professor's measured explanation, starts in the bacterial
kingdom inside each animal's four-roomed stomach. A cow's
grassy meal is plumbed down the anatomical pipeline that is
her esophagus, into her quadruplex stomach.

On the food's arrival, a horde of microbial minions cling
to the partially weakened plant fibers and then the microbes
launch an enzyme attack that breaks apart the cell walls.
"They are compelled to do this," Dr. Schaefer noted, "because there's no oxygen present, so they're always starved
for energy." With these fibers vanquished, other microbial

characters can move in and take hold of embedded carbohydrate and protein, busting them apart into tiny building blocks
of sugar, peptides, and amino acids. (If you've ever wondered
where the green in "grass fed" goes, this is the answer: into
that microbial soup.) Since a cow's big belly holds no oxygen,
this digestive offensive continues as a process of fermentation,
not unlike making beer.

All this biochemical shape shifting holds a key to the even-
tual richness that makes butter taste so delectable. Once the
grassy matter is broken down into its most naked elements—
carbon and hydrogen molecules that are strung together like
bracelets—other bacteria can swarm in and recombine these
elements into fat compounds called volatile fatty acids, or
VFAs. (Don't be misled by the word *volatile*; these are good
guys in the scheme of dairy things. Biochemists use the term
to refer to compounds that are quick to change.)

VFAs matter greatly to a cow's constitution, not just her
milk making. As little chains of carbon—six or less strung
together—they become the fuel, the biological octane that a
cow runs on. "The animal feeds the microbes that feed the
animal," Dr. Schaefer explained, neatly summing up the co-
dependence at work here. And we get the makings for butter.

Although the professor had demystified for me much of
the grass-to-butter phenomenon, another question came in its
wake: How do we account for the fact that milk fat content
and composition—and therefore its butter—can vary from
one breed of cow to another, given the same meal? Why is
milk from a Guernsey different from milk from a Holstein? I

PLATE II.

GUERNSEY COW.

THE CAROTENE-RICH MILK OF GUERNSEY COWS YIELDS AN
ESPECIALLY DEEP YELLOW BUTTER. (WIKIMEDIA COMMONS)

headed across campus to pose it to Dr. Laura Hernandez, one
of Dr. Schaefer's colleagues. Hernandez is a professor in the
dairy science department who specializes in lactation physi-
ology. She's an expert on the inner workings of the udder,
cream's construction site. Unsurprisingly, her office shelf is
lined with more than two dozen cow figurines.

"Only about half the fat comes from the diet," Hernandez explained. "The other fats in milk are mobilized from the
cow's own body fat and are assembled into milk fat in the
mammary gland."

Inside these glands, the resident cells act like matchmakers,
linking up the small fatty acids, one to another, to create longer chains of fatty acids. But the length of these bionecklaces

vary greatly. It's those variations in the length and type of these fatty chains that partly explain why one cow's cream is slightly different—or better—from another's. Although diet is a major reason why one animal's cream can trump others, anatomy is still a considerable factor. Given the same meal—and the health of the animals being equal—some breeds are just better at linking the constellations of molecules that give us more or better-tasting cream.

Even so, cow selection among dairy farmers looking to generate above-average cream is not a simple choice; picking one breed over another is based on many other factors besides milk composition: Climate, cost, frequency of milking, forage available, animal temperament, hardiness, and size factor in, as well as what products the farm aims to market. And when you live day in and day out with animals, there's some personal bias too. "In my experience, Jerseys are a bit too fussy and the bulls can be nasty," Steffan Schneider told me. The farmer in charge of Hawthorne Valley Farm, a four-hundred-acre biodynamic dairy, creamery, and vegetable grower in the Hudson Valley, discovered Brown Swiss cows on a trip to Wisconsin; gradually he switched from Holsteins to the toast-colored Brown Swiss. "They have a very calm temperament," Schneider said.

Since many large dairies succeed or fail based on the volume of their milk production, Holsteins continue to be the most common cow in our national farmscape. They've been bred to ably top the charts of milk output (as much as seventy-two thousand pounds per year) but not necessarily make the most or best butter. Although their churned milk fat can result in very satisfactory butter (mostly what's used for inexpensive supermarket brands), its cream is not the first choice of artisan butter makers (or cheese makers). These dairy crafters look to other breeds to source their dream cream, one that's high in milk fat, has a good proportion of milk solids, and has a fresh, rich aroma.

Breeds and their respective milks may have many distinctions, but increasingly these lines are being blurred, now that artificial insemination has been standard practice for several generations. "There are very few pure strains of cows anymore," admitted Schneider.

ANIMAL ANATOMY MAY BE the car that drives the making of milk fat for butter, but I soon discovered that the kind of fuel in the system also greatly affects what comes out of the churn. And I learned too that dairy farmers have a language unto themselves when discussing what to feed their milk-giving wards. Farmers I spoke with routinely tossed out words like *forage*, *silage*, *haylage*, *baleage*, and *alpage*, as well as the more exotic references to *forbs*, *silvopasture*, and even *browse* (a noun). All of these terms translate into a surprisingly detailed vegetarian menu of fresh or fermented foods for various ruminants.

Such lingo belied the impression I'd had about livestock feeding: that it was all very straightforward. Put the ruminants in a grassy pasture and let nature do the rest. What could be simpler, after all, than feeding an animal that eats directly off the wild earth? This is true in theory. But in practice, often a ruminant will need extra servings of grasses or grains to supply the special energy and protein needed for keeping the quantity and quality of her milk high. (Every milk molecule is built around protein; if a cow's dietary supply doesn't meet her udder's demand for this building-block protein, her milk supply quickly decreases.)

Hence the land itself demands a farmer's attention if a herd is going to depend on it for mealtimes. Such work involves skilled agronomy, with alternating steps such as rotational grazing, seeding, weed control, liming, and soil testing. One Irish dairy farmer told me, as I kneeled down to run my fingers through his impossibly thick soft pasture, that in actuality he considered himself a grass farmer. "If I take care of the grass, it'll take care of the cows." He watched that the cows clipped the grass in an area just to a certain level, before he moved them to another. "This keeps them distributing their natural fertilizer around the pasture," he explained. "By the time they return to that pasture in about a month, the grass has regrown and is ready for a new clipping."

The Irish butter I sampled on that visit was as yellow as a daffodil; its vibrant hue was a result of young, fresh, and plentiful grazing grasses. Such healthy new grass is loaded with hidden beta-carotene—a yellow pigment and antioxidant found in grass. (We don't see it in plants because the green chlorophyll masks it.) After a cow eats, the beta-carotene is stored in the animal's body fat. When that fat is mobilized to make milk, the carotene comes with it, lodged in the fat of the milk. But why is milk white? Because the pigment is concealed by a membrane that cloaks each fat globule in milk. With agitation, however—like the churning during butter making—the cloak of each membrane is broken and the pigment is released. Yellow beta-carotene becomes visible in the butterfat, and even more so once the buttermilk is drained off. (Some butters made from other animals' milk, like goat butter and water buffalo butter, are naturally white because these animals don't store beta-carotene in their fat the way cows and yak do. Instead, they convert it to vitamin A, which is colorless.)

Color isn't the only reason pasture is preferable for dairy products. In the interests of ideal flavor, for instance, some European farmers are prohibited from feeding dairy animals fermented stored hay (such as silage or baleage) or rations. Under the European Union's celebrity food certification program known as PDO (protected designation of origin), the making of certain local traditional dairy products—such as cheese and butter—is highly regulated, right down to what's allowed in the field or feeding trough. PDOs can specify that cows eat fresh pasture or dry hay exclusively. So it is in the region of Isigny in Normandy, France, where the local PDO butter can only be made from the milk of cows that graze near the sea marshes of the region; there the grass is rich in iodine and other trace minerals that lend Isigny butter a distinctive taste.

THE DUTCH SOIL REFORMATION

....

ONE OF THE REASONS THE TINY COUNTRY OF HOL-
land became the foremost maritime and dairy-producing
power in the world throughout the 1600s was because
of the unique soil Dutch farmers created for grazing.
Dutch cows of the seventeenth century were reportedly
bigger and gave "great store of Milk, of which is made
excellent Butter," as described by William Aglionby,
an English diplomat at the time. Industrious Dutch-
men created lush pasture by harvesting manure as well
as city street sweepings, bird droppings, and commercial waste, including ash from soap making. Piles of
this so-called night soil from urban regions were used
to constantly fertilize and replenish grazing soil. It's no
coincidence that this period in Holland's history was
called the Golden Age; not only was it marked by stupendous economic success, but according to Aglionby, it
earned Dutch people the nickname of "butterboxes" by
the envious English who claimed their rivals were "apt
to spread everywhere, and for [their] sauciness, must be
melted down."

Butter quality can also be affected by transhumance, the centuries-old practice of organized migration by dairy folk and their herds that continues in mountainous regions around the world, but especially in Europe. The transhumance is strictly seasonal and altitudinal; the animals are escorted up to wild mountain pastures for grazing from late spring until late summer to eat grasses, forbs (aka weeds) and wildflowers. When the threat of cold and snow begins to bear down at the end of the warmer months, the animals are herded back down to the lowland valleys or plains for the fall and winter seasons. Today transhumance is often carried out more practically, using trucks to transfer the animals between highlands and lowlands. But the traditional walking migration still continues in various rural villages. Where it does endure, the transhumance is often marked by a community procession and a celebration to honor the ruminants and their rich seasonal milk.

IN THE TRADITION OF TRANSHUMANCE, FARMERS IN
THE FRENCH PYRENEES PARADE THEIR ANIMALS TO HIGH
MOUNTAIN PASTURES. (MARTIN CASTELLAN)

Dairy folk have long recognized the organoleptic benefits (meaning the whole experience of taste, scent, color, and texture) that wild high-altitude pastures confer to milk, cheese, and butter. Now it's also understood that grazing on these alpine lands confers a nutritional bonus too. Milk from animals that roam these rich highlands contains significantly more of the so-called good dairy fat known as CLA (conjugated linoleic acid), which boosts the immune system and metabolism. (According to Dr. Hernandez, this can also happen in silage-fed cows if you optimize their nutrition.) But fortunately for us who live below the alpine level, the healthful X factor is not so much the altitude as the sumptuous diversity of the unspoiled pasture. Choosing butter derived from the milk of animals that chow down on a smorgasbord of spring and summer forage is healthier at any elevation.

By now it should be clear that nature is an uncanny architect of milk fat. Plants and animals together get full credit for creating the delicious richness that constitutes butter. Yet without man, there'd be nothing to churn this fat to the point of no return, where it separates into golden kernels floating in a white pool of buttermilk. Butter is mankind's invention; it wouldn't exist without our desire for it. And yet, like many prehistoric food inventions, its earliest occurrence was altogether unintended.

. . . .

TWO

Early Churnings

FROM ACCIDENT
TO PRECEDENT

. . . .

In cases where a leech has been swallowed, butter is the usual remedy, with vinegar heated with a red-hot iron. Indeed, butter employed by itself is a good remedy for poisons, for where oil is not to be procured, it is an excellent substitute for it. Used with honey, butter heals injuries inflicted by millepedes . . . For other kinds of ulcers, butter is used as a detergent, and as tending to make new flesh."

—PLINY THE ELDER,
Historia Naturalis, 79 CE

LIKE MOST FOOD ENTHUSIASTS, I'VE MADE ALL KINDS of gastronomic pilgrimages to distant places. But stepping inside the Cork Butter Museum in Ireland several years ago, I discovered what felt like my very own holy grail: a large pail of Irish butter more than a thousand years old. Peering through the glass plate that protected its crusty, petrified form, I marveled that this butter, which had been packed into a timber keg carved from the trunk of a tree, was made hundreds of years before Columbus sailed for the New World. At the time of its churning, Ireland itself was just beginning to emerge as a nation after centuries of tribal wars and Viking conquests. Such battles and raids, in fact, may explain why this butter was hidden in the peat bog; invaders couldn't steal it if they couldn't find it.

As ancient as this bog butter is, it's actually a relatively modern occurrence, given the prehistoric origins of butter making. Although the time and place when people first created butter is a subject of ongoing debate, most anthropologists agree that butter arrived on the scene with Neolithic people, the first of our Stone Age ancestors who succeeded at domesticating ruminants. Once these early families had milking animals under their control, the invention of different dairy products was an evolutionary next step.

We'll never know the exact details, but the probable scenario goes something like this: One spring morning a herdsman is milking his animals, using the customary pouch of a tightly sewn animal skin as a storage container. Stored in the shade during the day, the pouch of milk starts to ferment slightly. As the sun goes down, the temperature cools, chilling the milk overnight. Early the next morning, the shepherd sets out with his herd for a new pasture, harnessing the cool pouch of milk to one of his animals. Traversing the bumpy route, the milk is rocked back and forth, rhythmically, for more than an hour. At a cool temperature and slightly ripened by bacteria, the milk fat is in an ideal condition for churning. Before long the herdsman's dairy load separates into thick butter flakes floating in an opaque liquid (buttermilk).

A possible and less romantic twist on this scenario—based on the theory that cheese making preceded butter making—is that the leftover whey drained from sheep's cheese curds, rather than the whole milk, was accidentally agitated, which then turned into lumpy bits of butter swimming in whey. (This is still the way sheep and goat butter are made in some traditional dairies, as a by-product of cheese making.)

Either way, the herdsman may have cursed his lumpy liquid at first, but we know how the story ends. Marveling at the rich taste of the butter kernels, he thinks surely this stuff is the result of magic by the gods. He smiles (I like to think) at their edible benevolence.

Eventually this ancestor and his clan also discovered that this tangy dairy fat was not only useful for eating but also for cooking, fuel, and medicine. For early dwellers in hot climates of the Middle East, Indus Valley, and Africa, this breakthrough would soon be followed by the realization that when butter is long simmered, its water content is driven off and its milk solids sink, leaving a layer of butter oil (most commonly referred to as ghee or ghi) that keeps for many months at an ambient temperature. And wasting nothing that was edible, prehistoric dairy folk came to savor the leftover buttermilk—as either a refreshing drink or the basis of a simple low-fat cheese (as is still done in many dairy cultures around the world). Turning liquid milk into these various "value-added" products, prehistoric animal herders created world's first dairy processing industry.

You wouldn't recognize the world's earliest butters. For one thing, they were made from the milk of sheep, yak, and goats, not from cow's milk. Domesticated cattle came much later in man's conquest of various animals. From as early as 9000 BCE in the region of what is now Iran, communities relied on domestic sheep and goats, which are less intimidating in size and have comfort-loving dispositions that early man coaxed into submission. In the Near East, domesticated goats functioned as a virtual power tool and dairy plant for early man as well, defoliating the scrubby land as they grazed so it could then be cultivated. The animals turned this coarse plant diet into a ready source of good meat and milk. Goat's skin, being nonporous, also provided an excellent milk vessel.

Thousands of years later, man began to tame cattle species and other wild bovines for work. Although the doe-eyed bovine cow has become an international dairy icon, the ancient world was much less monopolized by this four-hoofed favorite. Other ruminants—like the camel, reindeer, mare, yak, and water buffalo—also played the valuable role of milk maker for thousands of years, particularly in regions of the world where a cow would never survive.

CHURNING OTHER MILKS

In the scorching, dry heat of the Sahara, the camel first became the only source of milk for nomadic desert tribes and is still the dairy animal of choice for desert dwellers. The Tuareg nomads of the Ahaggar (Algerian Sahara), for whom camel milk remains a staple food, have a saying, "Water is the soul; milk is life."

One account from the Food and Agriculture Organization of the United Nations, R. Yagil's *Camels and Camel Milk*, described a primitive Saharan method of making camel's-milk butter: "The butter is made by placing camel milk into a thin, hairless goat-skin for 12 hours. This skin is never washed with water . . . In winter the goat-skin is often placed into the ground near a warm fire to obtain the optimum temperature before making butter. This aids in the fermentation. Churning is done when the container is half filled with sour milk. Air is blown into the container and the top is tied off. It is hung on a tent pole and rapidly swung to and fro. This is done in the early morning and the amount of butter obtained is determined by the skill of the man doing the churning."

Camel butter usually contains many impurities, such as sand and hair, and it becomes rancid rapidly in the local climate. So over the centuries, nomads have turned it into a strained butter oil, like ghee, to improve its keeping quality.

MILKING A CAMEL AT A DAIRY IN RAJASTHAN.
(NICK KEMBEL)

At more northern latitudes, the yak was first brought under prehistoric man's control by the ancient Qiang people of China, who roamed the high-altitude Qinghai-Tibet Plateau more than fifteen thousand years ago. The large hardy animal was their salvation. Yak served a great many purposes—as a beast of burden and a source of milk, butter, hair, hides, and meat, as well as fuel; in regions above the tree line, yak dung was burned to make fires. The yak remains a vital means of survival and sustenance for dwellers and nomads living high above the tree line in the Himalayas and the Tibet Plateau.

West of China in what is now northern Kazakhstan, horses were the main source of food and drink for the ancient Botai people who lived in the region around 3700 BCE. Horses feed on grasses like ruminants, but they do not chew their cud, nor do they have a four-chambered stomach. Still, for early people, mares reliably produced a decent quantity of milk for dairy consumption. The Botai not only drafted the local steeds for transport, but they also routinely milked the mares to produce a Botain staple—the fermented dairy drink called koumiss.

In the Eurasian arctic and subarctic, wild reindeer (caribou) were domesticated at least three thousand years ago. Ancient reindeer herdsmen, the Sami people—Scandinavia's only indigenous race—were descendants of the tribes that followed the receding glaciers at the end of the last Ice Age and settled in the arctic region. A diary entry from Knud Leems, a nineteenth-century traveler gave an account of the local reindeer butter making, which had not changed since prehistoric times: "Butter is also made of the milk of the reindeer, of a white colour, but not so rich and well tasted as what is made of cow's . . . The Lapland woman sits on the ground holding a bowl in her lap filled with cream, which she stirs and works with her fingers till it thickens into butter." Handmade butter indeed: The Sami woman's quick, cold fingers served as a kind of churn. For these early arctic butter makers, reindeer milk offered a spectacular 22 percent fat.

A REINDEER GIVES A SCANT AMOUNT OF MILK,
BUT IT'S REMARKABLY HIGH IN FAT. (ART AND PICTURE
COLLECTION, THE NEW YORK PUBLIC LIBRARY.
"MILKING OF THE REIN-DEER." THE NEW YORK
PUBLIC LIBRARY DIGITAL COLLECTIONS, 1835.)

AS BUTTER MAKING BECAME less happenstance in
Neolithic communities, its crude technology slowly advanced.
The animal skin pouch filled with milk was moved off the
back of an animal and hung like a cradle from a tree limb, or
from a sturdy horizontal log supported at either end, or from
the center of a tripod of logs. The filled skin could be easily
rocked back and forth to agitate the milk for butter making.
This primitive animal skin method of making butter can still
be found in a few small, remote communities in the Middle
East and northern Africa.

The Sumerians of 2500 BCE used special terra-cotta jugs
for holding the milk and a plunger-type tool (called the dash
or dasher in English) for churning it. In many parts of Africa,

THE PREHISTORIC METHOD OF CHURNING BUTTER INSIDE A GOATSKIN CONTINUES IN SOME REMOTE NOMADIC COMMUNITIES. (FARRELL JENKINS / BIBLEPLACES.COM)

hollowed-out calabash gourds became the first butter churns; with their rounded bottoms, they were ideal for rocking the milk back and forth.

Just after the beginning of the Iron Age, butter making underwent a great regional boon with the expansion of another tribe of pastoralists, the Vedic Aryans, who flourished in the Indus River valley and northern India. *Makhan*, the traditional Indian unsalted butter made by hand from cultured whole milk *dahi* (yogurt), was a staple of these pastoralists, ancestors of today's Hindus. The milk of their water buffalo, by virtue of its higher fat content gave excellent butter that was then simmered into ghee.

Although butter was common throughout most of the developing world by the first century CE, there were significant exceptions. All along the Mediterranean, olive oil became the ruling food fat (as it still is). Oil made economic sense in the region, since the same terrain that allowed the olive tree to thrive—craggy limestone slopes, light soil, arid conditions—was highly unfavorable to cattle dairying. Sure-footed foragers like goats and sheep fared well on the scrubby pasture, but their precious milk was generally set aside for cheese making. Only a little butter was made from whatever fat residue was in the leftover whey. Butter also suffered a poor reputation along the Mediterranean because the ancient Greeks and Romans who ruled the region associated it with the "barbarians" of the north.

BUTTER IN BATTLE
. . . .

A LINE FROM THE FOURTH-CENTURY PLAY written by the Greek comic poet Anaxandrides, referred to the Thracian enemy (bloodthirsty allies of the infamous Trojans) as *boutyrophagoi* (butter eaters), as if eating it proved their vulgarity. Butter was a vital staple for these warriors, not just at the table but in the bath as well. "People in many cold regions where they lack olive oil use butter for washing themselves," noted the Roman Empire's most observant medical authority, Claudius Galen. Some early marauders also favored butter as a hair dressing, as revealed in the records of Sidonius

Apollinaris, a fourth-century Roman bishop and poet who decried the habits of occupying Gaulish soldiers: "I am forced to listen to the barbarous German language and to applaud, despite myself, what a drunken Burgundian sings, his head perfumed with rancid butter."

While the Greeks or Romans would not deign to eat the stuff, they did have a place reserved for butter in their medicine chest. Galen vouched for butter's curative properties: "We also use it as we use hard fats, mixing it onto poultices and other medicaments."

Anthimus, a Byzantine physician who authored *On the Observance of Foods* in the sixth century, specified the kind of butter used for healing: "Fresh butter is taken for consumption [tuberculosis]. But butter completely without salt, for if it has salt, it does not cure it as well. If it is pure and fresh with a little honey mixed in, lick it at intervals while laying down." (If nothing else, it was easy to take.)

The ancient Egyptians had very different corporeal uses for butter; they turned it into a cosmetic treatment for their dead. They devised various ways to give the shrunken corpse a plumper, more lifelike appearance by lining subcutaneous areas with various materials including sawdust, earth, sand, and butter. The materials were often inserted into the mouth or through incisions in the skin (not unlike modern Botox treatments!).

Meanwhile, on the other side of the ancient world, most early Chinese communities, except those in the far north, would rarely see, let alone taste, butter since dairying itself was an anomaly. Some historians theorize that dairying was rare in the region because people of Chinese descent are highly lactose intolerant. (But, the chicken-or-egg counterargument goes, perhaps they are lactose intolerant *because* they didn't develop a dairy culture. The enzyme needed to digest lactose naturally recedes as a person ages, but in dairy-rich cultures people have adapted epigenetically to digesting this milk sugar throughout their lives.) Other observers, like food science writer Harold McGee in his book *On Food and Cooking*, speculate that dairying never took off in China because in the region where Chinese agriculture began, the wild vegetation was toxic to ruminants. Even so, dairy wasn't completely unavailable or rejected in the Yellow River heartlands, the birthplace of Chinese agriculture. Influenced by roving Mongolian nomads to the north, who spread their dairy culture through trade with bordering communities, the early Chinese believed milk products to be nutritious in small, digestible quantities, especially when heated or fermented. Chinese dairy luxuries included a cultured skim milk, a fresh cheese similar to cottage cheese, clotted cream, and butter oil similar to ghee.

The heavy hand of conquest also influenced butter's reach in the early world. In the Anglo-Saxon territories of the early Middle Ages, butter was typically made from sheep's milk— a remnant of Roman occupation. Cows existed in the region but they were kept primarily to breed the oxen needed to plow fields, not for dairying. Sheep, however, could supply four valuable commodities: wool, tallow, milk, and meat. Sheep dairies were the existing system of milk supply for the Romanized Britons and butter making was a minor by-product of making cheese with ewe's milk. The amount of sheep's butter produced was precious little (about two pounds for every one hundred pounds of cheese), so only the nobility or local thane enjoyed it. Butter was therefore a luxury in Anglo-Saxon times; not until the high Middle Ages when wool and milk became more separate enterprises did the dairy systems in the region shift from sheep to cow, making bovine butter more affordable. Before long, butter became so popular among all classes that its production was more profitable than cheese making.

THREE

Sacred and Spiritual

BUTTER MEETS METAPHYSICS

· · · ·

Auspicious is the aspect of Vadhryasva's [a mythological warrior] fire. Good is its guidance, pleasant are its visitings. When first the people of Sumitra kindle it with butter poured thereon, it crackles and shines bright. Butter is that which makes Vadhryasva's fire grow strong; the butter is its food, the butter makes it fat. It spreads abroad when butter hath been offered it, and balmed with streams of butter, shines forth like the Sun.

—TEXT FROM THE
ANCIENT VEDAS

NOT MANY FOODS CAN CLAIM TO HAVE BEEN A CER-emonial linchpin for multiple spiritual practices spanning several millennia. But butter can. Since very early days, people have made butter more than just the sum of its agricultural parts, more than merely a staple. Beyond its utility, ancient cultures revered butter as a political, mystical, artistic, and/or symbolic tool. To understand why this might be, I sought out various experts, including Mary Young, a former

Buddhist nun living on a secluded retreat in upstate New York.

Young is an expert on Tibetan butter sculpture, having worked for more than six years on a film documenting its modern-day practice at exiled Tibetan Buddhist monasteries in Nepal and India. *Torma: The Ancient Art of Tibetan Butter Sculpture* is a visual trek through the making of *tormas* using "clay" made of butter, flour, and/or wax. These colorful figures created by monks are handcrafted in a range of shapes, sizes, and designs for use in tantric rituals and as offerings to the deities. Displayed on altars, impermanent tormas are essential to the practice of Tibetan Buddhism.

Showing me scenes of the torma sculpting, Young explained, "The monks work from before sunrise until late at night, every day, until the figures are complete." As I watched, the camera zoomed in to show the exquisite details of a tiny carved hand in a bas-relief of Marpa Lotsawa, the founder of one of the four main lineages in Tibetan Buddhism. The torma artist creating it—a young monk sitting cross-legged on the floor in a room full of other artistically inclined monks and nuns—cools his fingers and pieces of the sculpting butter clay in a bowl of ice cold water while working with them. His rendering of Marpa is just one of dozens of sacred images of Buddhist deities and lineage masters being carved on round medallions specifically for the holy festival.

There is symbolism in every aspect of the sacred butter sculpting, from the shapes and colors to the many figures portrayed. Each year, the community's beloved spiritual leader, the Seventeenth Gyalwang Karmapa, Ogyen Trinley Dorje, envisions all the pieces of the display months beforehand and sketches them out. "This makes them even more sacred," Young added. "We believe he is a fully realized Buddha, in the same lineage as the Dalai Lama. Devotion to the Karmapa is what drives the butter artists. It is their holy work."

I realized she uses the word *butter* loosely. Although real yak butter mixed with *tsampa* (roasted barley flour) was the traditional sculpting material used in Tibet for torma making (and still is in some monasteries), the extreme heat in India where many of the exiled Tibetan monks and nuns live makes real butter impossible to work with or preserve throughout a sacred event. Instead, torma sculptures for festivals are now generally made with ghee or margarine, mixed with paraffin wax and flour. Combined and kneaded by hand, the composite sculpting dough is then mixed with generous squirts of fine oil paint to give the tormas a rainbow of vivid colors.

Sacred butter sculpting in Tibet stretches far back to its pre-Buddhist shamanic history, but it was apparently first introduced into Buddhist practice in the region in 641 CE, the year Princess Wencheng of the Tang dynasty in China came to Tibet to marry its king, Songtsen Gampo. Being a Buddhist, among the many things she brought with her was a sculpture of Sakyamuni (Buddha), to be enshrined. To show respect for this grand gift and their new queen, the Tibetans copied the prevailing Buddhist custom in India of placing six offerings before the Buddha statue: two kinds of incense, divine water, fruit, the Buddha light (candle), and flowers. But fresh flowers were not in season, so the Tibetans—already skilled at butter sculpting—improvised by creating a bouquet of flowers from yak butter and flour colored with natural pigments. Presto, a ritual art form was born.

Tibetan butter designs became evermore intricate over the centuries, especially after 1409, the year that the Buddhist master, Tsongkhapa, established the first Great Prayer Festival to honor Sakyamuni. The story is told that Tsongkhapa dreamed one night of a land where thorns turned into bright lights and weeds changed into fresh flowers and many treasures. He regarded this vision as a cosmic gift. Wanting to share it with the people, Tsongkhapa organized a team of monks to sculpt his dreamland in butter, lit with thousands of small butter lamps. Every year now, the Tibetan Butter Lamp Festival held in Lhasa, Tibet's capital city, reenacts this message of "enlightenment" by illuminating the streets with endless rows of little glowing chalices filled with ghee made from yak butter or vegetable oil.

Butter sculpting is esteemed work for Tibetan monks, but it is an arduous honor. Over the centuries, working in subzero cold in winter, monks would dip their hands and arms in snow or icy water to avoid melting the butter as they shaped it. Sculpting took many months and the artists often suffered illness, frostbitten fingers, arthritis, and rheumatism. Yet Tibetan monks bore this hardship as part of their spiritual practice. Today, some torma sculptures are still made in extremely cold workrooms using yak butter. At the Kumbum Monastery in the highlands of China's Qinghai-Tibet Plateau, a towering outdoor yak butter sculpture as large as an oak tree sits inside the entrance during winter prayer festivals. When spring arrives, the painstaking daedal work slowly melts away, thereby

TIBETAN BUTTER CARVINGS, CALLED TORMAS, ARE SACRED
TOOLS IN BUDDHIST PRACTICE. (KO JUNG-FA, FROM *TORMA:
THE ANCIENT ART OF BUTTER SCULPTURE*)

symbolizing one of Buddhism's sacred tenets—the transient
nature of life.

Tibetan monks may have given butter its most resplendent
use, but long before they did, Buddhist masters in China had
derived inspiration from the golden fat, rare though it was in
that country. The act of butter making itself was considered an
ideal metaphor for spiritual development as early as the sixth
century. According to the Chinese Buddhist master T'ien-t'ai,
the dharma, or Buddhist teachings, could be understood in
terms of successive stages of soul transformation analogous to
the stages by which ghee ("liberated" butter) is derived from
milk. Just as milk comes from a cow, cream from milk, butter
from cream, melted butter from solid butter, and then finally
ghee oil distilled from the layers of melted butter, each dairy
product symbolizes a rung on the ladder of spiritual ascent.

As Buddhism spread to Japan in the first millennium,

butter gained yet another notch in its belt of spiritual celebrity through Zen Buddhist teacher, Hakuin Ekaku. The early master instructed students whose bodies were in a state of disharmony to gird their spirit and perform the following visualization (as translated by Norman Waddell):

> Imagine that a soft lump of butter, pure in color and fragrance and the size and shape of a duck egg, is suddenly placed on the top of your head. As it begins to slowly melt, it imparts an exquisite sensation, moistening and saturating your head within and without. It continues to ooze down . . . all the congestions that have accumulated within the six organs and viscera . . . will follow the heart as it sinks downward into the lower body. As it does, you will distinctly hear a sound like water trickling from a higher place to a lower place. It will move lower down through the lower body, suffusing the legs with beneficial warmth . . . it gradually fills the lower region of the body making [the student] feel as if he were sitting up to his navel in a hot bath filled with a decoction of rare and fragrant medicinal herbs.

If the visioning was diligently practiced, Hakuin promised that one's body and mind would be in perfect harmony, with remarkable side effects. His instruction was no less than a promise of transformation through butter meditation.

BUDDHISTS WEREN'T THE ONLY early spiritual believers to employ butter in their rituals. We know from archeological finds that the locals of Sumeria—a region that is now part of Iraq—were churning and celebrating butter at least as early as 2500 BCE. A well-preserved temple frieze testifies to their hallowed dairy culture; carved into its limestone surface are figures of cattle and sheep as well as people engaged in various creamery chores, including churning. Sumerian writings reveal that they revered their butter as well as butter making itself. As documented by Jeremy A. Black and colleagues in the *Electronic Text Corpus of Sumerian Literature*, they wrote passages like, "The rocking of the churn will sing for you . . . thus making you joyous."

From Sumerian clay tablets, we've learned that Dumuzi, the mythological dairy shepherd, was the instigator of a goddess love story that would serve to make butter central to life in the Sumerian walled city of Uruk. The powerful fertility goddess, Inanna, protector of the seasons and harvest, pronounced that she would marry the mythological grain farmer Enkimdu rather than her other suitor, Dumuzi. Apparently she favored the farm harvest over dairy products. But Dumuzi makes an impassioned case for the value of his dairy riches, including fresh milk, fermented milk, butter (or ghee), and various cheeses. His speech wins her over and they marry, thereby establishing the Dumuzi-Inanna cult, whose followers believed that the goddess would protect Sumerian storehouses and prosperity as long as she was generously supplied with dairy goods. The central rite of the cult was to bring regular offerings of butter to the temple to satisfy Inanna's dairy wishes.

Among the Vedic Aryans in the Indus River valley, butter

was also the centerpiece of religious ritual. In their Vedas, an epic collection of sacred texts (the foundation of much of modern Hindu mythology), there are copious references to butter's sanctity and symbolism (presumably in the form of ghee, given the climate). In one hymn, translated by indologist Wendy Doniger, the verse is accompanied by ritual sprinklings of ghee over the fire, causing the flames to crackle and dance:

> *This is the secret name of Butter,*
> *"Tongue of the gods," "navel of immortality."*
> *We will proclaim the name of Butter;*
> *We will sustain it in this sacrifice by bowing low.*
> *These waves of Butter flow like gazelles before the*
> *   hunter . . .*
> *Streams of Butter caress the burning wood.*
> *Agni, the fire, loves them and is satisfied.*

According to a classic Vedic analogy, ghee is hidden in milk like the divine Lord is hidden in all creation. Spiritual work and its rewards are symbolized by the willful act of churning, through which rich butter appears; when this butter is heated over fire (aka the sacred god Agni), the most hidden part of milk—golden ghee—is revealed.

Ancient Hindu mythology also describes the boyish mischief of Lord Krishna, who was famous for his childhood pranks, most notably his practice of stealing butter from the milkmaids of neighboring households and charming his way

IN ANCIENT HINDU MYTHOLOGY, VASUKI, THE SNAKE GOD,
WAS USED AS THE ROPE, AND MANDHARA, THE MOUNTAIN,
SERVED AS THE PLUNGER TO CHURN AN OCEAN OF MILK
INTO SACRED OBJECTS. (WIKIMEDIA COMMONS)

out of any punishment for it. He shared the golden booty with all, including the monkeys who hung about like sacred pets. Even today his devotees affectionately call Krishna *makhan chor* (the butter thief), and celebrate his birthday, traditionally called Janmashtami, with wild enthusiasm. In many places, especially in Mathura, where the blue Lord was born, grand exhibits portraying his childhood episodes are displayed with lights and images of the divine child. Pots of curd and ghee are hung high in the streets and human pyramids are formed to reach for their contents, reenacting the child Krishna's climb to steal the milk and butter from suspended pots.

Butter in sacred lore also turns up in the very first meal mentioned in the Bible. The passage describes an auspicious feast that Abraham prepares for three angels incarnate

THE YOUNG LORD KRISHNA'S PREDILECTION FOR
STEALING BUTTER IS CELEBRATED EACH YEAR AT THE
HINDU FESTIVAL OF HIS BIRTHDAY, JANMASHTAMI.
(HDNICEWALLPAPERS.COM)

(Genesis 18:1–8), one whom he presumes to be God. As part
of a few carefully chosen foods he serves, butter is clearly
considered worthy of a divine meal. The Bible verses describe
the honorable spread the old man offers to earn God's favor:
"And Abraham hastened into the tent unto Sarah and said,
'Make ready quickly three measures of fine meal, knead them
and make them caked upon the hearth.' And Abraham ran
unto the herd and fetched a calf tender and good, and gave it
unto a young man; and he hastened to dress it. And he took
butter and milk and the calf which he had dressed and set it

before them; and he stood by them under a tree, and they did eat."

Things turn out well for Abraham after this meal. As we know from the biblical narrative, he goes on to become the great patriarch of three world religions: Christianity, Judaism, and Islam. Just saying.

DIGGING THROUGH ANCIENT TEXTS was one way I uncovered the stories of our ancestors' metaphysical attachment to butter, yet others have literally dug into the earth itself for traces of early butter rituals. In Ireland, tracts of swampy turf have yielded hundreds of batches of buried "bog butter," some dating from as early as 400 BCE, up until the late nineteenth century. For thousands of years, Irish wetlands (and to a lesser degree, Scottish, Finnish, and Icelandic bogs as well) were used as butter mines, where covered wooden buckets, or firkins, packed with butter and wrapped in moss were sunk into the earth. Buried Celtic bog butter has also been found inside myriad vessels, from wooden tubes to animal bladders, while some lumps were buried without any apparent covering at all. Most of these have been accidentally discovered by men digging up the bog to dry as peat and sell for fuel.

Naturally cool, anaerobic, and highly acidic, a bog is an ideal medium for preserving certain kinds of organic matter. (Many ancient corpses have been found that are essentially mummified by the bog). Without refrigeration, Celtic dairymen probably relied on the bog to hide and preserve butter that would otherwise have spoiled in the warm spring and summer months, when cream for butter was most plentiful. The wet, airless conditions in bogs, along with the antiseptic qualities of the acidic turf, would have inhibited the butter from going rancid. So it made sense to bury butter in times of plenty to be retrieved in leaner times. It may have also been buried as a security measure, to hide a "food rent" material, such as butter, which would have been owed to an overlord. The surviving samples that have been unearthed were presumably misplaced, forgotten, or left behind as the result of migration and/or death.

More recently, however, another explanation for bog butter has emerged, claiming that some may have been buried as a pagan offering. Mapping the relative age and locations of early bog butter samples, experts have discovered that the majority of bog butters dating to the Iron Age have been found at important geographical boundaries. Historians have proposed that at least some buried samples were never meant to be retrieved but rather were deliberately placed as votive offerings. Depositing valuables in lakes, rivers, and wetland areas as ritual gifts to mythical gods and spirits was a common prehistoric practice—especially so in Ireland circa 450 BCE, when the Druids, an ancient priestly class, were alive and well. As with the Vedics and the Buddhists, butter was a vital symbolic element for the early Celts.

Freshly made butter, for instance, was essential for celebrating Imbolc (pronounced "EEM-olk"), the spring Druid festival that paid homage to the holy day of Brigid, the pagan goddess of fire, healing, and fertility. The action of making butter—that is, the phallic thrusting of the dasher in the churn—symbolized the blessing of fertility being sought during this celebration. The churn dash was also used as a frame to create an effigy of Brigid, which was then carried in procession from house to house. A bit of bread, cake, butter, and/or porridge might be left on the window sill for Brigid to enjoy as she passed by, perhaps with some feed for her mythical favorite white cow. In some homes, a place was set at the table for Brigid.

Like many ancient religious rituals, Celtic pagan practices involving butter were fundamentally about imparting a sense of control over destiny, health, and good fortune, as well as a means of dealing with the preternatural "faeries" that alternately terrified and awed country folk. It's also evident from early Irish archives that neighbors were not above suspicion either when it came to meddling with one's dairy success. A local "witch"—invariably a farmwife—could use magic to steal another's "milk luck" or "butter luck." Churnings that produced only froth or foul-tasting liquid were often believed to result from witchcraft. Because cream was considered "the top o' the milk," such things as the dew on the May morning grass or the surface water of the well, could represent a farm's cream. Walking across other people's land on a particular spring morning, a would-be thief could be indicted for "walking off the dew" and hence the milk luck. The first water to be drawn from the well on May morning was also regarded as a potent tool for charmed butter production; whoever skimmed the well water first could expect good milk and butter luck for the coming year. If it was a communal well, then the neighbor's dairy was also benevolently charmed. Legend has it that private wells were physically guarded from sunset on May Eve until sunrise on May morning to prevent any magical interference with the "top o' the water." (It's worth noting that the traditional Irish phrase to wish someone well, "Top o' the morning to you," has its origin in the dairy world; "the top" refers to the richest, loveliest part, as cream is at the top of milk.)

COME, BUTTERCHURN, COME

Buttermilk to the wrist, butter to the elbow;
Come, butterchurn, come.
Buttermilk to the wrist, butter to the elbow;
Come, butterchurn, come.

1. There's a glug here, there's a glack here;
There's a glack here, there's a glug here,
There's something better here than you'd expect,
There's something better than wine here.
Come, butterchurn, come.

2. The thrush will come, the blackbird will come,
The mist will come from the hill,
The cuckoo will come, the jackdaw will come,
The father osprey will come.
Come, butterchurn, come.

—TRADITIONAL IRISH SONG FOR CHURNING

Precautionary measures against having your dairy products jinxed were many and very exacting, according to the writer Jane Francesca Wilde—mother of the famed Oscar Wilde. Under her pen name, Francesca Speranza Wilde, she published *Ancient Legends, Mystic Charms, and Superstitions of Ireland* in 1887. Wilde's book became a cultural gem, a rare collection of oral interviews with the elder Irish peasantry of her day, who lived throughout the countryside. Among other folkloric beliefs, it recorded their practices for safeguarding dairy:

> To save milk from witchcraft, the people on May morning cut and peel some branches of the mountain ash, and bind the twigs round the milk pails and the churn. No witch or fairy will then be able to steal the milk or butter. But all this must be done before sunrise. However, should butter be missed, follow the cow to the field, and gather the clay her hoof has touched; then, on returning home, place it under the churn with a live coal and a handful of salt, and your butter is safe from man or woman, fairy or fiend, for that year. There are other methods also to preserve a good supply of butter in the churn; a horse-shoe tied on it; a rusty nail from a coffin driven into the side: a cross made of the leaves of veronica placed at the bottom of the milk pail; but the mountain ash is the best of all safeguards against witchcraft and devil's magic.

VEXED AND HEXED

····

*T*HE EARLY FARMERS OF IRELAND WERE NOT alone in their fear of supernatural threats to milk luck. There was also a large body of rules and rituals regarding cows and milk in the folklore of various countries, notably in Sweden and Norway. If the milk and butter inventory continued to suffer despite such practices, the farmer or community often resorted to blaming it on a scapegoat—usually a woman and her supposed witchcraft. (In fact, failed butter making appears in the transcripts of witch trials in Europe and the American colonies as one of the proofs that the indicted women had magic power over another's churn.)

Some of the ways early Swedish farmwives helped ensure their dairy luck against spirits and stealers by breathing into the milking pail before commencing to milk or passing the milk pail over a fire three times. More extreme measures also existed, particularly around the widespread belief that, by making a pact with the devil, a witch could virtually steal the milk of other farmers, without ever having to cross their property. According to Swedish lore, once that deal was struck, the person (invariably a woman) invoked the milk theft ritually, by standing naked on a tall pile of manure and calling out, "The milk is mine as far as my cry is heard."

Other folk versions of Swedish malevolence are migratory legends, turning up in other countries. Consider the *mjolkhare* (milk hare), for instance, which can be found in parts of Ireland and Norway as well. To appropriate someone else's milk and butter luck, a little woolly hare was woven out of sticks, wool, skin, clipped-off fingernails, and human hair. The milk hare was then "sent off" to a neighboring dairy to drink up all their milk, after which it raced back home and vomited up all the milk into the thief's own pails. The milk hare might also suckle directly from the cow's teats; legend has it that this often left small telltale scars and flecks on the udder. Apparently it was useless to shoot at a milk hare with an ordinary bullet; only a silver bullet could bring down the tiny beast, whereupon it would allegedly collapse into a pile of sticks and straw.

BUTTER ALSO TOOK ON a sacred role in the Middle Ages. Under the dicta of the powerful Roman Catholic Church, abstinence from butter on fast days became a hotly debated measure of religious virtue and obedience in medieval life.

Foods generally forbidden to medieval Christians during fast days included all meat and poultry, eggs, and dairy products (milk, butter, and cheese). Thomas Aquinas, the revered philosopher-priest of the thirteenth century, defended such abstinence on the basis that these staples "afforded greater pleasure as food [than fish], and greater nourishment to the human body, so that from their consumption there results a greater surplus available for seminal matter, which when abundant becomes a great incentive to lust." Fasting, which had originally been prescribed for monks as a means to curb their sexual inclinations and thereby keep their vows of celibacy, eventually become a mandate for every Christian, one that they were expected to practice frequently: By the early Middle Ages, fast days were observed on Wednesdays, Fridays, Saturdays, the eve of feast days, certain days of Advent, and for all the forty days of Lent before Easter—all together, roughly half the year.

These deprivations were of course much harder on Christians in central and northern Europe than on those in Rome and the Mediterranean region, where olive oil, fish, grains, and vegetables dominated the diet. (It's worth noting that many people of the oil-eating regions regarded butter with great suspicion in the Middle Ages. Accounts of medieval Provençal or Spanish travelers, obliged to pass through or visit dairy-rich foreign countries, describe how they took their own of olive oil with them, believing that butter made one more susceptible to leprosy.) Fasting in the southern olive- and fish-rich parishes still allowed for most of the staples people enjoyed, except for cheese and eggs.

Conversely, in the north, the prohibition against milk, meat, cheese, butter, and eggs—foods that provided basic sustenance where oil and fish were scarce—amounted to a forced starvation. In these regions, a duty to eat olive oil was as hard to digest as the foreign debts incurred by importing it. Especially given that many unscrupulous Italian and Spanish merchants dispatched oil of the worst quality to northern Europe.

Religious councils in various northern climes frequently wrestled with fasting restrictions, especially concerning butter since it was both a cooking fat and a food. Although French monks abstained from meat, lard, and tallow, they prepared their vegetables with butter or milk until it was emphatically restricted in 1365. According to Pierre Le Grand d'Aussy, the Council of Angers (that being the name of a French prefecture, not the emotion incited) knew "that in several regions even the clerics use milk and butter at Lent and on fast days, even though they have fish, oil, and everything that is necessary for this period. As a result we forbid any person whatsoever milk and butter during Lent, even in bread and vegetables, unless they have obtained specific permission." Those who disobeyed the prohibitions (especially against meat) were liable for a hefty fine or imprisonment or subject to severe corporal punishment by the whip or in the pillory.

But in 1491, Queen Anne, Duchess of Brittany lobbied Rome for permission to use butter, asking not only for herself but for the queen's household as well, since Brittany produced no cooking oil, nor did it import any. Ultimately the reprieve was granted and the whole of Brittany received the same allowance. A domino effect ensued, and by 1495 the same butter permission was granted to Germany, Hungary, Bohemia, and France.

Such dairy privileges, however, did not come without conditions; the butter eaters were required to perform certain prayers regularly and, above all, give alms to the church.

In parts of France and Flanders, where the churchwardens of various parishes asked that such alms be specifically applied to the repair or improvement of parish buildings, churches created *troncs pour le beurre*, alms boxes for butter, placed near the pews. A lasting monument to this period of spiritual extortion is the medieval Butter Tower, which majestically flanks the right side of the Gothic Cathédrale Notre-Dame de Rouen, France's largest church. The Butter Tower was added to the cathedral between 1485 and 1507, reportedly using the money that Catholics paid to the church for the privilege of eating butter on Lent and other fast days. No accounting records exist to prove whether butter dispensations actually financed the entire ornate 260-foot tower, or if the structure was sardonically named for the church's exorbitant butter permits. But we do know that in the thirteenth century the faithful paid a precious six deniers each time they were granted a butter allowance during fast days. Forfeiting six of them was worth the equivalent of fifteen pounds of salt or one nice fat capon.

In 1520, Martin Luther railed against such ritual profiteering; as described in Bridget Ann Henisch's *Fast and Feast*, the outspoken priest wrote in 1520: "In Rome they make a mockery of fasting, while forcing us to eat an oil that they themselves would not use to grease their shoes. Then they sell us the right to eat the foods forbidden on fast days, but they have stolen that same liberty from us with their ecclesiastical laws . . . Eating butter, they say, is a greater sin than to lie, blaspheme, or indulge in impurity." It seems hardly a coincidence that most of the dairy-rich countries producing and using butter were the same nations that broke away from the Roman Catholic Church in the sixteenth century. Paradoxically, the church's early fasting rules also eventually helped to promote butter among the oil-and-lard-loving people in southern European countries. Alberto Capatti, in his book *Italian Cuisine: A Cultural History*, explained that for the medieval peasant and working class in Italy, good olive oil was a luxury they could rarely afford. Lard was their common fat, but since products of the slaughterhouse were forbidden on fast days, they were left with no choice but to use cheap foul-tasting oil. When the church gradually gave in to allowing butter as a Lenten substitute for oil in the north, the practice eventually spread to the south, as it gave peasants an alternative to bad oil. Over time, the view of butter as "barbarian" fat gave way to its general acceptance. Italian recipes using butter began to appear, and by the sixteenth century butter had become something of a status symbol, especially among the Italian nobility living in cities in the south. The difficulty of obtaining and preserving a steady supply of butter in the hot clime made it all the more desirable as a luxury item. The church had unwittingly helped butter rise from the Italian food gutter to a place at the finest *tavoli*.

Remarkably, butter has held a heightened spiritual role throughout human history while simultaneously keeping its utilitarian place in everyday life. For as long as anyone can tell, butter has uniquely bridged the secular and the sacred, the scientific and the supernatural in vastly different cultures. Covering these dual narratives that stretch across time and place, I couldn't help but wonder, Why butter? Why did it become a global darling of both spirituality and domesticity?

Some of the answer resides in butter making itself. The craft was a great necessity for our ancestors but it was little understood. Preindustrial folk were no doubt puzzled that the simple act of shaking or rocking milk caused its invisible richness to suddenly bloom into floating morsels of butter. And yet the very same action failed to produce butter at other times. No matter how much the task was codified over thousands of years, butter making remained fundamentally a mystery until latter day scientists teased its molecules apart. And so, like many bygone earthly mysteries (rainbows, thunder, tides, etc.), its occurrence was deemed to be under the influence of temperamental gods and spirits. Butter seemed especially divinely brokered because it was such a gift for mankind. Not just a delectable food on its own, butter could be used for cooking, as medicine, for lamp fuel, as a lubricant, to preserve meats, and even for waterproofing. No wonder that long-held customs exalting butter continue to endure.

In remote regions of Ethiopia, among the nearly nude tribe in the Omo Valley, for instance, it's still customary to spread butter and red clay all over the skin of a bride-to-be, head to toe. She remains visibly lacquered in this mixture for several weeks while staying with her future husband's family. This ritual act indicates a level of commitment to the impending marriage, whereas the "engagement" period beforehand is often marked by a great deal of promiscuity by both the man and the woman.

The custom of ceremonially smearing butter on body parts is practiced in communities around the Himalayas as well. In the Dayara Bugyal region of northern India, an annual butter festival is held in which the participants sing, dance, and spread butter lavishly on their faces. Known locally as Anduri Utsav, the celebration marks the end of summer pasturing at the high altitudes, the time when local dairy families and their animals return to the valleys and give thanks for a safe milk harvest on the mountain *bugyal* (meadow).

Travel south along the Himalayas, to the remote Humla Province, and butter customs move from the face to the crown of the head. When a guest arrives or departs in the region, the locals smear butter on the visitor's head three times while reciting a blessing. According to Tempa Dukte, a Buddhist Lama priest I spoke with who grew up in the province, the butter is used to invoke three wishes for a person. "They are for prosperity, longevity, and happiness," Tempa explained. A similar ritual is enacted at local monasteries, where three pieces of butter are placed opposite each other on the rim of a glass; one represents a wish for an awakened mind, another for wisdom, and the third for unity (of body, mind, and spirit). Drinking from the cup, the monk consumes the butter pieces to fortify their quest for the three attributes.

Tempa told me how Tibetans also had a very ancient method of using butter to predict the future. This rite, known as *walchu*, comes from the Bön tradition, Tibet's oldest theosophy. The walchu is rarely performed since only a holy man in the community can enact it for critical soothsaying; he handcrafts a small torma sculpture of butter and flour and infuses it with "energy" for making predictions. Then he brings a large pot of water to boiling. "The torma is dropped in the boiling water," explained Tempa, "and if it floats, then a fortunate outcome is predicted. But if it simply melts, the prediction is not favorable."

FUELING INTENTION

....

*I*N TIBETAN BUDDHIST PRACTICE, BUTTER LAMPS are burned for three different reasons, depending on intention. One is the lamp that never goes out; its continuous light symbolizes the constant effort to eliminate the darkness of ignorance. Another type of lamp is lit for a personal celebration or challenge and is dedicated to qualities the person may need, such as clarity or strength. The last kind of butter lamp is burned as an act of contrition, to make amends for wrongdoing. For centuries, clarified yak butter was the fuel in these lamps but now cheaper *vanaspati* (vegetable oil–based) ghee is more commonly used.

On the fifteenth day of the first month of the Tibetan calendar (roughly equivalent to our February) the Butter Lantern Festival is a final celebration of Losar, the new year, which begins as darkness falls. In cities, the streets are filled with lanterns and votives (once upon a time fueled only by butter oil), many of which are suspended two or three stories above the ground. The effect is of a bright starry roof above the crowded streets, filled with Tibetans singing, dancing, and admiring the scores of brightly painted butter sculptures

SACRED AND SPIRITUAL

made by each household. As the butter lights banish darkness, they also embody the concept of turning an ordinary
substance into illumination, a transformation akin to man's
humble search for enlightenment. "If you wish for sublime realization," says Buddhist scripture, "offer hundreds of lights."

FOUR

Handmaidens of Flavor

WOMEN BUILD
THE BUTTER TRADE

· · · ·

The dairymaids would trip out with their stools and
buckets and wooden yokes, milk the tame cows where
they stood no doubt knee-deep in grass and buttercups
and return to the farm, swinging the heavy buckets
full of foaming milk from the yoke chains and trying
(or not trying?) to give the slip to the swains who, the
poets tell us, were ever trying to waylay them.

—JOHN SEYMOUR,
Forgotten Household Crafts, 1987

AH, THE VOLUPTUOUS DAIRYMAID, RIPE WITH FER-
tile innuendo. She has long fueled the romantic imagi-
nation of writers, poets, and painters, which can make it easy
for us to forget how stalwart these women actually were.
Yoked like oxen, they dispensed and hauled milk from the
fields where the cows grazed, beginning at dawn and regardless of the weather. But fetching milk was only the start of
their labors. Since milk was so perishable in springtime and
summer before the advent of refrigeration, these women

MARCELLUS LAROON'S *MERRY MILK MAID*,
LATE SEVENTEENTH CENTURY. (WIKIMEDIA COMMONS)

processed each pail full, every day, into butter and cheese. Because dairying was closely identified with female rites of fertility, birthing, and lactation, strong cultural taboos against men handling milk existed for centuries around the world, and so the business of butter making grew up squarely on the shoulders of hearty pastoral women.

The gender divide ran deep in the early dairy world, with butter and cheese making considered merely extensions of the many household duties relegated to womenfolk. Whereas men dealt primarily with "outdoor" work such as crop management and animal breeding, farmwives had a staggering list of domestic "indoor" responsibilities, from cleaning, child rearing, and cooking for the entire household and any helpers, to milking cows, baking bread, sending all grains to the mill, serving the swine morning and night, protecting the poultry, and gathering their eggs. In March and April, about the same time lambing, kidding, and/or calving began—and therefore, a peak supply of animals' milk was suddenly available—the wife was also expected to plant a kitchen garden to supply the household vegetables and herbs, as well as to sow her flax and hemp seeds, the plants of which she turned into fabric for sewing the family clothes. Yet that wasn't all. According to Sir Anthony Fitzherbert's sixteenth-century volume, *Book of Husbandry*, "It is a wife's occupation to winnow all manner of corns, to make malt, to wash and wring, to make hay, shear corn, and in time of need to help her husband to fill the muck-wain or dung-cart, drive the plough, to load hay, corn, to sell butter, cheese, milk, eggs, chickens, capons, hens, pigs, geese and all manner of corn. And also to buy all manner of necessary things belonging to her household, and to make a true reckoning and account to her husband, what she hath paid." The same treatise on wifely duties further advised: "Thou must make butter, and cheese, when thou may." Woe to the farmwife who had no daughters to help her.

The handmade, small-batch nature of early butter making by generations of women meant that butters of antiquity were wildly diverse artisan products whose quality and consistency could never be taken for granted. Results varied greatly from one farmhouse to the next, not to mention one region to another. With no formal training, women learned how to make butter from each other, just as they would other domestic arts.

IT WAS CUSTOMARY, BEFORE THE ADVENT OF
MILKING PARLORS, FOR WOMEN TO MILK THEIR COWS
IN THE FIELD, AS ILLUSTRATED IN THIS 1879 PAINTING,
THE DAIRY MAID, BY MANSEL LEWIS.

Butter making had great commercial value, yet it was a do-
main they controlled. Far be it from any man to interfere, as
one eighteenth-century agricultural writer, Josiah Twamley,
discovered when he tried to advise dairywomen about their
ways of working. "I am well acquainted, how unthankful an
office it is," he lamented, "to attempt to instruct or inform
Dairywomen, how to improve their method, or point out
rules, which are different from their own, or what had always
been practiced by their Mothers, to whom they are often very
partial."

Using their senses rather than science, dairymaids navigated the vagaries of milk, cream, and climate that often toyed with success at the churn. Their butter differed depending on the equipment and skill of the woman making it, as well as her taste preferences, the animal, the feed, and the amount of salt used to preserve the butter. The proud dairywoman would distinguish her local butter using various molds, prints, decoration, and packaging as a way of trademarking her product.

The flavor of butter produced could range from sublimely ripened golden batches, to supersalted butters preserved in brine, or highly fermented, oxidized versions that our modern palates would reject altogether as spoiled. The butter of manor dairymaids and farmwives also differed from modern types in terms of its cream's freshness. None would have been made from cream just a few hours outside the udder—what we call sweet cream butter. This version is a relatively recent product, ushered in by the invention of the mechanical cream separator in the late 1800s. Before that, dairywomen would pour each bucket of new cow's milk into "settling" pans or troughs and let it stand for half a day or overnight to allow the cream to rise to the surface, whereupon the maids gently skimmed it off for butter making. In the time spent settling, the raw milk ripened to varying degrees, depending on the temperature and ambient lactobacilli, veering away from sweet toward tanginess.

Preindustrial dairywomen in Europe also made butter from the milk of other ruminants, particularly sheep and goats. The fat in these milks does not easily or naturally separate on standing, like cow's milk does. Lacking a cream layer to skim off for butter making, goat and sheep milks were typically made into cheese or a yogurtlike mixture. Butter was then formed either as a by-product of the dairymaid's cheese making (by churning the leftover whey with its residue of fat) or by the reverse process—the whole milk yogurt was first churned to make butter and then the drained leftover buttermilk was turned into a simple fresh cheese. (Both of these techniques are still used by rural dairywomen in many parts of the world.)

Although a system of year-round lactation was developed as early as the sixteenth century to provide some milk through the winter, the lion's share was collected each spring and summer. Butter was therefore most plentiful when it was most perishable. Dairymaids devised a common method of preserving portions of it with salt or brine for many months to supply the winter market. First, they vigorously rinsed, washed, and pressed the butter to expel all the buttermilk. To store the butter in scalded firkins or tubs, the maid then held portions of it in hand and flung hard into the tub to ensure a tight pack. This was done in layers, which were each heavily salted and kneaded with her knuckles to drive off any remaining air bubbles. When it was time to eat the butter months later, women typically soaked the butter in cool water to leech out the excess salt.

Salted butter was also an important tool for preserving other foods for the winter pantry. In households that could afford it, butter was lavishly spread over cooked food as a seal to prevent spoilage. Sweet and savory pies were topped with a thick veneer of melted butter. With butter acting as a barrier, foods could keep for several weeks or months.

AS THE BUTTER ECONOMY grew, European producers competed for the reputation of making the most delicious and trustworthy butter. Food adulteration by hucksters and profiteers was rampant at the time and butter fell victim to various schemes, including mixing old rancid butter with new butter; adding stones, old turnips, and other dense objects into the butter to increase its weight; and using annatto or other colorings to make pale butter look like yellow "May" butter, which would garner a higher price. Much was at stake in the competition, for the sixteenth and seventeenth centuries were peak years in the age of European exploration across the Seven Seas, making new butter markets highly profitable.

At home on the Continent, big changes were afoot too. Cities were growing exponentially as populations moved away from the profoundly rural life that had once sustained them. No longer was the dairy consumer also its creator. Many of those who became town dwellers could not produce their own food and began to rely exclusively on food produced and delivered by those who remained in the country. In this burgeoning urban economy, the business of butter boomed, as did the job of dairymaid. Able-bodied women who were not married, or who were widowed, could find employment among a growing number of manors and large farms dedicated to dairying.

The position of dairymaid at a manor was considered a respectable one, a step up from the domestic servant since the sale of dairy foods was often more profitable than any other agricultural product at the manor. A dairymaid who consistently crafted good butter and cheese could always find work. In England, larger farms recruited teams of dairymaids; the standard allowance was one maid for every ten cows.

Beyond earning them job security, the seemingly mysterious methods by which dairymaids could turn simple liquid milk into solid rich butter and good cheese also gained them a rare measure of respect from men in the trade. Without dairy science or even written records to justify the steps of production that women managed simply by feel and eye, men had little understanding of how these foods actually resulted. As such, the enigma of milk processing elevated the status of a skillful dairymaid, at least up until the early 1800s when male-dominated dairy science began to revolutionize the industry. Before that, the dairy itself represented an inner sanctum of female territory, which partially accounts for much of the romantic, quasi-erotic notions attached to the dairymaid archetype. She was at once a paragon of domestic virtue and a hidden dairy cabalist. She dealt in purity within a world of fecundity. She supplied nourishment as well as pleasure—particularly in the form of butter. It's no wonder that of all of mankind's laborers, dairymaids have been the ones most often portrayed by poets and painters. Even the Dutch master Johannes Vermeer paid tribute with his now-priceless rendering of *The Milkmaid*.

THE PLEASURE DAIRY

....

*T*HE ICONIC INFLUENCE OF DAIRYMAID CULTURE
also led to one of Marie-Antoinette's most extravagant
indulgences—her *laiterie d'agrément* (pleasure dairy) on
the grounds of Versailles. Dubbed Hameau de Versailles,
it was part of a utopian hamlet complete with cottages,
watermills, and a farmhouse built for the nobility's
amusement. The pleasure dairy was a favorite retreat of
the French queen, where she and her ladies-in-waiting
would dress as dairymaids and play at making butter and
other simple dairy foods.

There were in fact two dairies at Hameau—the
queen's laiterie d'agrément and the more functional
laiterie de préparation, where skilled dairymaids created the ice cream, butter, and cheeses that were actually served at the pleasure dairy. ("Playing" dairy was
one thing; eating its results was another.) Both dairy
buildings were rustic and farmlike on the outside, with
exposed timbers and thatched roofs. But inside, the
preparation dairy was plain whereas the pleasure dairy
had fixtures made of gleaming white marble set against
walls meticulously painted with trompe l'oeil to re-
semble marble. The queen's collection of dairyware
included ornate porcelain milk pails, skimmers, dairy
spoons, and settling pans for cream, all custom made by

the most prestigious ceramic house in Paris. There were dairy costumes too; Marie-Antoinette allegedly liked to let her hair down and appreciated the less formal attire of milkmaids.

Was the laiterie d'agrément just a well-appointed stage for make-believe dairying, or did Marie-Antoinette and her courtly sorority actually make dairy foods? The historical record is ambiguous, though churning butter was noted. Crafting butter was simpler than making cheese and ice cream, and more immediately gratifying. But the real purpose of the queen's dairy was not production; it served as a handsome focal point for her gardens and a more intimate retreat for entertaining guests.

In 1787, Marie-Antoinette's husband, King Louis XVI, built her an even more sumptuous pleasure dairy at his Château de Rambouillet, but the French Revolution made sure that she wouldn't get to enjoy the place; the queen was executed soon thereafter, in part because of such extravagances.

Marie-Antoinette was not the first monarch to have installed a so-called pleasure dairy—though hers was the most controversial politically. Two centuries earlier, another imported French queen—Caterina de' Medici— inaugurated this royal architectural tradition as part of her creation of a model farm, known as Mi-voie, built in 1560, just beyond the grounds of Fontainebleu. Its centerpiece was a regal pleasure dairy incorporating a grotto and walls painted with mythical creatures and gilded astrological motifs. Unlike Marie-Antoinette's pastoral expression at Hameau, Caterina de' Medici's initiative was praised as an affirmation of the monarch's stewardship of the land and so it boosted her political popularity. Inspired by Mi-voie as well as the influence of a growing pastoral literary trend in the late 1600s that idealized rural life, France's nobility began to build other pleasure dairies on the outskirts of their estates.

Louis XIV even built a lavish laiterie d'agrément at Versailles as a gift to his grandson's wife, fourteen-year-old Marie-Adélaïde of Savoy, who reputedly took to dairying enthusiastically. As noted in Meredith Martin's *Dairy Queens*, Marie-Adélaïde enjoyed milking the cows herself and often served guests "butter that she churned with her own white hands, and that Louis XIV found excellent."

In the mid- to late eighteenth century, pleasure dairies began to appear in parts of England, Russia, and the region that is now Germany and Belgium. But more than merely fashionable, the pleasure dairy increasingly held political and cultural weight, as that rare place where aristocratic women of the early modern periodcould exercise female identity and power.

By the mid-1700s, dairying culture and butter making had been firmly transplanted in the New World. But not easily. The early colonists themselves barely survived, let alone their cows.

The first shipment of dairy cows in North America arrived

in Plymouth in 1624. Although indigenous milk-making ruminants, such as moose, elk, caribou, deer, antelope, and bison,
were plentiful on the North American continent, the Native
Americans had only hunted these animals, never attempting
to domesticate and milk them.

Being ill prepared for the harsh realities of the new-world
wilderness and woefully underfunded, the Plymouth Pilgrims
struggled to sustain themselves and their fledgling cowherd.
Many settlers and animals succumbed to starvation and disease in the early years. But remarkably, the colony endured,
and in doing so it proved to be an inspiration and catalyst for
the Great Migration, the period between 1630 and 1640 when
more than twenty thousand Puritans emigrated from England
to the New World, creating the thriving Massachusetts Bay
Colony. Between 1630 and 1633, dairy cows and other livestock were loaded on to almost every ship headed for the Pu-
ritan colony; dairy farming in North America would prove
essential for survival.

Immigrants from other butter-loving countries also staked
their claim to settlements in the New World, including the
French, Swedish, and Dutch. Like the English, these immigrants brought their dairy know-how and cows into regions
that had never before sustained a milk culture. In fact, the
landscape of the Northeast was not at all cow friendly in the
1600s. Thick virgin forests covered the New England area, except for salt marsh tracts along the coasts, freshwater marshes
inland, and the occasional open field that had been cleared
by native tribes to raise crops. Dairying in the New World
took a firm hold despite the terroir—and also, paradoxically,

because of it. By the summer of 1663, soil depletion and blight had caused widespread failure of wheat crops in Massachusetts, prompting many farmers to switch from growing grain to raising livestock and dairying. At the time, there was also a great demand for dairy products, including butter, from the people managing and working the vast sugarcane plantations in the West Indies. Intensive production of sugarcane, driven by slave labor, left the plantations increasingly dependent on the North American colonies for all their staples; ever-larger shipments of butter and other provisions were sent to the Caribbean islands to feed the captive African workers and their wealthy white masters.

The West Indians reciprocated by supplying the colonies with sugar as well as its abundant byproduct: molasses. Because it could be cheaply fermented and distilled into rum, molasses from the West Indies led to a proliferation of rum distilleries throughout the Northeast. The growing rum economy only boosted the demand for slave-driven sugarcane production, the result of which was a very reliable and lucrative market in the West Indies for the butter made by New England dairymaids. Farmers in Massachusetts, Connecticut, and Rhode Island responded by expanding dairy herds. It's no small irony that many of these descendants of the early Puritans—who had fled the "moral breakdown" in England just a few decades before—were now in a butter trade that depended on institutionalized slavery and alcohol consumption.

The West Indian market continued to be the principal buyer of butter made by New England's dairywomen until about the middle of the eighteenth century, when the rise of

new North American markets dramatically shifted the destination of dairy products. By the time of the American Revolution, twice as much butter was being shipped to east coast
markets in Nova Scotia, South Carolina, and Georgia, as was
making its way to the West Indies. Farms in the mid-Atlantic
region were producing butter exclusively; indeed, the agricultural expanse around Philadelphia became known as the
nation's Butter Belt, and that region took the lead from Boston in exporting American butter. The Butter Belt's robust
production, with women at its backbone, had one downside:
Farmers routinely dumped the buttermilk left over from
churning butter into the local rivers and streams, causing an
environmental plague. The question of what to do with all
that skimmed milk and cream eventually led to the widespread
production of cottage cheese, one of America's most popular
fresh cheeses.

Given the European roots of America's immigrants, farmstead butter-making practices in the early years of the United
States mirrored old-world techniques and traditions. "Man to
the plough, Wife to the cow" was a saying that also fit customs in the New World as women continued to be the primary milkers and butter makers on the farm. But eventually
gender roles began to shift more easily in the States simply
because American dairy farms were typically larger and could
accommodate more cows. Land was plentiful in the new nation, especially westward, and so by the end of the eighteenth
century, larger family farms also meant looser boundaries
around male and female dairy work. By necessity, men and
boys took up the milking stool and pail, helping to manage

the twice-daily flow of milk. But butter making still remained largely in the hands of women.

EVERY EPOCH HAS ITS resident epicures (alas, the folks we now call "foodies," with some derision). The eighteenth and nineteenth centuries were no exception, and dairymaids and wives who worked harder to cater to the predilections of the prosperous were generally well rewarded. Then, as now, celebrity butters were eagerly sought by the food sophisticates in Europe and North America. According to food historian Maguelonne Toussaint-Samat, in a popular French social journal of 1788, *Dictionnaire Sentencieux*, certain butters were declared must-haves: "There are only two types of butter which the fashionable dares mention: butter from Vanvre (Vanves) and butter from Frévalais" (both on the outskirts of Paris). The butter of these regions was very unique in that it was fresh and unsalted, so it was much more perishable than most other butters. The enterprising dairywomen of Vanves and Frévalais brought their expensive sweet cultured butter to Paris every Thursday where it was sold in precious rolls of three or four ounces, mostly for spreading on bread. Another Parisian specialty was perfumed butter, made by layering unsalted butter with a variety of flowers. Pieces of thin muslin cloth were placed between the blossoms and the butter, and the mixture was left to infuse for a day or more in a cool place.

The exalted butter that came from Denmark originated partly by accident. The Danes, in trying to extend the season of lactation for their cows, began adding rich rapeseed oil cakes to each milking cow's winterfeed. It turned out that these cakes had a very good sensory effect on their milk and hence on the texture and taste of Danish butter.

The United States also had its famed butter-making districts in the mid-nineteenth century. Before the days of centralized creameries, the dairywomen of Orange County, in New York State, and Franklin County in Vermont were esteemed for their skill and uniform quality in butter making. Franklin County butter was the gold standard of quality in Boston, and the butter from Orange County was a prized product in New York City.

In England, butter from the counties of Essex, in the south, and Yorkshire to the north, earned the most fame. Josiah Twamley in his 1816 *Essays on the Management of Dairy* also described "Cambridgeshire salt butter" as being a premium product that London cheesemongers would buy wholesale, rinse well to work out the salt, and then sell for a high price as fresh butter.

Twamley extolled the Yorkshire farmers who "perhaps make more butter from their cows than anyone . . . This is chiefly to be ascribed to the very great care they take of their cows during winter, as at that season they house them all, feed them well, and never suffer them to go out, except to water, unless the weather be very serene."

Although every country had its thriving butter regions in the nineteenth century, the southwestern corner of Ireland was unique in its domination of world butter commerce for the better part of a century, beginning in the early 1700s. With its temperate climate and rich pasture, Ireland has long been

IN ITS HEYDAY, THE CORK BUTTER EXCHANGE SHIPPED IRISH
BUTTER AROUND THE WORLD. (MARY EVANS LIBRARY)

ideal cow country. For centuries, its fertile land was divvied
up among a multitude of small tenant farms, all of which kept
a few cows and made butter primarily to pay their rent. In
the eighteenth century, the Cork Butter Exchange became
the destination for selling much of this butter. By pooling the
supply from a legion of farmstead butter makers, Cork eventually grew into the world's largest export butter market. In
its heyday, Cork had ships from Sweden, Denmark, Holland,
Portugal, and Spain regularly come to its port to stock up on
butter for their respective colonies.

Ireland developed its thriving butter monopoly largely because a group of local merchants instituted something never
before seen in global food trade: a rigorous and innovative
system of quality control. Before this new initiative, Irish
butter makers were paid more or less the same price for their

product by the city's wholesalers, regardless of quality. The merchants had a clear motive in revising the system—to gain control of the grading and pricing and eliminate the wholesalers while also offering a price advantage to "honest" dairyfolk who brought in fresh, lightly salted butter.

By the end of the eighteenth century, a vast network of country roads and carriage paths had developed in and beyond the southwest corner of Ireland, which led to and from Cork. Known colloquially as the Butter Roads, these arteries connected hundreds of small dairywomen to the Cork market where they could sell their homemade butter. To accommodate these distant suppliers, the Cork Butter Exchange was open day and night.

The Irish butter market, like its competition around the world, wouldn't have existed without the manual labor of women. All together, their ability to transform a daily tide of milk into tubs, balls, bricks, mottes, and prints of butter constituted a cottage industry of global proportion. Although their production varied in quality and quantity across the buttermaking world, the basic techniques and tools dairywomen used were nearly identical across time and place. It's easy to forget that the simple equipment women wielded to make butter also drove dairy trade, and more than any other tools they were proof of women's pivotal economic role on the farm.

. . . .

FIVE

Tools and Technique

VINTAGE BUTTER MAKING

. . . .

We had a very well made polished varnished wooden end-over-end barrel churn with small transparent glass windows to see if the butter was making, quite beautiful. The sound of the cream slopping and splashing within the churn actually changed note as the butter neared readiness so the churn could be stopped at just the right moment. We never tired of the magic of cream going in and butter coming out. Before the churn gave up its butter, the buttermilk was drained off from a plug in the bottom of the churn into a large deep earthenware glazed bowl, a delicacy on a hot day straight out of the bowl with a dipper beside it, a smooth slightly sour sharp taste which I liked and have never lost.

—SCORRIE, *"The Dairy," Rain on My Window, August 16, 2007, on growing up in the Orkney Islands during the 1930s*

BUTTER-MAKING HISTORY DOESN'T REVEAL ITSELF easily. You have to chase it, sometimes into places that are completely unexpected. That's how I found myself one frosty winter morning, standing outside a deserted self-storage unit on the suburban fringes of New Jersey. Leading me to the facility was its tenant, Sandeep Agarwal, butter artifact collector extraordinaire. Sandeep scours dairy and antiquarian fairs and websites for old butter-making tools and artifacts as zealously as other men hunt down sports memorabilia. He has amassed more than two hundred pieces, some dating back to the 1600s. On the morning we met, Sandeep explained that his collection (what he calls "Butterworld" on the rare occasions when he displays it) began with books. His family has been in the dairy business in India for five generations, making ghee. "I started to collect dairying books initially," he said. "Then I saw an old churn at auction and became more intrigued." Obsessed is more like it; when Sandeep flung open the corrugated door of his storage cave, it was stacked with boxes from floor to ceiling, each one containing a butter-making tool or piece of ephemera from a once-bustling creamery or dairy farm. Wedged in between were freestanding churns of various sizes, shapes, and age. Sandeep gently unwrapped some his more prized possessions, letting me examine them firsthand. There were delicate carved molds; churns of glass, metal, porcelain and wood; butter hands and patters; butter crocks and firkins; plus boxes we didn't even get to. It's one thing to read about such careworn old dairy treasures, but it was quite another to hold them in my hands, engage their moving parts, feel their heft. I felt as if I were stirring artisan ghosts—all of them women.

For a dairymaid or farmwife, butter making was a lengthy choreography of equipment and craft that began each time she set her three-legged stool beside a cow and commenced milking.

SETTING THE MILK

After the dairymaid had filled a pail with fresh cow's milk, she would strain it through a woven sieve (cloth or grass) into a large earthenware jug or other vessel until it cooled and lost its frothy head. The milk was then transferred again, this time to shallow "setting" dishes, or pancheons. The filled pans were covered with a cloth and left in a cool place for at least half a day or overnight, whereupon the cream would separate, floating like a soft ivory raft on top of the milk. In parts of northern Europe, a shallow slate trough with a plug on the bottom was also commonly used for separating the milk. The dairymaid poured fresh milk into the cool trough, covered it, and allowed the milk to set for the better part of a day or overnight. When the cream had risen sufficiently, the plug was pulled causing the milk layer to rush out into a container below. The cream remained, clinging to the sides of the trough; it was then scraped off and transferred to the churn.

But cream wasn't always separated for butter making. It was common practice in Holland and some other parts of Europe to churn whole cultured milk for butter making rather than skimming cream for the purpose. (This practice was also used at several big dairies in Pennsylvania and New York.) In terms of maximizing butter production in those preindustrial days, churning whole ripened milk was preferable to cream—90 to 95 percent of the butterfat in milk was captured as butter whereas the skimmed cream method utilized only about 80 percent (since not all the fat floated to the top). The downside of churning whole milk, however, was that it took

BEFORE ELECTRICITY WAS AVAILABLE, MANY LARGE
DAIRY FARMS USED ANIMAL-POWERED CHURNS TO MAKE BUTTER.
(CORNELL UNIVERSITY LIBRARY)

a lot more time, energy, and skill to make the butter come. Bigger operators devised methods of churning that didn't rely on manpower (or rather, womanpower); they would harness a dog, sheep, or horse to a treadmill, which in turn powered the churn.

At the typical family-run dairy farm, however, churning was done with cream and by hand. (Cream itself was also a valued staple in the farm kitchen.) Batches of cream were set aside for a day or more to ripen, or ferment, with the wild lactic bacteria that was naturally present on farm surfaces and on the skin of people who worked in dairy. In certain regions, a tangy cultured flavor was considered a mark of quality in butter. And the older cream generally yielded more butter than fresh cream (although, if left to ripen too long, bacteria would cause sour, rancid off flavors and/or very cheesy-tasting butter).

Before refrigeration, the more fortunate dairywomen had access to a springhouse for keeping cream and other dairy products cool. (The kitchen was usually too warm for making or storing butter, and cream cannot easily be churned if its temperature is above 70°F.) Usually constructed of stone in a shady location or built into a hill, with a spring-fed source of water running beneath it, the springhouse had a shallow trough dug into the floor, through which the cool stream passed; milk pans were set in the trough. The natural flow of cool water created a constant cellarlike temperature throughout the warm months when milking and butter making were at their peak (green energy, before it had a name). Nothing but fresh milk, cream, and butter were kept in this dairy hut, so as not to taint their flavor or aroma.

THE SUBTERRANEAN DESIGN OF A SPRINGHOUSE
KEPT FRESH MILK COOL BEFORE THE INVENTION OF
REFRIGERATION. (KEITH CHILDS)

BUTTER AND VIRTUE
....

We believe it is as easy to make good butter as that of an inferior quality. And we venture to say that it will elevate the moral tone of the whole family. We even think we can tell the character of the family by the looks of the butter, for the habits of attention and cleanliness that are formed by the making of good butter will be carried out in every particular.

—WILLIS POPE HAZARD,
Butter and
Buttermaking, 1877

SKIMMING THE CREAM

The dairymaid skillfully lifted the cream layer off of standing milk using a small skimmer and transferred it to a churn. The best skimmers were saucer-shaped, shallow, and perforated with a thin, sharp edge. As the cream was gently pushed to one side with this tool, it slid onto the skimmer; any milk collected drained out of the skimmer holes. (Dairy legend has it that the cream from a Jersey or Guernsey cow was so thick and dense that it wrinkled like a soft fabric as it was pushed along by the skimmer.)

After it became a well-established fact that the finest butter was made from the butterfat that rises first, leading butter makers in Europe divided skimming into two stages, at eighteen hours and then again at twelve hours, for first- and second-grade butter, respectively.

CHURNING

The process of agitating cream to make butter has inspired a vast collection of churns over the centuries. One of the oldest and most common styles used throughout the world was the plunger churn, which consisted of a tall wooden bucket with a tight lid that has a center hole just wide enough to fit a long wooden staff yet narrow enough to prevent cream from splattering out the top. The bottom of this staff, or plunger, was attached to either a base of cross boards or to a carved wooden base that was often perforated to boost agitation. The dairymaid pumped the plunger up and down until fat knobs of butter formed; the time that took varied depending on the cream's temperature, freshness, quality, and quantity, but twenty to thirty minutes was typical.

A later model was the paddle churn, which consisted of a container (wooden, ceramic, metal, or glass) with a paddle inside, sometimes perforated, attached to a center rod. The center rod connected to a rotating handle on the top or side of the churn that was turned continuously by hand until the agitation yielded butter. There were small jarlike versions for home use as well as large round and box-shaped paddle churns for dairy farm operations.

As butter demand increased in the eighteenth and nineteenth centuries, so did the size of butter churns and innovations to

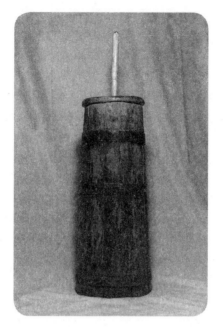

A PLUNGER CHURN IS ONE OF THE OLDEST AND
MOST COMMON RUSTIC TOOLS FOR MAKING BUTTER.
(LUCA PEARL KHOSROVA)

its design. (In the 1800s, patents were issued for new butter
churns every ten or twelve days. And that was only in the
United States!) One of the most popular designs was the barrel churn. The whole barrel would spin around like a wheel
by rotating its handle, or the barrel churn could be station-
ary with its handle operating rotating paddles inside. Some
square-sided versions of this design were called box churns.
When first introduced, this innovative churn won high praise
for its performance, as seen in an English manual for "country housewives" published by William Ellis in 1750: "A barrel
churn is so late an invention, that the uses of it are known

SMALL GLASS PADDLE CHURNS, SUCH AS THIS DAISY MODEL,
WERE A HOUSEHOLD FIXTURE IN THE LATE NINETEENTH CENTURY.
(LUCA PEARL KHOSROVA)

THE END-OVER-END CHURN (*LEFT*) AND SWINGING
CHURN (*RIGHT*) REPRESENTED A TECHNOLOGICAL LEAP IN LARGE-
BATCH PREINDUSTRIAL BUTTER MAKING. (ISTOCKPHOTO)

but in few counties in England. Buckinghamshire and Bedfordshire justly claim the first practice of this most serviceable dairy utensil, that every year comes more and more into fashion, for its being easily and quickly clean'd, as well as its being work'd with much facility and least waste of cream, and expeditiously producing the sweetest butter."

Swing churns and rocking churns were derivations of the barrel churn that operated like a cradle. (Manufacturers claimed that this gentle nursery-like action made for better butter.) One nineteenth-century version of the rocking churn, seen in Belgian artist Charles Petit's oil painting *The Butter Churn*, was also an unofficial amusement ride for toddlers. The small child could gleefully rock atop the churn while mother churned the cream.

The end-over-end (or over-and-over) churn was introduced around the mid-1800s to great enthusiasm. Made to flip the barrel or box-shaped churn over, top to bottom, this model was undoubtedly the most efficient means of making a significant quantity of butter. Better models came equipped with a small window to view the cream's progress and gauge the butter grains. In the corner of his storage, Sandeep showed me a large and rare model of an end-over-end churn made entirely from glazed stoneware—the best material for keeping cream cool. Smooth, white, and elliptical, it looked like an enormous egg suspended between two poles.

One of the oddest churning inventions was the Kangaroo-Jiffy Buttermaker made in New Zealand. It worked using three distinct motions: shaking up and down, shaking side to side, and tilting back and forth. The churn also gave a violent kick with each revolution, much like a kangaroo. The maker's instructions explained that if you strapped the cream container to the saddle of a galloping horse you would achieve the same motions, though why that was a selling point is a question that remains.

WORKING THE BUTTER

After the butter and buttermilk were separated from each other, the butter was usually well rinsed with cold water—the first step in purging more of the buttermilk residue. The cold water also served to firm up the butter grains, making them easier to handle. Next the butter was transferred to a bowl or tray to be "worked." The dairywoman pressed, turned, cleaved, kneaded, rinsed, and squeezed the butter mass, extracting the water and any lingering buttermilk, since this milky residue would cause it to spoil more quickly, especially in summer, before refrigeration.

The task of working the butter improved its texture, making it more cohesive, velvety, and spreadable. One seminal dairy manual of the day, by Willis Pope Hazard, advised that the moisture content of a properly worked butter was no more than "a very slight dew, and it should be of such a firm consistency as to slice down, hardly dimming the surface of a knifeblade." A well-trained dairymaid never touched the butter directly, instead using small paddles, one in each hand. They were known as butter spades, or butter hands, and were handcarved flat, spatula-like tools, with deep narrow grooves on one side. A similar tool, the wooden butter ladle, was slightly cupped and wide like a large shallow spoon with a blunt end. As the butter was worked with such tools, droplets of buttermilk surfaced and were rinsed away. Butter hands served other functions as well. They were also used to divide and shape butter into blocks or press into a mold. Some dairymaids were adept at also using the thin edge of butter spades to score the surface of butter bricks with geometric designs and patterns.

Handling the butter required not only finesse but also sound judgment as to when you were done with it; overworked butter could become greasy, or if too much buttermilk was drained, it would be dry and crumbly.

"You had to watch your cream. You did have to pay a lot of attention to the cream to get it so it was just perfect. You couldn't let it stand too long. You worked with it."

—MARY MORRELL, BORN 1892, OF TENNESSEE
(Learned to make butter when she was six on her family farm, where churning was done inside the springhouse. As an adult, she remembered reading aloud to her kids while she churned.)

Next the butter was spread out on a tray and sprinkled with salt, which was then lightly worked in. The degree of salting varied with the taste of the maker or her customers. In the mid-1800s, about a half pound of salt to ten pounds of butter was a fairly average proportion for butter that was to be promptly eaten. (That's about three times as much salt as in

most commercial butters today.) If the butter was to be preserved for several months, salt was added aggressively, rendering the butter virtually inedible. For this reason, preserved
butter was treated much like salted dried fish—repeatedly
soaked and rinsed in cool water to draw off much of the salt
before eating.

Many dairywomen worked their bigger batches of butter using a simple inclined V-shaped wooden tray with holes
for drainage at the narrow end. Freshly churned butter was
placed in the tray and a lever was moved back and forth to
squeeze and press the mass. The tray was tilted so the buttermilk that oozed drained out one end into a container below.

Most makers would have considered their work done at
this point in the process, except for portioning the butter. But
many German producers in Pennsylvania's Butter Belt region,
who fetched a higher price for their butter, employed a few
extra steps. After salting, their butter was spread again in a
tray and then propped up on its edge in a cool place overnight,
allowing the salt to thoroughly dissolve in the butter and any
remaining buttermilk/water to drain off. In the morning, the
butter was worked over thoroughly with the paddle in one
hand and a cloth soaked in ice water in the other until it was
dense and waxy.

PICKLED BUTTER

....

*I*T WAS COMMON PRACTICE BEFORE THE TWENTI-
eth century to store pieces of homemade butter in a
"pickle," or a brine bath inside a large crock or barrel to
preserve it for months, since dairy was more scarce and
expensive through the winter. *The White House Cookbook*, published in 1887, offered this method: "First work
your butter into small rolls, wrapping each one in a clean
muslin cloth, tying them up with a string. Make a brine,
say three gallons, having it strong enough of salt to bear
up an egg; add half a teacupful of pure, white sugar and
one tablespoonful of saltpetre; boil the brine, and when
cold strain it carefully. Pour it over the rolls to more than
cover them, as this excludes air. Place a weight over all
to keep the rolls under the surface." Before eating the
preserved butter, our butter-loving predecessors then
had to desalt their pickled product in fresh water for
several hours before it was palatable.

BRINGING BUTTER TO MARKET

Farm families who relied on butter making for income, branded their product with a custom-made stamp print, roller marker, or decorative mold that embossed the butter with a trademark design. Many a dairymaid took pride in "patting up" the butter into different shapes, known as prints, then stamping each with a design. Sandeep had a vast collection of these, including a delicate carved mold made in sections like a tiny folding screen with hinges; this allowed a square of butter to be embossed on all sides.

In summer, European dairywomen often wrapped their stamped market butter in green leaves, generally those of the garden orache plant. Provincially called butter leaves, the plant was sown annually in the garden just for the purpose of enveloping and protecting butter. Its fine-textured leaves were sufficiently large and had a pale green color that flattered the butter. If not available, grapevine and cabbage leaves were also used. Apart from lending eye appeal, the leaves allowed the butter maker to easily move her prints into and out of the market basket without leaving fingerprints.

In England during the late nineteenth century, butter was sold in a few places "by the yard." The maker came to market with rectangular baskets filled with narrow three-foot-long rods of butter. (Presumably the butter

MANY FARMWIVES USED PROPRIETARY HAND-CARVED BUTTER
MOLDS TO BRAND AND EMBELLISH THEIR BUTTER BEFORE SENDING
IT TO MARKET. (SANDEEP AGARWAL, BUTTERWORLD.ORG)

was forced through a pipe of some kind to create the shape.) When a customer ordered a "length" of butter, the seller measured it with a ring gauge and cut it crosswise. The advantage of this shape was that housemaids and wives could easily cut the butter into the nice round pats to serve at every mealtime.

According to a nineteenth-century account by Laura Rose, a Canadian visitor to dairies in England, you could tell which county you were in by the shape of the butter: "When she had the butter all vigorously kneaded, she measured it into pounds and rolled it into balls and then pressed it into Oxford prints; you could not dispose of a pound of butter in any other shape there. While at

Banbury, a few miles distant, they would not buy an Oxford print, the market there demanding plain rolls. That shows you the conservativeness of the English."

Among larger dairies in Europe, butter came to market as one large block, what the French aptly call a *motte de beurre* (mound of butter). These large heaps of butter, weighing between ten and twenty pounds, were made by lining a tapered pail or fruit basket with wet muslin, then filling it with firmly packed butter. At the market, the containers were flipped over, the cloth was removed, and the vendor cut thick or thin slabs of butter from the motte according to the customer's preference. Butter is still sold this way in many European provinces, especially in France, where butter mottes are typically on display in three varieties: *doux* (unsalted), *demi-sel* (lightly salted), and *salé* (fully salted).

In the United States during the early 1800s, butter came to market in various guises, depending on where you lived. The major eastern seaboard cities, such as New York and Philadelphia, saw tubs and bricks of international butters arriving from Ireland and Denmark, which competed with local butter neatly molded and hand-printed. But in small town America during the early to mid-nineteenth century, farm butter often came to market with very little panache; the dairy farmer's wife would simply load her tub of butter into the wagon or buggy, put on her hat, and set off for the village grocer.

The storekeeper would decide its value based on a sampling. Country proprietors in those days had to be wary buyers, given the propensity among suppliers (including farm women) to cheat the weight or quality of a product.

Butter presented in rustic tubs or as thick rolls wrapped in reused cloths were the common means of packaging for country markets and working class groceries of the nineteenth century in America. But selling butter in the lucrative, sophisticated city food shops demanded a more standardized shape and wrapper. Eventually hand-operated butter presses were invented that turned individual mounds of butter into standardized little bricks. Ironically, the trend has reversed today: Rough-cut butter in simple parchment paper sells to high-end food shops while the tidy uniform brand-emblazoned blocks of butter line the aisle of every supermarket.

By the late 1800s, when the dairy arts of women began to shift to the business of men, butter making on the farm and its simple tool kit were headed for obsolescence in both Europe and America. Within a generation, more than a thousand years of tradition would be dismantled, piece by piece. I was glad to stand among so many surviving relics in Sandeep's storage unit, many of which he had painstakingly restored himself. "After work, I like to spend time with these tools, cleaning and fixing them," he said. "Or I search for facts about their history so I can understand how all these instruments came together in the butter world." As we carefully re-packed his pieces and put them back among his other butter antiques, Sandeep explained that his plan is not to keep the collection padlocked away but to have it on permanent public display at a museum or dairy institution. "I enjoy finding these artifacts," he said, "but mostly I want to share with people the remarkable history of handmade butter."

The Revolution

MEN, MARGARINE BATTLES, AND BUTTER CANONS

. . . .

There are few that have not admired the fact of the
sound dairymaid, who with full, rounded arm, held
aloft the golden roll, and patted it into proper shape,
but of this there is no more. Her sweet voice at work
is displaced by the rattle of the wagons of the creamery man . . . the hissing of steam, the rumble of heavy
machinery mingled with the hoarse voice of creamery
men, as they attend to the details of rolling out tons
and car loads of dairy products.

—*Annual Report of the Nebraska
Dairymen's Association, 1887*

THE TOWN OF GREENWOOD, WISCONSIN, SITS ON MILES
of grassy pasture along the banks of the lazy Black River,
its roads winding through land settled by generations of farmers and cows. There are few signs of modernity here—that
is until the gleaming headquarters of Grassland Dairy comes
into view. With its skyscraping steel silos standing like turrets
beside a sprawling industrial campus, Grassland is a monolith
of modern butter making.

SIX

Inside this state-of-the-art milk-processing plant, I donned the requisite sanitized white jacket and hairnet, and then followed Trevor Wuethrich, the vice president of this family-owned megadairy, down the indoor avenues of the spotless factory. "We receive over five million pounds of milk a day," he said loudly over the clamor of machines, "from about eight hundred fifty different producers." (Industrial milk is measured in pounds because farmers are paid by weight; one pound equals slightly more than a pint.) Everywhere we turned, I was dwarfed by massive stainless-steel pipes, vats, and gauges—the anatomy of a modern dairy colossus.

Grassland produces forty-two thousand pounds of butter *per hour* using three continuous churns. These long muzzle-ended machines—which the French call butter canons—first pump cream into a cool top cylinder where it is mixed by high-speed blades so that in less than three seconds, butter granules form. (By comparison, churning in a commercial stainless-steel barrel churn takes between thirty and sixty minutes depending on the volume of cream.) The butter granules in the continuous churn are then forced through perforated plates while the buttermilk is drained off. The butter is instantly worked into a smooth mass by a double-barrel extruder before it emerges, pristine and ready to be packaged.

By any historical measure, butter's leap to this level of industrialization from dairymaid-driven production has been remarkably quick. For more than a millennium, butter-making customs and methods remained virtually frozen in time. But then, with the dawn of the Industrial Revolution, a stream of scientific ideas about dairy management began to percolate in Western countries. Before long, scientists, businessmen, and engineers had all descended on the dairywoman's workplace with a reformer's zeal. Like every other industry at the time, it was transformed. A more calibrated routine was devised for butter production, now managed by men yet initially still worked primarily by young women, many of whom were required to attend training classes at a local male-managed dairy school.

This was not an easy transition for many women, whose age-old methods were suddenly challenged. Historical records from the time are peppered with disparaging remarks about dairywomen's backward customs and how they interfered with the advancement of butter-making techniques. Historian Joanna Bourke noted in her 1990 article "Dairywomen and Affectionate Wives" that dairymaids and dairy mistresses were thought to stand in the way of progress, as evidenced by an 1885 report of the Commissioners of National Education in Ireland, which argued that "women confined to the narrow circle of home, without time for reading or opportunity of seeing improved methods, and frequently having no knowledge of the various qualities of butter required for the market, could scarcely be expected to contribute towards improvement in butter making."

Eventually, the new momentum in dairy science coupled with old-world chauvinism would eradicate women's authority and place in the dairy world. But it happened incrementally, as each new technical innovation erased a portion of traditional butter making.

The most groundbreaking of these was the centrifugal cream separator, invented by Gustaf de Laval in 1878. It revolutionized the dairy and butter industry by offering a radically faster and more effective way to separate milk fat (the cream) from milk.

De Laval's cream separator worked by centrifugal force. In this way, liquids with different densities—like cream and milk—could be separated from each other simply through spinning them. The continuous centrifugal cream separator had the capacity to process three hundred pounds of milk per hour. De Laval also perfected a small home model that women could easily operate to speed up their butter making. With the success of both the factory and family-size cream separator, farmers suddenly had a new cash crop: sweet fresh cream. By the end of the nineteenth century, de Laval had fundamentally changed the way the world handled milk—and the flavor and production of butter. Instead of waiting a day or more for cow's milk to levitate its cream layer, dairy folk could now produce butter in just a few hours with the cream separator. Fresh milk was run through the whirling device, and cream was collected from one of its spouts, chilled slightly, and then put in the churn. The resulting butter had a freshness rarely tasted before.

Now the butter market had a new variety, dubbed sweet cream butter. It's flavor was distinctly different from the more tangy, old-fashioned butter made from long-set, hand-skimmed cream. (Of note: A new, if relatively rare, trend today in the neoartisan butter world is to use "hand-skimmed" cream, produced by this old-world style of separating cream by letting the milk stand. Its practitioners claim that gentle handling of the fat globules creates a better product.)

DE LAVAL'S CREAM SEPARATOR—AND its many imitators that followed—instigated the rise of commercial cream-

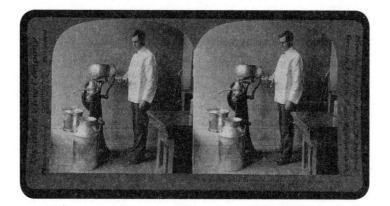

DEMONSTRATING HOW THE CREAM SEPARATOR WORKS, CIRCA 1919.
(LIBRARY OF CONGRESS DUPLICATION SERVICES)

eries (aka butter factories) in many dairy regions. It made economic sense to pool the milk of many farms and create a central processing place where it could be transformed quickly into butter; and so it was, for the first time in historym, that butter making was unceremoniously moved off the farm and into a factory setting.

The shift happened abruptly for some farmers, as noted in the diary of Emily Hawley Gillespie, an Illinois dairy farm-wife. On May 28, 1874, she wrote: "We commence to sell milk today to Mr. Clark. He is to pay us 80 cents for every 100 pounds and we are to give Mr. Morse 10 cents for carrying it, per 100 pounds." Three days later she added, "Well we think we do better to sell our milk than to make butter. We have now sold 254 pounds worth $20.32 and it has cost to carry it 21 cents." Increasingly Emily made budget notes about the butter she bought rather than the butter she made.

For many other women, butter making still lived in the rhythm of domesticity at the end of the nineteenth century, but as production started shifting to creameries, large farm churns gradually began to gather dust. Butter making for many farmwives changed from an activity that engaged them socially in the production and sale of butter, to a solitary task done in their homes only for their family's personal consumption. The social aspect of their work was largely transferred to men who delivered and sold the whole milk to the creamery and brought back buttermilk or skim milk to feed the livestock. As a result, dairywomen lost the ability to earn and control money from their butter making and, with it, a measure of status for the value of their work.

> "I have a memory from my 1960s childhood of our Dad buttering his toast and indicating with a shake of his head that any family that was reduced to using *margarine* was surely heading for trouble. I think he was nodding ominously toward the neighbor's house."
>
> —SHEILA CHAMBERS

Gradually, the traditional system of selling butter locally at farm markets and to butter agents began to disappear; creamery operators simply sold direct to retailers in towns and cities. The early transition of butter making from the farm to factories changed the very texture of people's lives and relationships, not merely their technology.

Though butter making became centralized at state-of-the-art factories at the turn of the century, it still remained a muscle-driven, hands-on craft. Automation didn't yet exist, but dairy equipment companies began to manufacture larger wooden mechanical rotating churns as well as specialized mechanical butter-working tables. Bigger equipment meant more muscle was needed, and so creamery work became increasingly populated by men. But it was not uncommon at other creameries not yet equipped with large churns to see a virtual battalion of dairymaids, each at their own churning station, vigorously spinning a small box or barrel churn filled with cream, one batch after another.

Refrigeration was another game changer. Now that men were able to bring artifical cold into the dairy and creamery, every step in the chain of butter making was affected. From chilling cream for easier churning and working the butter in a cooler environment, to preserving butter without the heavy-handed use of salt, refrigeration radically altered the butter trade in both production and distribution. Likewise, the development of refrigerated train cars meant that for the first time in history fresh summer butter could be shipped to long distance markets without the risk of it melting into a golden puddle en route.

Canned butter was also a new method of preservation, prompted mostly by the Alaskan gold rush in the late 1800s. Alaskan miners were willing to pay top dollar for good food that could withstand the journey to Alaska's remote artic wilderness. Butter in cans could stay fresh tasting and creamy for several months. (Canned butter continues to be a staple, primarily in military rations as well as for tropical markets around the world.)

AMERICA'S SACRED COW

———

It's a hot summer day in Iowa, but I've got my down jacket on. I'm dressed to accompany Sarah Pratt into her chilly workroom on the Iowa State Fairgrounds. There, over the course of the next week, I'll watch her transform six hundred pounds of butter into a life-size sculpture of a cow.

The Iowa State Fair butter cow is a tradition that dates back to 1911, when John K. Daniel was the first butter artist. The exhibit was created as a way to promote local dairy products, but it was such a hit with fairgoers that the butter cow has became a fixture at every fair since.

We enter the 42°F glass-paneled workroom, where the cow will eventually be on display for the public, and the first thing I notice is the smell: unmistakably of rancid butter. Sarah explains that most of the butter for sculpting is stored and reused every year with only a small portion of new butter blended in. It's a thrifty and conscionable practice, but it sure does stink.

I'm also surprised to find an armature inside the room, built roughly in the shape of a cow, made of wood and chicken wire. On this "skeleton" Pratt begins to smear a thick coarse layer of butter with her hands. (I had thought the cow was sculpted from a solid block of butter, à la *David*.) "The first butter layer has to penetrate the wire by at least an inch," Sarah explains, "so it can support the weight of butter layers on top of it." One year a previous sculptor's cow lost the bottom of her belly; it simply dropped off the wire frame during the fair. She quickly rebuilt it.

Pratt has a detailed photo of a cow pinned on the wall to use as her reference. "I usually sculpt a Jersey," she says. "Their eyes are so expressive."

On day two, the contours of the cow begin to take shape. Pratt presses thick wads of butter onto the first rough layer and then smoothes them. I get to help a little, pasting lumps of butter on to the rump of the cow with my bare hands; it's strangely satisfying.

The next day, Pratt starts to work on what she says is the hardest part of the sculpture: the ribs. We study the photo, discussing how the ribs taper and curve. While sculpting, she periodically ducks out of the cold room and stands in front of the display window, checking how the cow appears from that perspective. "It might look fine inside while I'm working on it, but from three feet below, where people are viewing the cow, the accuracy can be off."

As the week progresses, so does the cow's physique. The udder is added (with intricate veining); the ears are built around two metal rods; the tail is formed using special tools to make it look bushy at the end. Pratt isn't pleased with the head and decides to scale back the chin.

SCULPTING THE ICONIC IOWA STATE FAIR BUTTER COW,
SARAH PRATT APPLIES BUTTER TO AN ARMATURE OF WOOD
AND WIRE. (ELAINE KHOSROVA)

The legs are the last thing to be finished since the butter on them can crack if the armature shakes at all while working on the upper part.

Just days before the fair opens, the cow is complete. In ten days when the fair closes, the butter on the armature will be scraped off and put back into buckets for next year. I ask Pratt how she can stand to undo all her painstaking work. "I really can't," she admits. "I pay my kids or someone else to scrape it off."

At the same time butter was ascending the ranks of factory enterprise on the shoulders of men, so was its doppelganger, margarine. In 1869, as the price of butter soared in France, Napoleon III offered a cash prize to anyone who could create a cheap, plentiful butter substitute for the poorer classes and his military. (Napoleon was anticipating a war with Prussia.) A chemist, Hippolyte Mège-Mouriès, observed that since even starving cows produced butterfat in their milk, the fat must be coming from their own tissue. He reasoned that he could duplicate this corporeal milk fat by rendering oil from caul fat of beef (known as oleo). Mixing the animal oil with milk and salt, Mège-Mouriès formed a spreadable compound that approximated the character of butter. He named it "oleomargarine" (margaric acid being the name, at the time, of the chief fatty acid in the mixture). The chemist won Napoleon's prize, but he had little success in selling his ersatz butter in France. (Peace prevailed, dashing his hopes for butter shortages.) He sold his U.S. patent to the conglomerate U.S. Dairy Company. (Ironically, many big margarine producers also made butter.)

The company introduced margarine—colored yellow with annatto seeds—to the American public, and soon after entrepreneurs were keen to invest in margarine factories. By 1882, twenty million pounds of the beef fat-based spread was produced annually in New York State alone. (This original animal-derived margarine, by the way, was nothing like today's version of the stuff, which is made with hardened vegetable oils.) The threat to butter producers was immediately apparent. When colored, margarine was a close match for the average tub of butter, yet it could be produced at a fraction of the cost. Moreover, it was commonly mixed with butter itself to become "butterine," an even better-tasting cheap impostor. Consumers were increasingly won over to the substitute, especially poorer individuals and families who preferred it to the low-grade rancid (and often filthy) butter that was previously all they could afford.

In 1882, the vice president of the New York State Dairy Association, L. B. Arnold, testified to the U.S. House Ways and Means Committee that the availability of margarine had prompted creameries to improve their butter quality in order to stay competitive in the market. But, he warned, the makers of lesser butter—typically small farms—were being pushed out of the domestic and foreign marketplace by margarine products parading as butter. How long before even higher-grade industrial butter producers would feel the pinch of margarine's masked insurgency in the market?

According to Geoffrey Miller's study of margarine politics, "Public Choice at the Dawn of the Special Interest State," the dairy industry in New York and Maryland rallied its political might to drive the passage of a law in their states that required oleomargarine to "be marketed, branded, and stamped as such, under penalty of $100 and imprisonment for 30 days." So began a ninety-year battle of butter versus margarine, much of it fought on the grounds of state and federal legislative halls around the country.

The dairy industry upped its offensive, launching a stealth mission to destroy the margarine market by waging a slanderous disinformation campaign to scare consumers off the stuff.

IN THE LATE NINETEENTH CENTURY, THE MARGARINE VERSUS
BUTTER BATTLE WAS A COMMON THEME IN POLITICAL CARTOONS.
(LIBRARY OF CONGRESS DUPLICATION SERVICES)

It painted a lurid picture of margarine as a bogus butter made
from the "slag of the butchershop."

In 1884, a committee of dairy farmers in New York drove
the next major attack by petitioning the state assembly to
ban margarine outright. The new law, the first in the world
to criminalize margarine, stated that "no person shall manufacture . . . any article designed to take the place of butter."
State after state banned the product, but the New York law
was struck down as unconstitutional just six weeks after its
enactment. Appeals in other states won too, but the damage

had been done. By 1885, two-thirds of all margarine producers in the seven dairy states had gone out of business. Still, a year later the Federal Margarine Act mandated a two-cent tax on margarine and annual license fees for its production and sale. Margarine makers were forced to pay $600 a year; wholesalers, $480; and even retailers had to shell out $48 (the equivalent of almost $1,200 today) simply for the right to sell margarine. More restrictions followed: Less than ten years later, the Supreme Court ruled that states could ban colored margarine but not brands sold in their natural white condition.

By the turn of the century, thirty states had adopted the color prohibition. Some legislatures even demanded that margarine be dyed a different color altogether, such as red or black; five states passed laws requiring margarine be dyed pink! The color wars constituted an attack on the poor as well the oleo producers, for its effect was to stigmatize margarine and its users who couldn't afford real butter. Many low-income people resorted to buying so-called renovated butter—which some likened to axle grease. Also known as processed or packing-stock butter, it was made by recycling bad butter, the rancid and/or dirty stuff that was shoddily made and poorly stored. Production of renovated butter was not insignificant: In 1905, the United States produced more than sixty million pounds of the stuff. Apparently much of it was sold to England around the turn of the century, which earned all American butter a bad reputation and caused the English to seek out Canadian butter imports.

Makers of renovated butter claimed that their processing purified the butterfat and that there was nothing to taint the end product. And for most of the time that they operated (until the early 1940s), the renovators got away with that deception. The government, after all, was more concerned with disabling margarine makers than cracking down on butter sanitation. But in one notable case in the early 1900s, the New Orleans office of the Food and Drug Administration (FDA) called on a chemist to test a shipment of some of very foul packing-stock butter they had seized. The chemist was able to demonstrate that because there had been maggots in the cream that was churned, the maggot fat combined with the butterfat. Alas, the renovation process couldn't remove maggot fat.

The Europeans also defended their butter turf against the margarine insurgency with legislative weapons. Denmark was the first country on the Continent to pass margarine legislation in 1888 that forced the display of "warning" signs in shops selling margarine, outlawed the mixing of margarine with more than 50 percent butterfat, and added a ban on yellow food coloring in margarine. Without its mask of yellow, Danish margarine couldn't compete as a lucrative export to England. Great Britain and France limited the amount of butter that could be mixed with oleomargarine to 10 percent, whereas Germany and Austria forbid the direct mixing of butter and oleomargarine and required that all margarine be "earmarked" by mixing in 10 percent sesame oil. Denmark also required sesame oil in the production. Belgium went a step further, mandating its margarine producers add sesame oil and 2 percent dry potato starch to their recipe. There was no mistaking it for butter.

Still, all the statutory finagling in the world didn't protect

European butter makers as much as another simple tactic: increasing butter quality. Margarine and butterine were better tasting than low-grade butters, and much lower in price, so there was little question which one the budget customer would buy. If they couldn't beat margarine on price, then the only option was to win customers with flavor. Denmark's producers took this tack, abandoning the poorer markets to margarine and shifting to premium butter production.

"As for butter versus margarine, I trust cows more than chemists."

—JOAN GUSSOW

Margarine's threat had, in effect, greased the wheels of change in Denmark. In 1882, the Agricultural Research Laboratory was established in Denmark; within a decade, its forward-thinking researchers introduced pasteurization—a heat treatment for milk—to dairy farms as means of preventing butter rancidity. It was widely recognized that pasteurization was a trade-off: Killing the natural microorganisms with heat also resulted in a milder-tasting butter. But the market didn't seem to mind.

AS OFTEN HAPPENS WHEN new technology shakes up an industry, the butter businessmen who didn't adapt to these early twentieth-century dairy innovations were soon left in the proverbial dust. For more than a century, Cork's Butter Exchange held on to its position as the lead butter exporter to overseas markets. But by the late 1800s, changing tastes in butter (fresher, less salty) combined with greater competition from local producers in other countries; new winter butter sources in the Southern Hemisphere; the increasing availability of refrigeration and canning; and the advent of higher-quality butter from creameries; all had the effect of crippling Ireland's handmade farmstead butter export market.

The classic Irish firkin of salted butter lost much ground to clever Dutch and Danish entrepreneurs who had invented another system for improving quality and consistency: They purchased blocks of butter in bulk from farmers several times a week and mixed them all together to make a consistent product with uniform color, texture, and taste.

In addition, the Danish had also ingeniously perfected year-round dairying operations, in sharp contrast to the seasonal output in Ireland. Being able to supply fresh winter butter to the lucrative markets in Britain and Europe not only gave the Danish a greater profit on their product, but retailers came to rely on Danish butter and habitually stocked it. By contrast, Irish butter suffered marginal profits since it was only sold during the spring and summer months when prices were lowest. Adding insult to injury, the Irish producers often lost their position with grocers during the winter months and were forced to bribe their way back into the market each spring by offering a further discount.

In 1924, the Cork Butter Exchange closed its doors forever. In many ways, the end of Cork's butter reign symbolized the end of an era in peasant butter making, one that had existed for thousands of years.

At the same time, the technical revolution in creamery butter making continued. One of the reasons I wanted to visit Grassland Dairy—instead of say Land O'Lakes industrial creamery, which also churns out sweet butter by the ton continuously—was because its history as a family-owned company mirrors the pace of industry change in the twentieth century. Grassland's founder, John S. Wuethrich, who started the business in 1904, was the son of Swiss immigrants from the Alps who learned to make cheese and butter the old-fashioned way, with a paddle churn. Wuethrich's first churn at his Wisconsin creamery was a cedar barrel churn that rotated by a pulley system, fueled by a steam engine. When the churn was activated it tumbled the cream, like the motion of a clothes dryer, for about forty to sixty minutes. About 250 pounds of butter were churned at a time, from cream that Wuethrich himself collected each day from about twenty-five local farms.

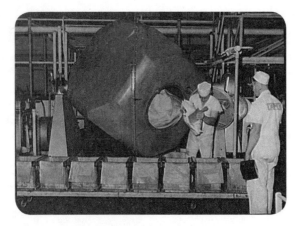

EMPTYING A GIANT MECHANICAL CHURN AT A LARGE CREAMERY
IN 1941. (LIBRARY OF CONGRESS DUPLICATION SERVICES)

After draining, rinsing, and working the butter, it was hand-packed into fifty-pound wooden tubs and shipped to markets in Chicago.

The company continued to use the steam-powered churn until 1930, when a new electric-powered cedar barrel churn was installed. State-of-the-art at the time, it was much larger and had baffles on the inside to provide more agitation to the cream and hasten the churning time.

The fact that Wuethrich was able to expand production at the onset of the Great Depression speaks to his shrewd business acumen. But it helped that in 1931 the federal government gave butter makers another boost in the butter versus margarine legislative battle. A new amendment to the Federal Margarine Act of 1886 was passed, closing the tax loophole for naturally yellow margarine. All yellow margarines were now subject to tax. The industry struck back defiantly—and creatively. Since there was no law against adding yellow food coloring to margarine at home, makers included little packets of yellow coloring with their margarine. Again, the consumer paid the price ultimately, this time with the inconvenience of having to mix the margarine and messy dye in a bowl by hand. This took time and effort and it wasn't unusual for the final product served to be either variegated or striped yellow and white. No doubt many a homemaker asked herself, "Why can't they just color the margarine yellow at the factory?"

Ironically after decades of fierce legislative wrangling to protect butter from margarine competition, the U.S. government ultimately paved the way for margarine's popularity by enlisting in World War II. Although the cheaper-priced oleo had already started to chase out butter a decade earlier with the economic hardships of the Great Depression, the advent of the war gave margarine a mighty retail boost.

Creamery butter became a rare commodity during the war in part because farm labor was scarce as brothers and sons went to the battlefront. But also, whatever butter was produced in the creameries was often diverted toward military needs. As the shortage deepened, butter and other fats were added to the list of war-rationed foods. By 1942, every American, including children, was issued a six-month book of ration stamps that totaled forty-eight points for each month. Ration points were assigned to various foods depending on how scarce they were. In June 1943, for example, three-quarters of a pound of butter cost six points, whereas a full pound of oleomargarine was only five points. Many households switched to oleo for its economy and longer shelf life. Although lard and cooking oils were removed from rationing in the spring of 1944, butter and margarine continued to be rationed until late in 1945.

Still, many wartime families preferred the taste of butter and quickly learned how to make the most of every allotment. One of the more ingenious tricks for extending butter during the war involved unflavored gelatin and milk. Knox Gelatine spread promised to "stretch your butter twice as far," according to the original recipe pamphlet distributed to homemakers. The technique was fairly simple for the homemaker. First she dissolved gelatin in water and combined it with milk and salt (and coloring, if desired). This mixture was whisked into very soft butter until well blended and then refrigerated until firm. The Knox spread looked a lot like margarine—shiny and smooth, but the taste was distinctly buttery (albeit with a slightly odd mouthfeel). Using the proportions given in the recipe, it did indeed turn one stick of butter into two, but with a caveat: This spread was for table use, not for cooking. Baking with it was a little iffy too, depending on the recipe.

Wartime may have crippled sales of butter and liberated margarine from regulation, but in its aftermath World War II led to a boom in churn technology as companies that had manufactured munitions switched to producing industrial equipment. Giant stainless-steel models were also fabricated postwar, many of which are still in use. When I visited Organic Valley's butter-making plant in Chaseburg, Wisconsin, an enormous steel barrel churn—about the size of a one-car garage—was being refilled with cream every hour and a half to churn out thirty thousand pounds of butter each day. Barrels this big require some physical adaptations, as I saw when the butter was ready to be removed. Instead of reaching inside and scooping the butter by hand as an operator would do with a smaller churn, the creamery staff steers a long stainless-steel "boat" (like a deep trough on wheels) into the round mouth of the churn and then slowly rotates the barrel so the one-ton mass of butter is moved to the top, whereupon it drops into the boat. It fell like an avalanche of butter.

By the late 1940s, the newly minted butyrator (continuous churn) came on the scene. Named like a superhero (from the Latin *butyrum* for "butter"), the title was altogether apt to dairy industrialists who could then employ these titanic churns to produce more than a ton of butter every hour. It has been a radical game changer in the industry. With each new decade,

MODERN COMPUTER-OPERATED CHURNS, SUCH AS THIS
IVARSON MODEL, CAN PRODUCE UP TO TWENTY-TWO THOUSAND
POUNDS OF BUTTER PER HOUR. (IVARSON INC.)

butyrator capacity has kept climbing; today, computer-
operated models can churn twenty-two thousand pounds of
butter per hour. (That's about six pounds per second.)

High-speed production makes butter quicker and cheaper,
but it doesn't necessarily make it better. One of the most
surprising discoveries I made on the trail of modern butter
making was that success actually has more to do with what
happens before and after churning. Agitating cream is the
easy part. As I learned at Grassland and other large creameries I toured, a good butter maker knows his job starts well
before he flips the switch.

. . . .

SEVEN

Molecular Butter

THE PHYSICS
OF MAKING FLAVOR

. . . .

One of the vivid memories of my Alsatian childhood
was going with my grandmother to her butterman in
the highland, tasting his butter, listening to their con-
versation about the minutiae of weather that went into
this particular summer's butter, just as, down on the
other side of the mountain, my vintner cousins were
talking about the weather affected this year's wine.

—MADO SPEIGLER,
personal communication, 2014

DR. BOB BRADLEY HAD JUST TASTED ONE OF THE
butters I brought him; he wasn't pleased. "First thing
you get is a slug of salt," he said, "and then there's some oxidation. It's a little cardboardy too." He turned his lanky frame
toward to his colleague, Marianne Sumkowski, waiting for her
reaction to the butter; she nodded in agreement.

The three of us were at the Center for Dairy Research
(CDR) at the University of Wisconsin–Madison where Bradley,
professor emeritus of food science at the university, is the

resident butter scholar, with more than fifty years experience in its researching manufacture.

It seemed every professional I queried on butter making directed me to Bradley, the Wisconsin oracle and author of the trade manual *Better Butter*. Bradley is also a highly trained butter grader and technical judge. He has the wherewithal to detect twenty different flavor defects in a sample of butter, as well as nine texture defects, three more for color and appearance, and two salt-related defects. (Who knew so much could potentially plague a simple stick of butter?) He agreed to show me how he judges butter—providing I brought the butter and he brought Sumkowski (another technical tasting pro and the dairy safety and quality coordinator at CDR).

Bradley and Sumkowski moved from one sample to the next, extracting a plug of butter from each. All the butters on the table were at a cool temperature, about 55°F; the coolness is essential to get a good deep bore and to accurately assess. The technique is simple: The trier is inserted, turned halfway like a key in a lock, and then pulled out. The long plug that's extracted—like a thick pinky of butter—is then put to a multisensory test.

Of the total points on a judging score card for a butter sample, its visible body and texture (as opposed to mouthfeel) are generally half as critical as the flavor. Graders give high marks for spreadability at a cool temperature. One simple texture defect is excess moisture, or "leakiness." Bradley explained that properly working the butter eliminates this defect, though butter that's been frozen and then thawed is nearly always leaky. Butter body is also downgraded if it's greasy, crumbly, or too weak in structure to allow a solid plug to be extracted. A "short" butter will often show cracks or separation, which is different from the defect of "ragged" butter.

On the palate, the texture of a fine butter should be somewhat waxy and cohesive, whereas a greasy butter will be slippery and oily. Butter should be relatively slow to dissolve so that you can fully taste all the flavorful compounds in butter that are released as it melts on the tongue. Salted butters are generally downgraded if they have any grittiness, although the presence of crunchy sea salt crystals—a longstanding tradition in Brittany—is now a popular variation among artisan butter makers.

The natural color of butter depends on the amount of green feed—silage, grass, or alfalfa—in the animal's diet. More green translates into deeper yellow butter owing to the beta-carotene in the plants. The later into the summer growing season, however, the more mature and tough the grass usually is, which is harder for the cow to break down digestively. As a result, less of the beta-carotene becomes bioavailable than it is with tender springtime green grass, which is why spring grass-fed butter often shows the most vibrant golden hue. (Some breeds of cow also mobilize more beta-carotene from their tissue, resulting in more golden butter.)

It's a little known fact that U.S. dairy manufacturers are allowed by law to add a flavorless natural coloring agent, such as annatto, to their butter without having to declare it on the label, whereas all other foods have to reveal coloring agents on the label. This special dispensation harks back to those last-century battles with margarine. So a deep yellow golden color in butter is no guarantee that it came from the milk of happy pastured cows.

Old dairy trade magazines catering to farmers and creameries were once filled with ads for yellow butter coloring, typically made from vegetable oil and crushed annatto seeds. The hues were sometimes so intense that the churnings looked more cheesy than buttery. Most manufacturers today do not adjust the color of their butter; paleness has become quite acceptable, if not the norm. But that could change as golden grass-fed butter grows in popularity.

Before tasting each sample, Bradley sniffed it for any telltale off odors. Ideally, butter should have a milky fresh scent with a hint of sweetness and diacetyl—the main compound that accounts for "butteriness." Cultured butters may also have a whiff of pleasant acidity, similar to crème fraîche. Some off odors, such as an oniony or garlicky scent, can transfer from the animal's feed if they've been grazing on wild chives or ramps. Poor storage near anything smelly will also spoil a butter's aroma, as will prolonged storage; eventually the butter will go rancid, causing it to smell sour and musty, like an old sneaker.

When I asked Bradley about the trace of "cardboardiness" he detected in one sample, he explains that oxidation is the culprit. "When oxygen links up with the unsaturated fatty acids in butter, the result is aldehydes, [which can] yield an odor like cardboard."

Bradley and Sumkowski shifted from eyeballing each sample to tasting them. "You swish it around your mouth and look for points of perception," Bradley explained. "Sweet and salty on the tip of the tongue, acid on the sides, and bitter way back. And then you've got this olfactory system in the back of your nose, so you try to get the aroma of the butter, as it warms on your tongue, back up in there to detect any defects."

In unsalted butter making, it is common to add lactic acid—considered a natural flavoring—which also works in place of salt as preservative by lowering the pH of the butter. Whether it's stirred in as an additive or the result of natural culturing, lactic acid can be a great flavor enhancer if present in the right proportion. Tasters are looking for that balance relative to the style of butter.

Diacetyl also needs to be just right; too much of this good thing actually makes butter taste coarse and acrid. Diacetyl naturally occurs in butter as a result of ripening or fermentation, but some manufacturers boost flavor by adding extra diacetyl in a sort of cocktail mixed with lactic acid. (On the ingredient label, added diacetyl can simply be listed as "natural flavoring" because it's the result of the fermentation of milk or whey and therefore not from an artificial process.) To the untrained palate, a diacetyl-enhanced butter is hard to recognize—it'll just seem exceptionally buttery. But professional tasters can often spot it because it has a slightly concentrated flavor and lingering aftertaste.

Rancidity is a flavor defect as well as an aromatic one. Bradley explained that when my sweet fresh-tasting butter turns into a spread smelling faintly of baby vomit, it's because lipase—an enzyme in dairy products that thrives at room temperature—has split the short chain fatty acids in butter. Their cleaving causes the formation of butyric acid, which has a rank flavor and odor that gets increasingly stronger over time.

Some flavor characteristics that would have downgraded butter a generation ago are now considered interesting, if not tasty. "Whey" flavor, for example, is a mild cheesiness found in certain butters made from the leftover fat in whey, a by-product of cheese making. Many people, including myself, like this bit of sharpness; in fact, we're willing to pay extra for whey cream butter. Likewise, a slight grassy, herbal note is now hailed as a commendable trait by butter aficionados who want complexity, rather than a simple clean creamy taste. (Still, industrial butter makers regularly "steam-strip" cream to reduce the presence of "pastoral flavors.")

BECAUSE IT IS EQUALLY delicate, perishable, and highly reactive, milk fat is a complicated mistress. Given all that can potentially go wrong with butter flavor and texture, it seems a wonder that most of our butter these days is very good quality, if not exceptional. Modern refrigeration and sanitation have a lot to do with that. But being able to craft a really fine textured and full-flavored butter (as compared to the nice but rustic, plain DIY version) also depends on key steps that happen before and after churning. Because it is equally delicate, perishable, and highly reactive, milk fat is a complicated mistress.

The best butter begins with quality cream. For sweet butter, it should be very fresh, with low acidity (a pH of 6.6 or higher), with no off odors or tastes. Better yet if it comes from the milk of cows fed on a mixture of good grasses.

BEFORE MODERN MICROBIAL TESTING, BUTTER MAKERS
WOULD ROUTINELY SNIFF FRESH CREAM TO CHECK FOR DEFECTS.
(LIBRARY OF CONGRESS DUPLICATION SERVICES)

(Flavorwise, the source of animal feed is potentially more significant for sweet butter since that style is such a clean slate for
subtle tastes; cultured butter, however, often has other things
going on with acidity and developed lactone flavors such that
the nuances of an animal's diet can be more masked.)

After the cream is sourced, next comes a sequence of
crucial steps that are key to optimizing the texture of butter.
Texture is critical to every butter experience, but managing
the texture of butter is tricky business because of the unstable
nature of cream. I used to wonder why some brands of butter
had an exquisite density—almost a velvety chewiness—and
smooth spreadability that I could never come close to achieving in my own kitchen butter making. Now I know the reason.
Smooth-textured butter is the result of manipulating the structure and ratio of fat molecules in cream, which are either hard

and crystalline or soft and fluid. By warming and cooling the cream—a process known as physical ripening or tempering—the consistency of its fats can be remodeled to create a more spreadable butter.

Naturally hard milk fat, which is typical from cows on winter feed, has a lot of crystalline saturated fat and short-chain fatty acids; it will yield a rock-solid, stiff butter if not tempered. On the other hand, cream high in soft, unsaturated fat will result in loose, greasy butter. This is often the case with milk fat in summertime if cows are feeding on fresh grass.

Tempering begins after the cream is pasteurized at a high temperature (a legal requirement in most countries). If the butter maker has winter cream, physical ripening generally involves a cold/warm/cold sequence of temperatures over the course of twelve or more hours. With soft milk fat, the tempering follows a warm/cold/less cold sequence. Overall, the aim is to have 40 to 45 percent of the milk fat crystallize so there's some rigidity in the butter, but not so much that it's a brittle product. The magic of good tempering is that it also causes the liquid portion in the center of each fat globule to migrate to the outside surface, where it helps the fats to adhere to each other during churning. The result is more cohesive butter.

Many smaller butter producers operate without the equipment necessary to perform these fine calibrations. But in these small plants, the cream is still ripened for many hours (often twelve hours or overnight) at a single temperature that's adjusted seasonally for the softness or hardness of the milk fat. It's less exact, but it does measurably improve butter texture and the amount of fat lost in the buttermilk.

While physical ripening is done for all butters, making a traditional cultured butter also requires a simultaneous "biochemical ripening" to develop its tangier, more complex flavor. A double whammy of cream intervention. For the biochemical process, the maker adds a cocktail of lactic-acid-producing bacteria to the cream and allows it to gradually, precisely ferment during part of the tempering process.

Given the long artful tradition of culturing cream for butter making, I was surprised to learn that many so-called cultured butters on the market today are not the result of skillful, slow ripening with lactic bacteria. Instead, they are simply sweet butters that have been injected, after churning, with natural flavor compounds, such as diacetyl and lactic acid distillations, to give the taste of cultured butter without the inconvenience of making it. Known as the NIZO method (for the Netherlands Institute for Dairy Research, where it originated), it was developed in the late 1970s when the industry was struggling with the oversupply of naturally acidic buttermilk generated as a by-product of real cultured butter making. Using the NIZO method, this problem was solved; watery skim cream (oxymoronic but correct) discharges from the churn instead of acidic buttermilk, since the acid flavorings are added to the butter after churning and draining. Using NIZO, creameries could also process milk rapidly since there was no need to inoculate the cream and allow it to ferment for twelve to twenty-four hours. And neither did they need to carefully monitor the microbial action during fermentation.

Such instant-cultured butters can be hard to distinguish from the real thing, especially for an untrained taster. In fact, not even in professional and competition butter tastings are these categories of cultured butter differentiated, despite the fact that one is merely flavored while the other is fully fermented. Neither does their packaging tell them apart. Both list "lactic acid cultures" in their ingredients, but there's no telling if these were added before or after churning. Some American artisan producers are taking aim at this obfuscation by labeling their slow-ripened butter as "vat-cultured" or "naturally cultured." Otherwise, the only other way to know which type you're buying is to do a little brand research (or consult Appendix A at the end of this book).

BETTER BUTTER APPELLATIONS

In the eurozone, select butters wear a premium badge on their label that certifies they're produced according to longstanding traditions. In France, for instance, a seal of AOC (appellation d'origine contrôlée) on a package of butter guarantees its old-world pedigree. Beurre de Charente-Poitou from southwestern France has an AOC certification that specifies it can only be made in the regions of Charente, Vendée, or Vienne, and the cream for the butter must be ripened for fifteen hours using a specific starter culture; no coloring agents or preservatives are allowed.

In the Isigny-sur-Mer region of Normandy, located between the seawater of the English Channel and the

VINTAGE BUTTER PACKAGING
FROM THE RENOWNED FRENCH DAIRY
REGION OF ISIGNY.

fresh water of the Bessin and Cotentin marshes, pasture grows on soil rich with clay and silt. The milk cows produce from this grass has a particular minerality and high butterfat, which give AOC Isigny butter a unique flavor and color. The AOC Beurre des Deux-Sevres can only be awarded to butters made from the milk of cows grazing within nineteen miles of Échiré, a village on the Atlantic coast of France. Generally known as Beurre d'Échiré, it is made in traditional teakwood churns rather than modern stainless steel, and the butter has a generous 84 percent butterfat (most eurozone butters are 82 percent). Its texture is dense and velvety like a chocolate truffle.

Beurre de Bresse, made on the far eastern side of France, is the most recent butter to be awarded the AOC designation. Made in a traditional batch churn, butter from Bresse is noted for its soft texture and nutty, herbaceous flavor.

The French AOC certification now operates alongside the European Union's similar PDO certification scheme. Beurre Rose from Luxembourg has earned the PDO title, as has Beurre d'Ardenne, made in Belgium, which was relatively late to develop a butter-making culture (locals generally spread lard on their bread up until the early 1900s). The famous sweet Mantequilla de Soria made in north-central Spain is an unusual PDO butter, one that looks like a box of frosted cake at first glance. Made only from the milk of specific breeds of cow that graze on high-altitude pastures, the butter is sweetened with sugar syrup and gently worked for one to two hours until its soft texture allows it to be pressed through nozzles that swirl the butter into shallow boxes. Also from Spain is the PDO Mantega de l'Alt Urgell la Cerdanya, made in the Spanish Pyrenees; its celebrated taste comes from the diet of high-meadow pasture the cows eat, as well as a two-day-long fermentation process before churning.

FOR MANY AMATEUR BUTTER makers and do-it-
yourselfers, the moment when cream suddenly yields butter
is often pretty amazing, even a little magical, not unlike put-
ting a runny batter in the oven and having a dense cake come
out thirty minutes later. But we know, of course, that both
transformations happen for good scientific reason, not by any
impenetrable process.

In the case of cream becoming butter, the switch occurs
because of the construction of milk-fat globules, those crystalline and liquid fats, which are encased in a thin membrane.
This delicate outer shell is what keeps the globules dispersed
in the watery portion of cream, or what scientists call a fat-
in-water emulsion. The purpose of churning is to create the
opposite kind of emulsion—water in fat—which is essentially
how we define butter, biochemically speaking. (As my editor cleverly interpreted this, churning is like "turning cream
inside out.")

When we agitate cream through whipping or concussing
inside a churn, we start to create a "foam" (aka whipped
cream) as the mechanical action introduces lots of air bubbles
that attract the fat globules. (This is why churns are only half
filled; air is essential to the process.) Because of their molecu-
lar affinities, the fats will cluster around the surface of every
air bubble. As we beat more air into the foam, more physical
pressure is put on fat globules, particularly their thin outer
membranes. As they're squeezed, needlelike crystalline fats
penetrate the membrane and cause it to rupture. At the same
time, the ruptured fat globules are tumbling against the baffles and walls of the churn, which causes some of the internal

liquid fats to leak through the membrane. This viscous fat acts like sticky glue, making the fat globules adhere to one another rather than remain dispersed. (This is why a ratio of crystalline and liquid fats is a big deal; one type breaks the membranes, while the other causes the fats to cling together.) At this stage, the butter has "come." The cream has separated into floating butter grains and buttermilk. With more rapid churning, the fats coalesce and the butter particles become about the size of popcorn kernels. Now the churn is stopped and the buttermilk, which represents about 60 percent of the volume in the churn, is drained through a fine sieve.

At a commercial creamery, after the churn is drained, the butter maker takes a few samples of the butter, blends them together, and then analyzes the portion for moisture. By U.S. law, butter has to be at least 80 percent fat; the remaining 20 percent is mostly water with a small fraction (1 percent) of milk solids, which include protein, lactose, and minerals. Water may be mixed in to adjust the ratio of fat. If the butter is to be a salted kind, it is added at this point. The churn is then switched on again, at a lower speed, in order to work the butter into uniform mass.

The finished butter is then wheeled or piped to a station where shaping and packaging happen. Generally this step is automated in commercial operations, but in many artisan butter plants it is still done by hand. Plain parchment paper is the oldest butter wrapper and still very common today, but it is the least effective in protecting butter from odors and oxidation. "You can see the effect of porous packaging by scraping the butter surface with a knife after unwrapping," Bradley noted. "It the butter is lighter yellow below the surface, then moisture has been lost through the parchment cover. Oxidation and off flavors from storage may have developed." Paper wrap that has been laminated with a thin layer of wax or plastic is better, but the best covering is paper laminated with foil. It seals the butter effectively.

ALTHOUGH BUTTER IS MOSTLY a fine matrix of fatty acids and water, there are invisible organic agents embedded in these substances that also exert a profound effect on flavor. Lactones existing in tiny concentrations in butter, impart the characteristic sweet flavors we look for in its taste. When butter is heated, lactone precursors convert to lactones and create an even deeper flavor (which is one reason why butter melted on foods is instantly tastier than if it is eaten in solid form and allowed to slowly dissolve on the tongue). Methyl ketones also develop with heat and act synergistically with lactones to create the rich dairy savoriness unique to buttery foods. Methyl ketones and lactones commingle with the so-called Maillard reactions in baking (the toasty browning of sugars and proteins). Altogether, these volatile compounds are what make buttery pastries and baked goods so irresistible.

Diacetyl is the quintessential buttery-nutty flavor maker that's naturally present in all butters, but its concentration increases with fermentation—as when cream is cultured for butter making. However, diacetyl isn't very stable in cultured products; the longer these products are stored, the more the diacetyl is decomposed. Yet another reason to eat your butter fresh.

Dimethyl sulfide originally comes from the feed of cows. It helps to smooth the flavor edges of diacetyl and other acidic substances in butter that can be sometimes harsh or overpowering.

Aldehydes are a family of compounds that have a love-hate relationship with butter flavor. At low concentrations, they lend a creamy seductive note to its taste, but at high concentrations—caused by too much oxidation (as when a butter ages or is poorly stored)—they can impart off flavors.

By now it should be clear that when you deconstruct butter and its production, you venture into some pretty complex, if not wondrous, territory. As scientist Harold McGee, a renowned authority on food chemistry, noted in *On Food and Cooking*: "The coming of butter is an everyday miracle." Even more so if it's superb butter. Like the one and only sample that brought a smile to Bradley's face as we ended our tasting. "It's lightly salted, cultured, with a little grassy note," he said. "That's as nice a piece of butter as I've had in a while."

EIGHT

. . . .

Role Reversal

THE GOOD DIET,
WITH FAT

. . . .

The danger of simplifying a medical issue for public
consumption is that we may come to believe that our
oversimplification is an appropriate representation of
the biological reality . . . In the case of diet and heart
disease . . . every one of the complications that arose
has implicated carbohydrates rather than fat as the
dietary agent of heart disease.

—GARY TAUBES, *Good
Calories, Bad Calories, 2007*

FOR DECADES JULIA CHILD SERVED AS BUTTER'S BEST
promoter, urging us to whisk, slather, spoon, and spread
it to our healthy heart's content. Julia is gone now, but she
a butter-touting successor in Sally Fallon Morell, president
of the Weston A. Price Foundation (WAPF). At a sold-out
conference on traditional diets held in Maryland in 2015, I sat
in the crowd listening to Morell rally for the return of butter
and other natural saturated fats in our meals. With a Power-
Point of charts, photos, and reports, she also warned us of the

perils of consuming industrial vegetable oils and their highly touted polyunsaturates. After making her impassioned case for pasture-raised animal fats, Morell finished with a tip for avoiding the oily pitfalls of food service fare: "When eating out, order simple foods—and put butter on everything." The crowd laughed. But Morell wasn't kidding.

> "I always give my bird a generous butter massage before I put it in the oven."
>
> —JULIA CHILD

For more than fifteen years, Morell has been president and spokesperson for WAPF, a Washington, D.C.–based nonprofit funded by its members and "dedicated to restoring nutrient-dense whole foods to the American diet," according to its website. Its mission is founded on the 1930s research of Weston A. Price, a nutrition pioneer who traveled the world to compare the eating habits of healthy isolated peoples in nonindustrialized regions to those of their degenerating countrymen in more developed areas. The primitive diets of these robust communities—ranging from remote enclaves of Swiss and Scottish to Eskimos and Africans—differed radically from each other, but they had some basic factors in common. A liberal intake of animal proteins and fat characterized the whole lot, as did the absence of refined or processed ingredients. Plant-based foods in their natural or fermented state were another commonality, as were raw dairy products.

Based on Price's comparisons and many subsequent (if

marginalized) studies on the effects of Western refined and high-carb diets, WAPF has long been urging Americans to reject refined grains and sugar, avoid those unnatural poly-unsaturated seed oils, and return to traditional nose-to-tail pastured animal products, including organ meats, eggs, raw milk, and butter.

These days WAPF's position on animal fats is hardly considered radical, what with the revival of artisan dairy and meats as well as the recent absolution of eggs in our diet by the FDA. Now we know about the dangers of trans fats in hydro-genated products and of the growing tide of scientific critiques against government-prescribed low-fat, high-carb diets. Re-discovering natural animal fats in our cooking is no longer a far-fetched idea. But back in 1999, when Morell launched the foundation, most people in the mainstream considered her diet advice—published in a hefty cookbook called *Nourishing Traditions*—pure quackery if not irresponsible propaganda. Public health and nutrition experts were vehemently anti–animal fat and -cholesterol at the time (and would continue to be so until very recently), owing to the prevailing belief that animal fats were the culprit for skyrocketing rates of heart disease in America.

Back in the early 1980s, I was a fresh college graduate with a degree in dietetics, trained by the experts to join in the anti-fat battle. Our tactic seemed logical: Don't eat fat and you won't get fat; avoid cholesterol and you prevent its deposit in the arteries.

If only it were that simple. More than thirty years later, heart disease is still the number one killer and Americans are fatter than they've ever been, despite the fact that they're eating 10 percent less fat in their meals, as advised by the U.S. Department of Agriculture (USDA). Even the fact that one in every four Americans over the age of forty-five gulps down statins (cholesterol-lowering drugs) every day, hasn't helped rid us of heart disease. Americans also buy a plethora of reengineered lean, low-fat, and fat-free foods in order to trim fat, cholesterol, and calories from their diets. Yet obesity and its twin condition, diabetes, have reached epidemic proportions. Cardiac bypasses and stents have become routine treatments as the implacable (pardon the pun) scourge of heart disease continues.

How can this be? Why isn't the ban on butter and other fats making us healthier? Those are long overdue questions if you ask Dr. Fred Kummerow, who has been studying the relationship of dietary fat to heart disease since 1957. His interest began as a young researcher at the University of Illinois in the mid-1900s, when he persuaded a local hospital to give him autopsy materials from twenty-four patients, several of whom had died from heart disease. Kummerow was surprised to discover that artificial trans fat—a man-made fat found in hydrogenated oils and margarine—had accumulated in tissues all over the body, including in the arteries and especially near the heart.

Kummerow followed up with many studies and became a trailblazer in the research of dietary trans fat. Alarmed at what he was finding, he lobbied the American Heart Association (AHA) in the late 1960s to include warnings about hydrogenated fats in their next set of guidelines. The stakes were potentially high since by this point in time margarine sales had surpassed butter sales. And margarine had replaced butter in all kinds of processed foods and commercial baked goods; there were lots of trans fats circulating in the American diet.

Despite originally agreeing with Kummerow and his warnings, the AHA did an about-face, apparently bowing to pressure from the edible-oil industry to avoid any worrisome reports on trans fats. Although the first printing of brochures for the AHA's 1968 dietary guidelines contained facts about hydrogenated oil, those were destroyed and a new version was released; it made no mention hydrogenated fats. Butter took the bad rap.

More than three decades would pass before findings from Kummerow and other trans-fat researchers were widely accepted in the heart-health community. But it would take another twenty years for health policy to actually change because of it: In 2013 the FDA finally announced that partially hydrogenated oils are not "generally recognized as safe" for use in food and that eating trans fat raises blood levels of LDL (low-density lipoprotein), the so-called bad cholesterol, increasing the risk of coronary heart disease. All those tubs of margarine the public had consumed instead of butter to prevent cardiac disease actually had the exact opposite effect: Margarine increased the likelihood of a heart attack.

Not surprisingly, the numbers of cardiac patients and incidents kept rising throughout the 1970s, '80s, and '90s. Of course, there were other contributing factors too—like smoking, obesity, high blood pressure, inactivity, genetics, and stress—but no one suspected margarine. Except Kummerow and his like-minded colleagues, whose dissenting voices could barely be heard above the increasing din over the supposed perpetrator of heart disease: animal fats.

The indictment of animal fat and its dietary sidekick, cholesterol, began in the 1950s, largely because of a dogged campaign launched by one researcher, Dr. Ancel Keys. An American physiologist based at the University of Minnesota, Keys had came to the study of cardiovascular disease sideways. Early in his career, Keys published the seminal *Biology of Human Starvation*, which documented the physiological, psychological, and cognitive effects of starvation during and after World War II. But it was during his sabbatical year at Oxford, and related travels in 1951–52, that Keys became fascinated with the cultural differences in diet and disease risk. Because rates of heart attacks had risen acutely in the United States, especially among male executives, Keys was intrigued by the comparably low rates of heart attack in the Mediterranean countries he'd visited. These populations—many still recovering from the deprivations of World War II—also ate a diet low in fat, especially animal fat owing to food scarcity at the time. After surveying diet and heart disease mortality statistics in men from the United States, Canada, Australia, England, Wales, Italy and Japan, Keys became convinced that the higher the fat intake, the higher the heart-disease rates.

He presented his findings at a World Health Organization (WHO) conference in 1954, proclaiming, "No other variable in the mode of life besides the fat calories in the diet is known which shows . . . such a consistent relationship to the mortality rate from coronary or degenerative heart disease." Keys fiercely defended his theory with a graph plotting the percentage of fat consumption in seven countries (though England and Wales were lumped together) along one axis and their rates of degenerative heart disease along the other. As the dots converged, the conclusion seemed irrefutable: Eat more fat, suffer more heart attacks. But in a dramatic critique of Keys's hypothesis in 1957, Jacob Yerushalmy, a biostatistician at UC Berkeley, and Herman Hilleboe, the New York State commissioner of health, revealed that Keys had chosen to illustrate data from only seven countries, even though data were available from twenty-two countries.

Keys had left out places like France, Holland, Switzerland, Norway, Denmark, Sweden, and West Germany, where the populations ate 30 to 40 percent of their calories from fat yet whose death rates from heart disease were roughly half that of the United States. Moreover, there wasn't any mention of more extreme fat-consuming populations like the Native Inuit in Alaska, who ate more than 50 percent of their calories from animal fat yet appeared to have half the rate of heart disease of the United States. When the other fifteen values were plotted on the graph, Keys's clean rising curve practically vanished amid a sea of random dots. And had Keys plotted fat consumption in all the countries against overall longevity, he would have found that the higher-fat-eating populations lived longer!

Such is the confounding power of epidemiological statistics where so many variables are intertwined. No doubt the higher fat consuming populations lived longer because they were generally in developed countries with abundant food

supplies and more advanced healthcare, but that's speculation, not science. Which leads to the other salient criticism of
Keys's study: It established only an association between two
phenomena (fat consumption and heart disease), not a clear
cause and effect. What if something else in the subject's lives
was leading to heart disease? After all, the Japanese, who had
low rates of heart disease did eat less fat than Americans, but
perhaps they also consumed less sweets and pasta or smoked
less.

Keys was not derailed by these criticisms of his diet-heart
hypothesis. He felt they just complicated the central message:
Steer clear of animal fats, like butter, to keep cholesterol levels
low and thereby avoid heart disease. Even in 1957, when an
AHA committee issued a report authored by Irvine H. Page
and colleagues discrediting diet-heart researchers like Keys
and others for taking "uncompromising stands based on evidence that does not stand up under critical examination," the
indictment against dietary fat did not go away. In fact, three
years later, Keys was drafted on to a six-man AHA committee
that issued another diet report in 1960. Though the evidence
against fat hadn't changed in the intervening three years, the
committee officially supported Key's hypothesis and strongly
recommended that Americans at risk of heart disease (middle-aged men mostly) reduce the fat in their diets and replace
saturated fats like butter with polyunsaturated fats (vegetable
and seed oils). It flagged high cholesterol as the leading heart
disease risk factor, even though the evidence on that point
was very contradictory. John Gofman, a renowned lipid researcher frequently posited that many coronary artery disease

(CAD) sufferers had low cholesterol, and conversely, a great number of people with high cholesterol never developed heart disease. Keys claimed such statistics were misinterpreted or based on faulty data. Although he would admit that the benefits of lowering cholesterol had not yet been established, Keys insisted it was merely a matter of time until they were.

By the late 1950s, Ancel Keys became the public face of the low-fat fraternity when *Time* magazine enshrined him on its cover in January 1961 under the banner "Diet & Health." In the accompanying article, Keys presented his version of the ideal heart-healthy diet: 70 percent of calories from carbohydrates and 15 percent from fat (with protein making up the balance). Only in a single paragraph did the story mention that Keys's hypothesis was still being debated among researchers.

Except for allowing some portion of olive oil in the diet, Keys and his colleagues proclaimed that a diet low in all fats—but especially restrictive of animal fats such as butter, cheese, eggs, and beef—was the solution to preventing heart disease. The possible nutritional deficiencies of a low-fat diet were never considered. Our bodies depend on fat-soluble vitamins, cholesterol, and fatty acids to run all kinds of internal systems optimally, especially in the brain; among children, this fat function is even more essential. But policy makers and health experts eagerly embraced Keys's one-size-fits-all approach. Indeed, his diet-heart theory was such a best-selling headline that the media virtually ignored any of Keys's critics.

One notable alternative theory at the time was proposed by Dr. John Yudkin, a professor of nutrition and dietetics at Queen Elizabeth College of London University. Yudkin claimed there was a clearer correlation between the rise in heart disease and the rise in refined sugar consumption. In his experiments with rodents, chickens, rabbits, pigs, and various student volunteers who were fed a diet high in sugar and carbohydrates, he consistently found increased blood levels of triglycerides (a class of fats), which was then, as now, considered a risk factor for heart disease. (Other leading researchers had made the same discovery in the late 1950s, but in the shadow of Keys's work, they were largely ignored.)

When Yudkin outlined his results in his 1972 book, *Pure, White and Deadly*, he proposed that sugar might have a stronger causal link to heart disease than fats. After all, he noted, people had been eating high-fat foods like butter for centuries, while refined sugar was had been a rare treat for most people until the mid-1800s, when it became widely available.

As Julia Llewellyn Smith reported in the *Telegraph*, the British Sugar Bureau promptly sent out a press release dismissing Yudkin's claims as "emotional assertions," and similarly, the World Sugar Research Organization described his book as "science fiction." An aggressive campaign by the sugar-dependent food industry discrediting Yudkin's theory ensued, with denunciations from several high-level scientists, including Ancel Keys who called Yudkin's evidence "flimsy indeed."

But the primary criticism leveled at Yudkin was that his theory often relied on observations of, rather than concrete explanations for, rising heart disease as it related to sugar. He could state it was happening but not why. That was because several of sugar's metabolic pathways that would have explained his hypothesis had not yet been discovered. His findings were about a decade too soon. By the end of the 1970s, Yudkin's sugar theory had taken its lumps, and butter had lost an important ally. Few scientists dared to pursue further research into the heart disease-sugar connection for fear of being similarly dishonored. Nor could they find much funding for such research even if they wanted to, since studies that shook the foundation of the fat hypothesis were highly unpopular. (Conversely, the vegetable oil industry generously funded scientists whose work could be used to promote their product's polyunsaturated fats.) Sugar consumption began to soar, especially when engineers in the food industry found that various forms of sugar (e.g., fructose) compensated for the flavor lost when fat was removed from foods. Consequently, low-fat and fat-free products, spiked with sugar, began to line supermarket shelves everywhere. Likewise, hydrogenated vegetable fats began to pervade the modern Western diet in the guise of more margarine choices, processed food, and innocuous-sounding vegetable shortening. (Who didn't have a can of Crisco in the pantry in the 1960s? It was a standard ingredient in American postwar recipes well into the late 1980s.) Margarine took on the shining specter of a health food. Butter continued to take a beating from its impostor, first on price and then on health perceptions.

Over the course of the next two decades, the diet-heart hypothesis appeared to be evermore bulletproof, especially after Keys published the initial findings of his landmark trial—the Seven Countries Study—in 1970. He undertook this study after issuing his controversial 1955 report at WHO, no doubt to prove his theory conclusively. From 1958 until 1964, his Seven Countries Study documented the food patterns and heart disease rates of 12,700 middle-aged men in Italy, Greece, Yugoslavia, Finland, the Netherlands, Japan, and the United States.

When the results came in, Keys touted a strong correlation between the consumption of saturated fats and death from heart disease. In eastern Finland, where the men ate a diet high in dairy products and meat, deaths from heart disease topped the charts at 992. By contrast, on the Greek islands of Crete and Corfu, where the local diet had little meat but plenty of olive oil, only nine men died of heart attacks. In between these extreme results were 66 deaths among the rural Japanese, 290 for the Yugoslavian and Italian men, and 570 deaths among American railroad workers. For the heart-healthy Greeks, saturated fat (not total fat) comprised only 8 percent of calories, compared to 22 percent for the cardio-afflicted Finns.

The study was lauded as proof positive of saturated fat as the culprit in heart disease, despite one aberration: Why did the Japanese, who had very little fat of any kind in their diet, have more heart disease than the Cretans in Greece whose diets were about 40 percent fat? Keys postulated that the abundant amount of monounsaturated fat from olive oil in the Cretan diet actually protected against heart disease. Now Keys's hypothesis had a fresh—and more palatable—twist: It extolled olive oil. So-called good fat was born, as was the trendy Mediterranean-style diet.

Despite its celebrated debut, the Seven Countries Study had a major flaw, similar to his WHO study. The countries themselves in the study were not chosen at random but were ones that confirmed the diet-heart hypothesis. Had Keys included France or Switzerland, for instance, the results would have been inconclusive; both populations eat an abundance of saturated fat yet have relatively little heart disease. (Remember the so-called French paradox? There's a Swiss one too. And even a Masai paradox. In fact, Norway, Denmark, and Sweden each consumed nearly as much fat—plenty of it saturated—as Americans, yet had less than half the rate of heart disease.) With selective thinking, Keys and his colleagues had managed to avoid what Thomas Henry Huxley called "the great tragedy of science: the slaying of a beautiful hypothesis by an ugly fact."

Before long, a sharp line was drawn between a small but vocal group of conservative scientists who believed the body of evidence was conflicting and required more exacting trials and practicing clinicians who felt they had a duty to give their patients medical recommendations based on the latest research. To wait for final scientific proof of the diet-heart hypothesis seemed a formality they could ill afford as long as heart disease continued to claim lives.

This sense of urgency was largely the reason why Keys's hypothesis suddenly graduated on January 14, 1977, to accepted nutrition dogma. That was the day Senator George McGovern's Senate Select Committee on Nutrition and Human Needs issued the first publication of the government's *Dietary Goals for the United States*, which urged Americans, among other things, to cut fat and boost carbs. In a 2014 article in the cardiology journal *Open Heart*, Zoë Harcombe and colleagues recounted that one of the scientists opposed to the antifat message, Dr. Robert Olson, from St. Louis University, pleaded before the committee "for more research on the problem [of heart disease] before we make announcements to the American public." But, McGovern responded, "senators don't have the luxury that a research scientist has to wait until every last shred of evidence is in."

And so, falling in step with the AHA, the committee endorsed a low-fat, high-carb diet for all Americans. With several notable exceptions—like the American Medical Association, which argued against the recommendations—the health establishment supported the report, adopting an even more aggressive stance against cholesterol and saturated animal fat.

"It is hard to overstate its impact," award-winning investigative science writer Gary Taubes said of the McGovern report in his 2007 book *Good Calories, Bad Calories*. According to Taubes, the *Dietary Goals* writers "took a grab bag of ambiguous studies and speculation, acknowledged that the claims were scientifically contentious, and then officially bestowed on one interpretation the aura of fact."

But policy makers were convinced that their actions were at least prudent, if not prophylactic. As D. Mark Hegsted, then director of the USDA's nutrition committee at the time, said rhetorically, "The question . . . is not why should we change our diet, but why not? What are the risks associated with eating less meat, less fat, less cholesterol?" He, like many others, could not imagine any dangers in shifting the fat-carb equation.

In the meantime, the food industry rolled out newly labeled

"cholesterol-lowering polyunsaturated" margarine. A blitz of "no cholesterol" or "low cholesterol" claims on other foods would soon follow—and persist seemingly forever. (The grocery shelves continue to be full of them even though the warning against dietary cholesterol was officially reversed with the government's 2015 Dietary Guidelines for Americans.)

As the low-fat offensive advanced in the late twentieth century, butter made a steady retreat from many American tables. By 1992, when the USDA reissued its low-fat, high-carb diet recommendation in an infamous graphic known as the Food Guide Pyramid, annual per capita butter consumption had tumbled from eighteen pounds in 1930 (when there was, by the way, very little incidence of heart disease) to just four pounds by the early 1990s.

FOR THE PAST FOUR decades, many health experts have claimed that there is plenty of solid evidence to support the bad rap butter and other saturated fats (like meat, eggs, and cheese) have gotten. They've pointed to a bulwark of clinical trials and massive population studies that supposedly confirmed the diet-heart hypothesis, including the oft-cited Seven Countries Study, the Framingham Heart Study, the Oslo Diet-Heart Study, the LA Veterans Administration Trial, the Finnish Mental Hospital Study, the Sydney Diet Heart Study, and the Women's Health Initiative. But on closer inspection by a new generation of researchers, many of these studies and others have been found to be inconclusive at best, if not deeply flawed in their methodology.

The 2014 *Open Heart* meta-analysis, authored by Harcombe

and colleagues, examined all research studies that were available to government decision makers in the United States and
Britain when they made their first official dietary recommendations to the public in 1977 and 1983, respectively. Of ninety-
eight potential studies selected for review, only six met the
inclusion criteria of being a randomized control trial (RCT),
the gold standard of research. When all the findings were compared the authors found that "there was no statistically significant difference in deaths from coronary heart disease [between
the control groups and intervention groups]." Although mean
serum cholesterol levels were measurably reduced in the intervention groups, this didn't result in significant differences
in CAD or mortality in general. The *Open Heart* study con-
cluded: "Dietary recommendations were introduced for
220 million US and 56 million UK citizens by 1983, in the absence of supporting evidence from RCTs."

But what about more recent studies and RCTs? Given that
the antibutter, low-fat diet recommendation has been reissued
time and again for more than thirty years, surely there must be
convincing new evidence stacked up by now?

That depends on where you look or whom you ask. The
answer, we now understand, is vastly complicated by a population that has great disparities in age, gender, body type, eth-
nicity, and lifestyle (smoking, exercise, drinking, etc.). Over
the past decade lipid scientists have made new and startling
discoveries in fat and carbohydrate metabolism that are cast-
ing a virtual floodlight on the mechanisms of heart disease. As
the variables become more obvious, so does the evidence that
fat consumption can't easily be singled out as the primary risk

factor. Now with better lipoprotein science at hand, researchers are gradually dismantling the simplistic (if not erroneous) assumption that saturated fat is categorically bad and rebuilding a much more nuanced and individualized understanding of what causes heart disease. In the process, butter is getting a long overdue pardon.

I heard it firsthand, when I spoke with Dr. Thomas Dayspring, director of cardiovascular education at the Foundation for Health Improvement and Technology, in Richmond, Virginia. A wizard when it comes to detailing fat metabolism, Dayspring is also something of a hero in the growing low-carb, high-fat community of dieters, even if he himself doesn't subscribe to any particular food regime. In his online lectures and videos, Dayspring rails against outdated restrictions on foods like butter based simply on their saturated fat content. "There are many people," he told me, "who when they increase their saturated fat intake, do not get elevated levels of LDL-C or LDL-P [types of cholesterol]. A lot depends on your genetic response, how a given body handles saturated fat. You really need a metabolic workup to decide which kind of nutrition would be best for your particular genotype." Nonetheless, I asked Dayspring, could the USDA Dietary Guidelines restricting saturated fat consumption to 7 percent of calories still be considered a good prophylactic policy for a diverse population? "I do not think so," he responded bluntly. "I think that fat intake has to be highly individualized and I think it's absurd to restrict fat as an absolute recommendation across the board. There's a large part of the population who are insulin resistant and diabetic for whom restricting dietary fat is terrible advice." (Fat is the only food substance that doesn't raise insulin levels; carbs certainly do, but so does protein to a lesser extent.) "Only those who are eating fat that sends their LDL cholesterol and particles through the roof," he added, "should be given such restrictions. If saturated fat is not doing that for a person, why would I ever tell them to stop eating it? It would make no sense to me."

While Dayspring's clemency of saturated fat is rooted in the diversity of our individual reactions to it, Ronald Krauss, director of atherosclerosis research at Children's Hospital Oakland Research Institute, says that it's also the diversity of saturated fats themselves that makes a blanket butter restriction unwarranted. "The effect of particular foods on coronary heart disease cannot be predicted solely by their content of total SFA [saturated fatty acid]," he explained in a presentation delivered to the California Dietetics Association in 2013, "because individual SFAs may have different cardiovascular effects." For instance, many of the shorter chain fatty acids in milk fat (where butter comes from) have been found to have important immune response functions that can prevent heart disease. And some saturated fats, such as the stearic acid in butter, do not raise LDLs; their effect is neutral.

AS THE FIFTY-YEAR-OLD INDICTMENT against saturated fat and heart disease finally weakens under the weight of better nutritional science, butter has returned to the grocery list. (Americans have increased their butter consumption by 25 percent since 2002 and it continues to climb. To wit: Some food manufacturers have reformulated their products so they can boast "made with real butter.")

While it's great to enjoy butter without the extra serving of guilt, the good news regarding this food isn't just about doing no harm; butter has actual health benefits too. In every pound of butter (especially organic and grass-fed brands) there's a payload of fat-soluble vitamins and other constituents that support good health. Vitamin A and its precursors, which are critical to many functions in the body (good vision, a defensive immune system, and skin health), are abundant in butter, but it's the concentration of vitamin D, E, and K_2 content that have been most recently lauded.

For generations, vitamin D has been readily available through our skins' response to sunlight. But as we spend significantly less time outdoors these days, and use more sunscreen when we do, vitamin D deficiency is markedly increasing in developed countries (afflicting as much as 75 percent of the population in the United States). As a result, experts are finding that without adequate vitamin D, a host of chronic diseases can develop or worsen, including depression. Not widely available in foods, except those with fat that are specifically vitamin-fortified (like whole milk), Vitamin D is present in butter, and even more so in the butter from grass-fed animals. The same is true for vitamin E, an antioxidant in butter that thwarts the damaging effects of oxidized fats and free radicals that can lead to heart disease and cancer. As with most vitamins, vitamin E works best when consumed in whole foods rather than as an isolated concentrate.

Other health-affirming aspects of butter specifically apply to grass-fed or "pastured" butter. Such labels are not merely about marketing the bucolic image of cows grazing in lush green fields; butter made from the milk of 100 percent grass-fed cows is actually nutritionally superior. In practice, many dairy cows get both grass and grain in their diets, given the seasonality of pasture, so labels on butter can be misleading. If a cow spends just a minimal amount of time in the pasture, her butter qualifies for the premium "grass-fed" label. But a true grass-feeding operation will let the animals graze freely for most of the year and supplement only during the winter with haylage.

In addition to storing more vitamin A, true grass-fed butter is also rich in health-promoting CLA—conjugated linoleic acid, a type of polyunsaturated fat. In research studies, CLA has exhibited potent antioxidant activity, especially in the prevention of cell damage that can lead to heart disease, diabetes, and cancer.

The same feed-based variation happens with vitamin K_2, a relatively new superstar in the wellness world. Not to be confused with its better-known cohort, vitamin K_1, long appreciated for its blood-clotting business, K_2 appears to play a much wider role in the body. Promoting healthy skin, forming strong bones, preventing inflammation, supporting brain function, reversing arterial calcification (aka "hardening of the arteries"), and helping to prevent cancer all seem to fall under the busy job description of K_2.

The majority of commercial butters sold in the United States are from cows that are confined to a man-made diet of grains with little if any fresh grass, so their dairy products are not a rich source of K_2. To gain the most vitamin perks, seek out a verifiable grass-fed butter (and be prepared to pay a little extra for it!).

Dissecting butter's nutrient composition certainly strengthens the case for its return to the table (in moderation, of course). But most experts now agree that chasing or avoiding single nutrients like saturated fat, vitamins, antioxidants, high-density lipoproteins, and so on is neither a wise nor practical way to make dietary choices. We thrive on the dynamic network of nutrients in a whole food, not by separating them. Even though the message for the last fifty years of nutritionism has to been to isolate and banish certain "bad" things in foods, this deconstruction of our diets has been of little help to the average person who, in the end, simply wants to know what the heck to eat. As a result, diet and nutrition experts are fixating less on quantifying nutrients and denying foods and instead on promoting servings of specific food choices that support good health.

The bottom line: We can enjoy butter in good conscience, albeit with temperance; it is, after all, rich. It does us no good to eat any fat with abandon. Nor does buttery overindulgence equate with more satisfaction. Indeed, one of the best lessons learned from my career in food and cooking is that gratification is something of a paradox: Too much of a good thing often diminishes the pleasure we derive from it. (Would you really want to eat your favorite dessert every day?) Call it the Goldilocks principle. Balance isn't just right for your body; I think it also assures real satisfaction.

NINE

. . . .

The Modern Buttersmith

SMALL BATCHES, BIG FANS

. . . .

The special thing about our butter is how its taste ages out, changing over time from the cultures. If you taste it right out of the churn, it's more sweet with a lot of bright lactic flavor. After a month, it has developed a secondary, slightly nutty, baked-bread kind of taste. After 120 days, the butter has a really interesting sharpness, but it's not spoiled.

—ADELINE DRUART,
production manager,
Vermont Creamery, 2014

*J*E SUIS ELANÉ . . . *EYLANE KHOSROVAH,*" I SUD-denly heard myself saying in a confused French accent, having dialed through to a shop in Brittany. Frantically I was searching my memory for bits of high school French in an attempt to understand the fast-talking man at the other end of the phone. A man I'd been trying to track down for more than a month: Jean Yves Bordier, France's most unorthodox butter dignitary. Despite the choppy phone dialogue, the call was a success. Eight days and about three thousand miles later, I found myself at the doorstep of his small shop at 9 rue de l'Orme in Saint- Malo.

Walking across the store's Breton-blue threshold, a sensorial butter trip began. From a granite table in the middle of the rectangular boutique, a sharp drumming sound beat the air as a "butter patter" went to work. Customers clustered around the table to watch as the patter wielded a ribbed boxwood paddle in each hand to cleave a wedge of butter from a giant motte of fresh-made butter. He checked its perfect weight on a scale and proceeded to firmly thwack and smack at it with the paddles, rotating and shaping all sides of it at rapid-fire speed. In just seconds, a tight yellow palm-size brick of butter emerged. The patter passed it to an assistant who hand-wrapped the edible bullion in folds of white parchment paper.

A sweet lactic scent of butterfat—the unmistakable whiff of eau de dairy—lingered near the front of the shop where customers at the retail counter lined up to sample the house butter and flavored variations. The choices were many: delicately smoked butter tasting of cream and campfire; a vivid sweet pepper version the color of terra-cotta; a butter with sea salt crystals and another mixed with flecks of truffles; green-tinged butter embedded with local Brittany seaweed; and a putty-colored version made salty and chewy with olive puree. Sweet butters are also in the lineup, some mixed with honey, others with citrus. Next door, the shop's adjoining cafe offered a butter-tasting course, with a sample tray of seven of these flavored butters.

La Maison du Beurre—the House of Butter—has been

operating under various owners since 1927. But the bustling destination it is today—part dairy shrine, part market/cafe—didn't exist until 1985 when the business was bought and re-imagined by Bordier. Some in the trade claim that he's more marketing genius than true artisan, but at a time when standardized, cheaper industrial butters have supplanted many smaller, traditional farmstead producers, Bordier has raised the appreciation for traditional *beurre de baratte* (butter from a batch churn) made slowly with natural lactic acid cultures.

"You have to realize what's special about our butter process," he said (through my blessed translator). "Whereas industrial producers bring in cream and six hours later a bar of butter goes out, in our fabrication, almost seventy-two hours elapse from when the cow is milked and the butter leaves our creamery for the market. We allow time to do its work so the cream will mature and acquire aromatic complexity."

His brand, Beurre de Bordier, is recognized far beyond the walled city of Saint-Malo. To be fair, there are other celebrated French butter artisans, including Rodolphe Le Meunier—a star *affineur* (cheese ripener) in France—who markets a highly celebrated slow-ripened beurre de baratte from Normandy (available in the States). And another of Bordier's countrymen, Olivier Martin, based in the Pas de Calais, is the maker of very popular Au Bon Beurre butter. Martin's blending of cream from Jerseys, Holsteins, and Norman cows, he says, is what makes for the fine flavor of his butter.

But Bordier was earliest on the scene, doing it well before such butter was trendy. With a strong following among star-studded chefs and food media, Bordier ships to white-tablecloth restaurants and fine markets throughout Europe, as well as to the United States, Singapore, and Japan. If there were a Rolls Royce of French butter, Bordier's brand is it. But Bordier says he never intended to make an exclusive product as much as an exceptional one.

At his white-tiled production facility in Rennes, about an hour from the retail shop in Saint-Malo, fifty-kilo urns of cultured batch-churned butter arrive in the morning, made with pasteurized cream from surrounding farms in Brittany and Normandy. In France, Bordier could use raw cream for his cultured butter, but because it travels long distance, it has to be more resistant to spoilage. (If ever you're in Paris, don't miss the chance to taste raw cream butter at a Pascal Beillevaire cheese shop. Its private-label butter, officially called *beurre cru baratte à l'ancienne—raw butter made in the old style in a barrel churn*—comes unsalted, salted, and in a *demi-sel croquant* [crunchy] version made with fleur de sel.)

When the bulk butter is delivered to Bordier's facility, it's carted to a white-tiled workroom for the "spa" treatment— a long, deep massage using Bordier's signature retrofitted Wonka-like machine, called the *malaxeur* (massager). Used on larger farm creameries in the nineteenth century, the malaxeur was designed to work the butter texture into a silken mass. At other times, it was used to blend not-so-good batches of butter with better batches to create one homogenous product. Bordier explains that it chases off excess buttermilk, finely distributes the remaining beads of moisture, and "lengthens" the butter's taste by creating a dense yet creamy texture.

Back in the day when it was state of the art, this malaxeur

may have been animal-powered via a treadmill on which a draft horse kept pace. Bordier has had it retrofitted for electric power. Now his malaxeur is the centerpiece of his butter workshop and likely the only one of its kind operating in the modern butter world.

After the butter is rendered silky and smooth, it is either shipped to the patting counter at Bordier's retail shop or it moves to another corner of the Renne facility where a team of employees in hairnets and lab coats will shape it into elegant portions. With paddles in hand, working side by side around islands of stainless-steel tables, Bordier's staff instantly sculpts knobs of butter into small discs, pyramids, cubes, logs, and bars with rapid-fire speed.

Of course, this could all be done by machine. But Bordier believes in the hands-on method. "I am a bad businessman," he joked. "I spend way too much time doing things. In a fast-food world, I am a slow food operator . . . but doing it this way pleases me, and I have made a living." Today his company—which is now owned by the Brittany-based food company Triballat—produces more than one hundred thousand pounds of butter annually, with the demand steadily increasing, despite its premium cost. "I can sell my butter at a certain price and support a certain number of people. Which is nice and good," he stated, adding, "but I don't hold any grudge against the industrialists. There is a lot of milk flowing every day. It has to be transformed. We have a lot of people to feed."

IT'S A GOOD TIME to be a butter lover. Choices are plentiful, diverse, and storied. We can buy one butter for its personality, another for its utility. This side-by-side availability of artisan butter and machine-made brands has never really existed before. At least not in mainstream markets. Sure, there have always been the dairy outlanders, the do-it-yourselfers who made their own butter in the shadow of sprawling postwar commercial dairy plants, but they have been the exception.

Now an ever-growing community of buttersmiths is forging a revival of man-made selections. This low-tech category of churned cream is often described as table butter. Distinguished from utilitarian supermarket butter used for cooking or baking, table butter refers to those small-batch independent brands that are best relished as is—with nothing more than a little raft of bread to transport it from hand to mouth. It's not that you can't bake or cook with these table butters, but their subtle flavor nuances (what you paid extra for) are often lost in the process.

Artisan butter, like other handmade foods, is on the rise for many reasons, some practical, some ideological. Many young crafters have realized that producing a niche specialty food product is more financially viable than getting a good job in a post–Great Recession economy. Career butter making has also been spurred on by the latest health findings that exonerate butter in the complex battle against heart disease battle (as detailed in the previous chapter); sales prove that the public appetite for butter is continually growing. Many new butter makers also view their work as agricultural policy in action; at the very least it can support the value and infrastructure of the local family farms that supply them cream. Dairy artisans see themselves on the side of sustainability practices, organic production, and better treatment of animals.

The ranks of those who buy artisan butter are growing for many of the same reasons. But people are also buying it simply because it can be genuinely flavorful and unpredictable, because it tastes and looks different than the uniform sticks they grew up with. And it's an indulgence that, relatively speaking, costs very little.

Most twenty-first century buttersmiths have cherry-picked old and new methods, like Bordier, to improve productivity and quality without negating the human x factor. However, small-batch butter making is not necessarily a guarantee of excellence; great butter is the result of great intent, not merely its downsized doing. In the ranks of men and women who do it well, several have been early or key players in the hands-on butter revival. Like Bordier, they're passionate and innovative butter makers whose story has shaped butter's narrative. Although I've listed many excellent producers in appendix A of this book, this chapter profiles a few of the groundbreakers and rule breakers in the modern butter world. They all operate very differently, yet collectively they've raised the discourse, and the bar, on butter.

I FIRST MET ALLISON Hooper, co-owner of Vermont Creamery, when I was working the cheese beat, on an assignment to cover her award-winning chèvre. When my focus switched to butter, Hooper was one of the first producers I visited in Vermont because, like nearly every dairy product she has launched, her premium butter was first in its class in the American market. Hooper has a real knack for predicting what we want before it exists.

She credits her college exchange experience in Europe during the early 1980s with supplying the inspiration for the creamery's butter start-up. During one summer between semesters, she stayed with a farming family in Brittany, earning her keep by helping them with various chores, including churning cultured cream to make butter. "We collected the cream all week long from the daily milking, adding it to a bucket in the refrigerator, where it all naturally fermented. By the end of the week, the cream had essentially turned into thick crème fraîche. We'd put that in a small electric churn, shaped like a washing machine, and make butter. It was fabulous—tangy, high fat, lightly salted." Each portion of this farmstead butter was shaped using a wooden mold engraved with a cow, then wrapped in parchment paper and sold at the local market. "That's what was in my mind," Hooper recalled. "I wanted to re-create that butter."

At the time Hooper that began her foray into butter making, she was already operating Vermont Creamery, a small goat-cheese-making operation she had launched with business partner, Bob Reese. Their celebrated *crottins* and minilogs of fresh chèvre were among the first to be introduced to Americans, goat cheese being exotic fare in the United States in the early 1990s. That business (which today has grown into a multimillion-dollar enterprise) was likewise inspired by Hooper's French farm experience and entrepreneurial hunch. She had made delicate goat cheeses during her summer in France and was sure they could find a market in the States.

Shifting to cow's milk to produce butter, however, was a

very different kind of enterprise. But having made a few small batches of cultured butter at home, Hooper was confident that Bob (the numbers cruncher) and she could build a commercial operation. In the process, she hoped to turn America on to the slightly piquant version that was so popular in Europe. "With goat cheese, we had created these horrendous categories that no one could pronounce. At least people knew what butter was," she joked.

Their early optimism was rewarded: While driving through Middlebury, Vermont, one afternoon, Hooper and Reese spied an old commercial stainless-steel churn sitting outside at a dairy farm. They stopped to inquire about it; after a brief negotiation, the partners bought the used churn for three thousand dollars and hauled it back to their creamery. Suddenly Hooper had the capacity to make five hundred pounds of cultured butter a week, but who would buy it? No one was doing this style of butter in the States at the time. Hooper was churning rich 42 percent butterfat cultured cream into luxurious tangy butter, like she had done in France, but store managers would taste it and say, "Yeah, this is great, but there's no real category for it."

Having dealt with the same kind of resistance when first marketing her goat cheeses, Hooper knew that her most viable first customers were chefs. In particular, French ones. She contacted a chef from Brittany who was working in New York City and asked him to sample the butter. He did and was ecstatic with its flavor, claiming that it tasted like the butter of his childhood. The chef was eager to help Hooper succeed, so he introduced her butter to his French chef friends at

Lespinasse, La Côte Basque, Le Cirque—the best restaurants in New York at the time. Before long, batches of cultured butter were being transported from the company's makeshift rustic headquarters in Vermont to some of the most elegant tables in Manhattan.

"It is impossible not to love someone who makes toast for you. People's failings, even major ones such as when they make you wear short trousers to school, fall into insignificance as your teeth break through the rough, toasted crust and sink into the doughy cushion of white bread underneath. Once the warm, salty butter has hit your tongue, you are smitten. Putty in their hands."

—NIGEL SLATER, *Toast*

Ironically, that high-class placement proved easier than getting her butter into the corner market. Good as it tasted, Vermont Creamery's butter had practical flaws that hindered its retail readiness. For one thing, the company's tubelike plastic packaging wasn't consumer friendly. "We sold it in an eight-ounce plastic chub, like the goat cheese, with metal clips at either end," said Hooper. "People wondered, 'How do I get in this thing?' [It's now sold as a foil-wrapped log.] And it didn't have marks to measure by the tablespoon . . . and no one knew what cultured butter was. Overall, we had a long way to go. Our butter only sold to a very special consumer."

Funny enough, it was the European competitors who eventually helped their butter gain a place on American store shelves. As imported butters from Europe—many with high butterfat, less salt, and cultured flavor—began to show up in specialty food markets, a new category of butter was gradually recognized and the Vermont outlier (by then more conveniently packaged) was able to claim a spot among them.

Adeline Druart, the production manager at Vermont Creamery who grew up in France, gave me the technical reason their cultured butter is unique: "We hold our cream for an extra twenty-four hours to ripen it with three special bacterial cultures. Two of these bacteria turn lactose into lactic acid, which adds tanginess but also, critically, changes the pH [acidity] of the cream to make it the right environment for the third bacteria to work."

IN CONTRAST TO HOOPER'S expanding butter distribution across the country, the other pioneering Vermont butter maker I visited keeps her production willfully small, distributing it to just five celebrated American restaurants. Diane St. Clair and her husband, Alan Clarisse, operate Animal Farm, a tiny dairy and one-woman creamery in Orwell where she's been making butter since 2000. Every week during milking season, St. Clair sends her small-batch butter, churned from the cream of her eleven cows, to the kitchens of the French Laundry in the Napa Valley; Per Se in New York City; Boston restaurants No. 9 Park and Menton; and the Inn at Little Washington in Virginia.

St. Clair and her husband started out with just one family cow and no intention of starting a butter business. "But the cow gave so much milk," she said, "that I wound up making butter and cheese." Without any training in making cultured butter, she turned for instruction to a handful of antiquarian, out-of-print dairying manuals, some written more than a century ago. She wanted to reclaim some of the practical skills of American farmstead butter making lost in the ramp up to postwar industrialization. From the writings of various bygone dairy experts and plenty of trial and error, St. Clair developed a process of culturing her hand-skimmed cream with a generous glug of naturally fermented buttermilk left over from the previous batch of cultured butter. Using this self-perpetuating model of culturing that has been practiced for centuries, every batch of butter begets the next one.

St. Clair thought her homemade butter was pretty remarkable, but she wanted an expert opinion. Having recently read about Chef Keller's hallowed restaurant, the French Laundry, she sent him a note asking if he'd judge her butter. When he agreed, St. Clair shipped him a sample and Keller quickly responded with a request to buy all the butter she made; price was not an issue. Keller also asked her if she could double her cowherd to produce an ample supply for his restaurant. And when he opened Per Se in New York, he convinced her to get four more cows. (St. Clair also named her best performing dairy cow Keller.)

Through her association with Chef Keller, Diane St. Clair became America's first celebrity butter maker. Food media across the country pounced on the story of the collaboration between a world-famous urban chef and a small-time female dairy farmer from a remote farm in Vermont. Indeed, it's a perennial tale whose appeal doesn't seem to wear out despite the fact that Animal Farm's butter is relatively unavailable to most of us. Though not a populist butter, it was nonetheless one of the first to create a steady interest in the revival of artisan butter making.

MY FIRST INTRODUCTION TO Swedish butter maker Patrik Johannson was through YouTube. Another food journalist had put me on to him, saying Johannson was doing some unorthodox things with butter. (Not, ahem, in the Marlon Brando way.) In the process, this Swedish maker was creating what some in Europe regarded as the Michelin of butters. Described as intensely buttery, more acidic and yet fresher than standard butter, some reviewers claim it's positively addictive. Not surprisingly, this insurgent butter is made by a man who calls himself "the Butter Viking." (It was in fact the early Vikings who helped spread butter-making practices throughout northern Europe.) Chefs are sold on his product, and on Johannson himself—a flavor sleuth with a highly developed culinary sense of "what if?"

In the videocast of his presentation at a European food symposium, I learned that Johannson was a former IT man who nine years ago began churning cultured butter for an elite handful of European restaurants, including Noma in Copenhagen (voted tops among the 50 Best Restaurants in the world). He makes traditional butter, but most of the attention he has garnered is from his one-of-a-kind "Virgin Butter." Technically, it's illegal to even call this product butter because it has only 40 percent butterfat (half that of standard butter). Yet its taste virtually explodes with tart-sweet butteriness when served correctly: cold from the fridge, spread on warm bread. When I caught up with Johannson months later for an interview, he explained, "Virgin Butter has a lot of moisture because I don't drain the churn at all. Its texture is fluffy and spreadable, though slightly grainy." Straight from the fridge it just tastes mostly acidic like a rich yogurt, owing to the seven different bacterial cultures Johansson uses to ripen it. But once spread on warm bread, as it is tableside at Noma, it releases a lush cascade of buttery, tangy flavor. "I analyzed the best properties of butter and enhanced them," Johansson said, crediting his systems analysis training for helping him understand the interlocking flavors of butter.

Johansson didn't plan on being a butter man when in 2005 he quit his urban job and together with his wife and their two small children moved to the country outside Gothenburg to live more simply as self-reliant homesteaders. The couple first created a small business by "boiling down the ocean" to sell their own brand of natural sea salt crystals, which helped sustain their isolated life style. In the meantime, Johannson had also begun tinkering with his grandmother's manual churn. He remembered her butter-making steps and was intrigued by the physical process, then even more so by the biochemistry of culturing cream before churning it into butter.

Over the course of the next year, Johannson made countless batches of butter before submitting it to the scrutiny of restaurateurs. He also produced some early oddball riffs, including "dew drop" butter inoculated with the bacteria in morning dew, as well as his triumphant "Kings" butter, invented specially for a dinner in Gothenburg to honor the visiting king of

Sweden. "I wanted to make a new butter with lots of everything when it comes to taste, both super creamy and buttery," Johannson recalled. Using his own chilled, lightly salted crème fraîche (cultured for three days) as a base, Johannson slowly melted his regular butter and using the tip of a knife, dropped individual "pearls" of butter on to the soured cream. As the butter pearls cooled down and solidified, he carefully folded them into the crème fraîche, until the cream portion was lavishly studded with delicate butter pearls. Johannson urged people to eat it directly off a spoon; bread was superfluous. The visiting king reportedly said, "I'm not a big fan of butter," as he went for his fifth helping.

But Johannson's most unorthodox butter experiment was his "boy" and "girl" butters. One day when he was delivering his butter to Noma, he brought some cream along with the intent of making two gender butters using lactobacilli from the skin of the restaurant staff. Asking the women to dip the back of their hands into one pail of cream, and the men's hands in another, he inoculated both creams with gender-specific bacteria. After allowing the he-and-she samples to culture for more than a day, Johannson churned them separately to make two butters. "The boy's butter was really awful," he said, "but the girl's butter was one of the best."

In addition to selling his Virgin Butter, the Butter Viking and his more recent partner, Maria Håkansson, also make a best-selling traditional high-fat butter, drained of excess buttermilk in the usual way. "My grandmother taught me to beat the butter long and hard so it would be more yellow and fatty," Johannson admitted, "but that's not our style." Wanting a

EMBOSSED BUTTER WITH HERBS FROM PATRIK JOHANNSON,
A.K.A. THE BUTTER VIKING. (PATRIK JOHANNSON)

lighter texture, he stops the churn as soon as the cream separates into flecks of butter floating in buttermilk.

Nor does he wash his butter grains, as his grandmother would have, since that would rinse away the lingering film of buttermilk that adds complexity to his butter's flavor. "I'm not worried about shelf life," he said, knowing how quickly his small deliveries of butter disappear. It's all about taste. And he also cares about presentation. Before delivery, Johansson's high-fat butter is pressed in a wet piece of hand-knit wool woven with various patterns; when the wool is removed, it leaves a beautifully embossed "knit" surface on the butter.

As of this writing, Johansson and Håkansson had just relocated their creamery to the Rew Valley on the Isle of Wight in England, in hopes of serving a much larger audience with various creative butter products. "The London chefs really get it," Johansson enthused.

IT'S COMMON PRACTICE FOR all vat-cultured butter makers to lavish attention on the cream that breeds flavor-making bacteria. But at the CROPP (Cooperative Regions of Organic Producer Pools) creamery in Chaseburg, Wisconsin, butter begins with minding the cows well before the cream. The company's limited-edition cultured pasture butter, sold under the Organic Valley brand, is made exclusively with the cream of organic milk from Wisconsin cows grazing on fresh May-through-September organic pastures. Indulged with a banquet of natural green grass to feed on between late spring and early fall, these roving cows give milk that contains a biochemical bounty. Compared to conventional butter derived from feedlot grain-fed cows, the pasture butter has as much as four times the amount of desirable fatty acids (CLAs and omega-3s) as well as a greater pool of subtle flavors, aroma, and healthy nutrients. It also looks different: It is bright yellow, strikingly so, especially in the spring when color-making carotenoids in tender new grass are more digestible. "I'm always asked if we add coloring to our butter," said Steve Rehburg, the plant manager, as he toured me around the creamery, "but no, never. It's just what happens when cows have lots of good pasture."

Marketing this seasonal butter is also a means of selling agricultural awareness to consumers, which is a big part of the company's philosophical DNA. As George Siemon, CROPP's CEO, once said of the cooperative's aim, "We are a social experiment disguised as a business."

Organic production does not require an all-pasture diet, only that the feed itself is always organic and the cows enjoy some regular time outdoors. The organic label also guarantees that the milk comes from cows not treated with antibiotics and hormones. So the cream for the pastured butter comes from farmers within a three-hundred-mile radius who have made a commitment to both organic methods and full-time pasturing as the season allows.

Rehburg explained how Organic Valley's technique for using lactobacilli to develop flavor—the result of in-house experimentation done years ago—differs from most other cultured butter makers: "After pasteurization, we use two creams. We blend a vat of fresh sweet cream with a vat of cream we've cultured using lactic bacteria. Combining the two gives us the flavor profile we want and makes the butter workable in our system. It has the right moisture and consistency." The pasture butter is churned and drained longer than most to give it a generous 84 percent butterfat content.

"There's an art to knowing when and how much buttermilk to drain," Rehburg noted. "It's crucial to have a certain level of moisture in the butter but not too much." By contrast, in large industrial plants that use a continuous-type churn, ideal moisture levels are automated. In addition, the butter makers at Organic Valley do not wash the finished butter with water as do other commercial producers; like Johannson, they claim that much of the "cultured" flavor is in the buttermilk so it makes little sense to strip it out completely.

When I ask about the busy creamery eventually switching to a continuous churn, Rehburg answered, "One batch at a time, one churn, is more in line with who we are. It's the right footprint for us. We just keep churning batches every day until we run out of time or cream."

BUTTER MADE WITH NOTHING more than fresh, uncultured cream and an optional pinch of salt is what's favored on most tables in the States, Canada, Great Britain, Ireland, Australia, New Zealand, and Iceland—the so-called sweet butter lands of dairy country. Uncomplicated to make, sweet butter is also the first choice of many entrepreneurs who've recently taken up the artisan butter trade. In the States, the number of small-batch, sweet butter choices has been on the rise for at least the last ten years, especially as struggling family dairy farms diversify beyond milk to stay in business. In the Northeast, where I live, it's easy to find regional butters in each state (I've spent a small fortune buying every one I meet). In other countries, however, where the economics of family dairying is more stable, butter making has remained largely an industrial product. That's why I was surprised to discover Abernethy butter, handcrafted in Northern Ireland by Will and Alison Abernethy. Postwar Irish butter has long been synonymous with the mighty Kerrygold brand, a much-loved butter produced by the tonnage. It's practically unpatriotic to offer another butter in Ireland.

And yet, as Will and Alison discovered entirely by accident, there's a foodie contingent in their locale with an appetite for handmade butter, reminiscent of their great-grandparents' homespun butter. With no culturing involved, the Abernethy's butter is nothing more than liquid cream spun into soft gold. Their small-churn butter began selling so well after just three years on the market that Alison left her job in nursing to help her husband manage the rising demand for their product.

It was Alison's father, Norman Kerr, who taught Will how to make butter by hand four years ago, when a bout of ill health prevented Kerr from continuing his favorite pastime: demonstrating churning at the local country fairs. An avid rescuer of forgotten household tools and crafts, Kerr would "make a wee bit to show how it's done and people went mad for it," Allison said. When he became temporarily bedridden, Will and Alison took over the butter act. Seeing how people clamored for the handmade butter, the Abernethys decided to sell some in the local shops. When a well-respected local chef, Derek Creagh, tweeted about the couple after discovering their butter at his local butcher's shop, Heston Blumenthal tracked down the Abernethys, asking if they would supply butter to his iconic Fat Duck restaurant. So did chef Marcus Wareing, of Marcus restaurant in Knightsbridge and the elegant brasserie, the Gilbert Scott, in London. In such celebrated company, it wasn't long before a throng of food devotees was seeking out Abernethy butter.

Norman Kerr's small hundred-year-old potbellied metal churn now stands in the corner of the Abernethy's mini-creamery, which is housed in what used to be a granny flat on the farm. These days the hand-cranked churn is only trotted out for butter-making demonstrations at shows and events. A larger barrel churn that holds thirty-five liters of cream—a modern electric version of the end-over-end churn—gets all the action in the creamery as the couple tries to keep pace with requests for their butter.

Will's butter making starts each day at 6 a.m. with a walk down the lane with his collie, Fudge, to pick up two forty-liter milk cans of fresh pasteurized cream dropped off by nearby Draynes dairy. Dromara lies in a temperate region of rolling grass-clad hills, ideal for dairying. There's no shortage of farms to supply cream. Starting out in their retail butter venture, Will and Alison tried lots of different local creams, churning each sample. "The consistency, color, and flavor from Draynes was the best," Alison said. "They only use milk from their own cows. The other dairies use milk from hundreds of farms." Tasting their butter, I savored the simplicity of it—so creamy, fresh and nutty—and marveled that each four-ounce piece of Abernethy butter is shaped, one at a time, into a neat little jellyroll with a ribbed surface—evidence of Will's skill with a classic pair of grooved wooden butter hands.

ABERNETHY BUTTER IS HAND-ROLLED INTO LOGS USING TRADITIONAL BUTTER WOODEN PATS. (ABERNETHY BUTTER)

Like all of the steps in his process, he learned from his father-in-law how to roll the butter. It's a labor-intensive last step, but one that's reminiscent of farmstead butters from centuries past. Back then, the refined shape or design of a butter marked its provenance and implied an assurance of quality. Today, in Dromara, that's true once again.

BACK IN THE STATES, I drove to the heart of Pennsylvania's Amish and Mennonite farm communities to learn more about the sweet butter made at Trickling Springs Creamery. Newly built in the style of an old-fashioned clapboard country market with a front porch and scattered picnic tables, the creamery building is part food shop, part production facility. It supports many fifth- and sixth-generation farms in the area by collecting local milk for organic and grass-fed products that are sold in big city outlets in the east. A young woman in her traditional Mennonite dress and bonnet was operating the stainless-steel churn on the day I visited.

I made the trip to Trickling Springs because the creamery produces one of the more unusual high-fat butters on the market. It has a whopping 91 to 93 percent butterfat, making it chewy and dense—ideal for leaving out at room temperature for table butter (also great for making ghee). It never wins any contests because most butter judges find its consistency just too unorthodox. But tasting a little wedge of it straight up, I found the flavor to be deep and lingering, and the texture firm yet ultrasmooth. The high butterfat content comes from mechanically pressing the butter after churning to drain much of its buttermilk.

Another kind of unusual butter prompted my drive north to Stirling Creamery, located about two hours east of Ontario in Canada's dairy country. The ninety-year-old creamery produces an uncommon style of butter made from the bits of fat leftover in whey, called whey cream. This fat is a by-product of cheese making, typically cheddar cheese production. Generations ago, whey cream butter was easy to find. But back then it was considered a second-class product and there were prohibitions against mixing whey cream with fresh cream in premium butter making. Even now, whey cream butter in the United States can only ever earn an A grade from the USDA—not the gold standard AA—but its fans, like me, don't care. The sample that Stirling's vice president of marketing, Greg Nogler, handed me was one of the better whey cream butters I'd tasted: Slightly tangy, with a distinct savory-nutty flavor layered with a little sweetness, its texture was dense and creamy. It's similar to cultured butter yet more boldly flavored with an umami-rich fullness. Stirling Creamery also makes four other premium butters in traditional batch churns—unsalted and salted versions of either 80 percent or 84 percent butterfat (lauded as one of the "World's Great Butters" by *Saveur* magazine)—but its whey cream butter stands out for its brighter yellow color and deeper, tangier flavor.

Alcam Creamery in Richland Center, Wisconsin, has also been making whey cream butter since 1946, capitalizing on the daily tide of whey that results from Wisconsin's cheese-making empire. Picking up whey cream from eighty-five different cheese plants, Alcam produces butter under thirty different private label names. But most of these do not label it as whey cream butter, for fear it will confuse customers. So this style of butter is out there—it's just not easy to spot.

AS THE SMALL-BATCH BUTTER trade continues to develop on both sides of the Atlantic, one of the more fascinating consequences is the resurgence of other animal butters, made from goat's or sheep's (aka ewe's) milk cream, or from blending these different animal creams with cow's cream. You can instantly see and taste the difference between these butters and the standard cow product. When my long-awaited sample of ewe's butter from Haverton Hill Creamery in Petaluma, California, arrived in the mail, it had the signature paleness of butter made from sheep's milk. The previous two sheep's-milk butters I had tasted had an almost grayish caste to them, but Haverton Hill's butter—nestled snugly in a small white cardboard eight-ounce tub—had a warmer color, more like unbleached flour.

This was the first surprise. The second was its smooth, matte texture. Earlier sheep butters I'd tasted had an off-putting greasiness to them, a fact I mentioned to Missy Adiego, who, together with her husband, Joe, runs their sheep farm and Haverton Hill creamery. Missy was very familiar with the greasy issue, but she assured me when I placed my order that their butter was not like that. "Yes, we had some very fatty-tasting sheep butter before we started our creamery," she conceded. "But at the time, we were convinced it was possible to do better." It turned out to be a good hunch, backed up by some months of R&D to get the butter just right. "First the cream has to be really fresh," she explained. "We made some with previously frozen sheep's milk and there was a huge difference. It was really sheepy tasting."

For sheep's-milk butter making, the percentage of milk fat in the cream has to be between 36 percent and 40 percent; otherwise it won't churn correctly. "We found that out the hard way, after our first month of making butter," Missy admitted. "Suddenly the churning didn't work." They called various experts in Wisconsin to try to figure out was going wrong. Turns out they had been churning cream that was about 68 percent milk fat, which, ironically, is too much fat to form butter. So now they test the fat in the milk before every churning.

They also ripen the cream for twenty-four to thirty-six hours before churning, which is what helps mitigate the greasiness. Its flavor is ultrarich and interesting, with none of the heavy gaminess I'd tasted in other versions. But there is a very subtle taste of "sheep," a pleasing flavor if you're a fan of artisan sheep's-milk cheeses. There is nothing else like it.

JUST AS THE ADIEGOS have mastered sheep's-milk butter making, Al and Sarah Bekkum of Nordic Creamery in Westby, Wisconsin, have succeeded in the artisan goat's-milk butter category. Their traditional cheese and cow butters have a loyal following, but for the goat butter Al now makes—which won an award at the 2013 American Cheese Society contest—demand far exceeds supply. Tasting Al's white pristine goat butter you can understand why. It's creamy yet lighter tasting than cow's-milk butter, but with a mild goaty tang.

Al Bekkum is large, sturdy man of Norwegian descent, somewhere in the early years of middle age, who is used to the rigors of farming and dairying (not to mention parenting— he and Sarah have six kids). So I was surprised to hear him confess that making goat's-milk butter almost had him beat. "It's a crazy beast of a thing until you've done it for a while," he admitted. "In the churn, the butter doesn't easily expel its moisture so getting a firm consistency is a challenge." Because the milk fat in goat's cream has a lower melting point than that in cow's, Al also had to cool it way down for churning— about twenty degrees lower than for making cow's butter. Sometimes, to avoid these production challenges, he makes a mixed-milk butter with cream from cows, goats, and/or sheep. It's a hybrid butter I've not see anywhere else in the market. Tasting a batch, I wondered why not; it was buttery and yet also more than that. It's delicious complexity lingered.

I didn't (yet) travel to where it's made, but I also knew of the first, and one of the best, American goat butters. It's made by Meyenberg in Turlock, California, which pioneered the category of commercial goat dairy products more than eighty years ago. In the 1980s, the farm began to make goat cheeses, but its European-style butter didn't follow until 2004. Made from the cream of goats on pasture, it has some of the zing of goat's cheeses, but with less pungency. Distinct from cow's-milk butter in taste and appearance (it's snowy white), Meyenberg goat butter is the only one available nationwide. (Try it next time you're making Southern-style biscuits; its unique taste delicately broadens the flavor beyond the usual taste of wheat, buttermilk, and salt.)

FAR AWAY FROM THE markets and media of our new-fashioned butter scene, there are remote artisans whom you will never see, making butters you will never taste. But their contribution to butter's narrative is no less significant. Because their methods are primitive, in fact, they represent a rare living link to our ancestral food customs, one that may not exist at all in a generation or two, given how technology and communications are changing even the most remote areas. To taste these old-world butters firsthand and see how they were made felt like a great imperative to me. I'm no anthropologist, but attention is a means of preservation.

That's how I became witness to the centuries-old practice of Bhutanese yak herding and tasted its butter—as detailed in the prologue of this book. From that Himalayan experience, I am left with a memory of earth and people that is much more remarkable than the actual yak butter itself, which was simply mild (when fresh) and not as sweet as cow butter. Pursuing butter, I've learned, is not always about chasing deliciousness; sometimes butter leads to something more profound.

My butter journey to the Punjab region in northern India in 2014 also left some indelible impressions. In search of traditional butter making using the milk of water buffalo, I was led to a small village and the home of Ajita, a sari-clad elder with a dark creased face and one gold front tooth that gleamed when she smiled. For more than sixty years, she had been making butter from the milk of water buffalo that the family kept roped outside their concrete home. (These are very ornery creatures I quickly discovered—like giant horned

YAK BUTTER-MAKING METHODS IN THE HIGHLANDS
OF BHUTAN REMAIN UNCHANGED FOR CENTURIES.
(ELAINE KHOSROVA)

guard dogs without the bark.) I had read that water buffalo's butter was superlative, that the Indians considered it much more delicious than cow's-milk butter. But because the cow is more docile and such a prolific milker compared to the water buffalo, cow's butter is gradually replacing traditional buffalo butter.

Years ago I had tried a water buffalo butter from Italy, but it was underwhelming. Perhaps because its milk wasn't cultured overnight into a thick yogurtlike consistency before being hand-churned—as is the custom in rural India, where

IN A PUNJAB VILLAGE, BUFFALO'S-MILK BUTTER
IS CHURNED IN A PLASTIC BUCKET USING A ROPE TO
SPIN A WOODEN PLUNGER. (ELAINE KHOSROVA)

the cream is not separated. This practice comes from ancient
Ayurvedic healing traditions that stipulate ghee must be made
from the butterfat of fermented whole milk.

As I stood by, Ajita poured the thick frothy fermented
milk into a tall plastic bucket, a salvaged container that had
once held some kind of industrial product. Then she inserted
her churning instrument—a long wooden pole with a cross
plate at the bottom. A thick rope was wrapped around the top
of the pole, like a neck scarf. Ajita held both ends of the rope
and began pulling them alternately, which made the pole spin
and rise up and down slightly. It was a method of churning

I'd never seen before. (Generations ago, before plastic, Indian women used the same pole method but with a large ceramic pitcher as the churn; they would sit on the floor bracing the churn with their feet and pull on the ropes that wrapped around the narrow neck of a center pole.)

Occasionally Ajita would pour a little hot water into the bucket to hasten the churning if she thought the milk was too cold. After twenty minutes or so, another woman who lived next door took over. It's a vigorous project. I too stepped in to help, only to pull a bit too vigorously on the ropes and cause the milk to overflow onto the floor. The two women shooed me away.

After more than a half hour of churning, tiny white flecks of butter began to appear. (Natural buffalo milk butter is not yellow.) Using her hand, Ajita scooped out the tiny bits of butter into a bowl and worked them together into a solid mass. I vividly remember the moment when my husband and I were handed a spoonful of the butter to taste. Most of Ajita's neighborhood had come over to silently watch us, rare Western visitors in their tiny remote village. As the butter dissolved on my tongue—into rich waves of creamy, tangy, nutty, buttery flavor—the audience read my pleasure. With nodding heads and smiles, they knew what I then realized: It was one of the best butters I'd ever tasted.

TEN

. . . .

Working It

BUTTER, THE INGREDIENT

. . . .

Now for the making of puff paste of the best kind, you
shall take the finest wheat flour after it hath been a little
baked in a pot in the oven, and blend it well with eggs,
whites and yolks all together, after the paste is well
kneaded, roll out a part thereof as thin as you please,
and then spread cold sweet butter over the same, then
upon the same butter roll another leaf of the paste as
before; and spread it with butter also; and thus roll leaf
upon leaf with butter between till it be as thick as you
think good: and with it either cover any baked meat, or
make paste for venison, Florentine, tart or what dish
else you please and so bake it.

—GERVASE MARKHAM,
The English Housewife, 1615

SPIN THE BOWL! KEEP SPINNING THE BOWL! OTHER-
wise you're gonna get scrambled eggs!" As chef-instructor
Joe DiPerri barks this lesson at his flinching culinary students, their stainless-steels bowls, balanced over pots of near-
simmering water, whirl in jerky unison. At the same time,
each student furiously beats a whisk inside their bowl, trying

to whip its two ingredients: egg yolks and water. It's an ambidextrous skill, like when you pat your head while rubbing your belly. "The harder you whip, the more volume you create! Got it?" DiPerri says. A deferential chorus of "Yes, Chef!" rings out, platoon-style, from the sixteen students, all dressed in uniform whites and toque. It's a familiar fashion for me; almost thirty years ago, I had worn the same uniform when I was a pastry arts student for eight months, here at the Culinary Institute of America (CIA) in Hyde Park, New York. Now I was back to observe this butter-centric class that hadn't been part of my pastry study.

It's day eleven in what will be a three-year-long stint for these new enrollees at the CIA, and this morning each fledgling cook is trying to make that golden paragon of French sauces—hollandaise. It is a classic emulsion sauce, where technique meets alchemy. Emulsions defy logic by blending that which seems unblendable: fat and water.

Hollandaise sauce, made with egg yolks, water, melted butter and lemon juice, plus a pinch of seasonings, is best known for being draped over poached eggs and English muffins on brunch-time plates of eggs Benedict. But it's also, more notably, a pillar in the cooking world, one of just five so-called mother sauces (or *sauce capitale*) in French cuisine that spawns many saucy offshoots.

The trickiest parts of making hollandaise are controlling the temperature and gradually whisking in the butter so the ultrarich sauce doesn't "break," or separate. DiPerri, a robust middle-ager with a well-fed frame, patrols the room, issuing orders and the occasional joke or tease to his students. "Isn't

CHEF AUGUSTE ESCOFFIER IS CREDITED WITH REFINING
THE TAXONOMY OF BUTTER-BASED "MOTHER SAUCES" AND
THEIR DERIVATIVES IN THE EARLY TWENTIETH CENTURY.
(WIKIMEDIA COMMONS)

it nice that no one's towel caught on fire today!" he declares.
Though loud and commanding, he's a good-natured teacher,
quick to praise students when they do well. One by one he
tells the aspiring chefs in the class when their beaten yolk mixture is thickened enough so their pot can promptly come off
the stove. The next step for the students is to whisk a steady
stream of clarified butter into their egg mixtures. "It should
be creamy and dreamy," DiPerri says rousingly, "like cake
batter . . . like Betty Crocker! Got it?"

"Yes, Chef!"

With the butter and egg blended, now the group seasons their sauces with lemon juice, salt, a little cayenne and a dash of Worcestershire. As one slim dark-haired student, Connor Dineer, is finishing his sauce, I ask if it's the first time he's made hollandaise. "Yes!" he says, beaming through thick owl-rimmed glasses. "It's so exciting!" I recalled the same thrill when, as a culinary student, I made croissants for the first time.

Dineer and his classmates plate a ribbon of hollandaise over steamed broccoli and carry it, like a sacred offering, to the chef's desk. DiPerri is looking for each rendition to be a glossy, velvety smooth sauce with no hint of separation and a balanced buttery-lemony taste. He is pleased. After congratulating the class, the chef then tells the students—with what I detect is a soupçon of glee—to pour a glug of melted butter into each of their crocks of hollandaise, causing the sauces to break. Small gasps and groans erupt. "Now you're gonna learn how to fix your broken hollandaise!" DiPerri says, grinning.

Over the next three weeks, these students will make hollandaise again (this time flying solo, without the chef's cues) as well as the four other fundamental sauces of classical French cooking: béchamel, velouté, espagnole, and tomato sauce. All combined, these sauces lead to hundreds of derivations in the classic French repertoire.

With the exception of tomato sauce, all the mother recipes incorporate butter. It is this intrinsic connection to the backbone of classic cuisine—sauce making—that has made butter virtually synonymous with French cuisine. The fact that today each class of brand-new students at the CIA begins their long training with these classic emulsions and sauces demonstrates just how vital butter still is to the foundations of gastronomy.

> Fresh butter stirred into a sauce just before serving is the simplest of enrichments. It smoothes out the sauce, gives it a slight liaison, and imparts that certain French taste which seems to be present in no other type of cooking.
>
> —JULIA CHILD,
> *Mastering the Art of French Cooking (1961)*

SAUCE MAKING MAY BE one of butter's more gloried applications, but there are many other ways this dairy fat serves us in the kitchen. In fact, it's hard to think of another ingredient that boasts as much versatility. As a flavor-lifting cooking medium, butter can be put to work in the sauté pan and on the griddle as well as in the saucepan. It can be browned, whipped, smoked, clarified, salted, spiced, or herb-seasoned. And then there is butter's stupendous role in baking. Because it can be creamed, rubbed in, cut in, or layered with other ingredients, we get to choose from a vast range of sweets and desserts. Tender cakes, flaky delicate pastries, chewy bars, snappy and soft cookies, as well as luxurious buttercreams all owe their invention to butter.

Butter even turns up in the beverage category. There's classic hot-buttered rum of course, but modern mixologists have also expanded dairy at the bar with what they call butter-washed cocktails. The technique is a simple one: Melted butter is combined with a choice of spirit and left to sit for a few hours. Then the mixture is chilled until the butter solidifies on top and is skimmed off. The spirit remains infused with the flavor of butter.

"Bulletproof coffee" is also new on the butter beverage scene, though it was inspired by the very old butter tea tradition of Tibet. Invented as a power drink, bulletproof is made by blending hot coffee, grass-fed butter, and flavorless MCT (medium-chain triglyceride) oil. Whether or not this mixture lives up to its claims—faster weight loss, more energy, better brain focus—continues to be hotly debated, but anyone who has sipped bulletproof coffee agrees: It's the emulsified butter that makes it tasty.

Incredibly, butter is built for all these culinary options. And yet its most common use is the simplest—straight off the stick as a ready-made spread on bread and rolls, toast and biscuits. What other food can play so many supporting roles in sweet or savory recipes yet still show up irresistibly solo at the table?

Butter works as a culinary multitasker because of its unique constitution; as a matrix of fats, water, and milk solids, these components work together—and separately—to great effect. The milk solids in butter, which are usually embedded in tiny droplets of water, contain proteins and phospholipids that serve as the invisible binder between fat and water that creates an emulsion. Any water-based sauce can therefore be thickened and enriched by simply whisking a cool knob of butter into it just before serving. (The only caveat is that the heat must be low—(below 140°F)—to prevent the sauce from breaking.) The professional name for this technique is *monter au beurre*, to "mount" a sauce with butter.

> Believe me, there's a big crock of softened butter on almost every cook's station . . . In a professional kitchen, it's almost always the first and last thing in the pan.
>
> —ANTHONY BOURDAIN,
> *Kitchen Confidential, 2000*

And then there is *beurre monté*, a very different preparation that resides mostly in celebrated restaurant kitchens. Beurre monté is remarkably simple in theory—butter melted without separation. Yet in practice it's a delicate maneuver. As an emulsion of water in fat, butter naturally wants to come undone when heated (hence the separation that happens automatically with clarified butter). To keep the emulsion intact, yet melt the butter, chefs use a ploy that involves a little water and a lot of patient whisking.

Starting with a few tablespoons of water heated to a simmer, chefs whisk a pound or more of butter, piece by piece, into the liquid over low heat. As the butterfat is slowly incorporated, it stays suspended in the water, so the emulsion holds. The result, assuming the heat and technique are just right, is a creamy, fluffy butter bath. Because its water and milk solids are embedded, beurre monté has a deeper flavor and more versatility than butter that's simply clarified.

Chefs rave about beurre monté as a cooking medium for meats, seafood, and poultry because it heats foods more gradually than braising in other liquids. And the buttery flavor is a luxurious bonus. This liquid emulsion of butter is also ideal for holding and infusing meats; a sautéed pork tenderloin, for example, submerged in beurre monté maintains an ideal temperature, doesn't dry out, and is imbued with butteriness.

Chefs also use it regularly as a basting sauce. Just a few spoonfuls of beurre monté keeps meat or poultry moist, seasons it, and lends the roasted or grilled protein a lovely burnished browned color. The merits of beurre monté are many indeed, including its easiest use—as a creamy dipping sauce for bread.

EARLY ON IN MY career, I spent nine years as a test kitchen editor for a national magazine. It was a great gig, spending every day toying with ingredients and recipes and getting paid for it. (I lived off the leftovers too.) Although I came to the job with a degree in food and nutrition, my special interest was baking; I had done an eight-month stint at the CIA studying pastry arts after college and then worked as a dessert chef before being hired as a recipe tester for the magazine. As such, butter was my stock in trade. I couldn't have baked without it. But, it being the 1990s, when the low- and no-fat mania was in full tilt, my baking work at the magazine often required than I slim down recipes and use oil instead of butter whenever possible. The results were nearly always a compromise in flavor and texture. Although I groaned about this practice ("Why not have a smaller portion of something truly scrumptious rather than a big slice of ho-hum?"), the job of thinning out baking recipes taught me well that butterfat— or the lack of it—affects taste on many sensory levels.

Butter's own rich flavor make sweets and desserts irresistible, but it also enhances the taste of other ingredients in the recipe. Spices are spicier, chocolate is more chocolaty, lemon more zingy, and so on. Fat carries other flavors within a dish and holds them longer in the mouth for a lasting, lingering release. A water-based flavor, conversely, might be intense at first, but it doesn't have any staying power. Some argue that this is why people are inclined to eat too much of various low-fat, high-carb products—there's just less satiety from starch than from fat. Butterfat melts and coats the mouth for a full, rounded and complete flavor experience, then gradually recedes. Margarines and vegetable shortenings—which are designed to replace butter in baked goods—lack the same superb flavor, and because they're formulated to melt at a higher (more workable) temperature, they often leave a waxy, gummy residue in the mouth.

In addition to being a first-class flavor vehicle in baked goods, butter also makes possible a range of textures, depending on how it's combined with flour and sugar. The method of creaming butter and sugar to make a cake, for instance, is a means of aerating the blended ingredients to get more tiny gas bubbles in the fat before egg and flour are added. The tender, springy melt-in-your-mouth texture of a cake comes partly from those superfine gas bubbles that are trapped in butter's web of soft and crystalline fats. (This can't happen with a vegetable oil.)

Aerating the fat also makes chemical leavenings work better. Baking powder, for example, functions by releasing carbon dioxide that expands the bubbles *already* in a batter; it doesn't form a single new bubble. This means that the creaming step in cake making, which distributes air bubbles in the butterfat, is crucial. Don't rush it. Bruce Healy, a French pastry expert and coauthor of *The Art of the Cake* (1999), has experimented a lot with each step in mixing a cake batter to determine how they relate to cake volume. He claims that maximum aeration of the butter and sugar is the key to a buoyant texture. It's more important than the time taken to add the eggs, flour, or liquid. (A good five to eight minutes is generally recommended for creaming, depending on the type of electric mixer being used.) Formerly a theoretical physicist, Healy notes that the ideal temperature of butter for creaming with sugar is 65°F. Much higher than that and butter will start to melt during beating; a lower temperature makes it harder to aerate.

Cakes also get their soft texture from another butterfat effect: tenderizing proteins. The gluten protein in wheat flour and the protein in eggs will toughen the structure of cake if fat and sugar are not around to soften their scaffolding. But too much fat and/or sugar can make a cake collapse under its own weight. A light moist cake demonstrates an exquisite balance of four central ingredients.

Unlike cake, cookies have many textures that we enjoy— chewy, crumbly, crispy, and crunchy. But what makes a cookie a cookie, regardless of texture, is a relatively high proportion of fat and sugar to flour, with very little, if any, liquid (except from eggs). Butter provides flavor, richness, moisture, and in some cookies, a pliant body. (It does the same for crumbly, short French tart doughs—*pâte sucrée* ["sugar" pastry] and *pâte sablée* ["sandy" pastry]—which are essentially cookie doughs rolled out and fitted into a tart pan.)

When butter melts during cookie baking, it lubricates the particles of flour, sugar, and if present, egg. As it melts it also causes the cookie to spread and flatten, especially drop cookies. (Shortbread cookies and those that are rolled out and cut in shapes, spread very little because of the high ratio of flour to moisture.) Because butter melts at a lower temperature than margarine or shortening, it allows the cookie to spread earlier and longer, allowing for a thinner cookie.

Butter's role in producing flaky baked goods is perhaps the most complex part it plays in baking. In a piecrust, for example, fat creates flakiness and tenderness at the same time. Yet the action that leads to the former is completely at odds with the method for making the latter. (No wonder so many people are intimidated by pie baking.) To render flakiness in a pie, the butter must be dispersed in tiny flecks and pieces to create layers in the dough. Once in a hot oven, the butter pieces melt into the flour particles at the same time the water in butter is driven off as steam, pushing the layers apart. Conversely, dough tenderness (sometimes called shortness) occurs when butter coats the flour rather than remaining dispersed. When butter is rubbed in to flour, it coats the particles and prevents the gluten in flour from overdeveloping, which causes toughness.

With butter doing these two separate jobs, technique is paramount in making flaky pie dough; the baker has to work in the cold butter both finely—for tenderness—as well as in fragments—for flakiness. (It helps to use low-gluten pastry flour.)

Puff pastry, or *feuilletage* in French, is a more elaborate flaky construction, but it's based on the same principal of layering cool butter in a simple dough of flour and liquid (called a *détrempe*). In this case there are alternating sheets of both—what amounts to a "dough-fat sandwich," as food science writer Harold McGee calls such fat-laminated pastries. In the standard method of making puff pastry, the rich doughy sandwich is rolled, folded, and refrigerated for a total of six "turns" over the course of several hours. The goal is to distribute the layers of butter evenly throughout. The reward for this patient process is pastry that is stacked with microscopically thin leaves—729 layers of flour dough separated by 728 layers of butter. When it's baked in a hot oven, the butter melts and its expanding water vapor steams apart the multi layers, causing the height of the pastry to increase by four to six times.

Given the dynamics of liquid in this scenario, it would stand to reason that a standard American butter that has 16 to 17 percent water (80 percent butterfat, by law) would be better to use for flaky pastries than a European-style butter that has more butterfat (82 percent or more) and consequently less water. But this isn't so. Professional bakers prefer working with a higher-fat butter (sometimes called *beurre sec*, or "dry" butter) because it makes flaky pastries crispier. (Plugrá brand, made by Keller's Creamery in California, is an 82 percent butter that's popular in many U.S. pastry kitchens, though on the

**THE DELICATE LAYERING OF PUFF PASTRY IS CREATED
BY STEAM FROM BUTTER'S MOISTURE. (SHUTTERSTOCK)**

West Coast, Crémerie Classique, made by Larsen's Creamery in Oregon, is the pro's 82 percent butterfat choice.) The
higher moisture levels in standard supermarket butter tend to
toughen pastries since water develops gluten. In fact, special
butters are made in France for professional bakers and pastry
chefs that are almost pure butterfat. *Beurre concentré, beurre
pâtissier,* and *beurre cuisinier* are all made by slowly melting
regular butter and then separating out its water content by
centrifuging. The distilled butterfat is then either recooled as
is or separated into fractions that melt at varying temperatures, according to the professional's needs.

In the butters available to home bakers, a 2 percent difference in butterfat composition doesn't sound like much of
anything, yet it can make the difference between ho-hum and
splendid results in baking. Butter with a greater ratio of fat

also creates more tender cakes and cookies, and frostings that are creamier and less likely to separate. These butters are also easier to handle at room temperature because they're dense and firmer.

Despite their advantages, higher butterfat choices in U.S. markets can still be hard to find—or recognize. Sometimes they're labeled as European-style butter, as in the case of the new Land O'Lakes version, which debuted nationwide in 2015. It has 82 percent butterfat; sample it side by side with the regular Land O'Lakes butter and you'll see the difference.

When choosing a higher butterfat brand for baking, go with an unsalted version; its flavor is sweeter and you can more easily control saltiness in the recipe. But without salt, freshness is key since these butters more easily spoil. It's not so easy to ascertain which butter is freshest when standing in front of a dairy case full of them, since expiration dates on butter are no guarantee. If a butter hasn't been properly handled and stored after it left the creamery, its sell-by date is meaningless. Your best recourse is to buy butter that's well packaged (foil wrappers or small sealed tubs are ideal), displayed in a closed-door refrigerated section, and sold in a market where there's good turnover.

Once you've scored good butter, keep it well wrapped in foil or plastic, away from other ingredients that have odors. Unless you go through it quickly, it's best to tuck it in the back of the fridge away from sudden changes in light, temperature, and moisture. Salted butter keeps longer than unsalted in the refrigerator—at least four months if it's well protected.

Unsalted butters are more perishable, though properly stored they'll keep well for two months. Freezing butter will keep it from spoiling for many months, but it can make butter slightly grainy, less spreadable and cause its moisture content to be a little "leaky." When industrial butter makers routinely freeze many tons of butter during peak production in the spring and summer, they "microfix" the butter before sending it to market; this mechanical process reestablishes the physical structure of butter that is compromised with freezing. Honestly, I've never been able to detect much performance difference in the butter I've frozen and then thawed for baking, but it's still good insurance to use fresh butter whenever you can.

When recipes call for softened butter, it's ideal to pull the butter from the fridge hours before it's needed and let it temper naturally (65°F is best). Soft butter should be malleable, but should never reach the point of being greasy and slack. If you need to hasten the process of softening, cut the butter into small pieces and leave them out at room temperature; they'll warm up relatively quickly. A microwave can be used too, but it's riskier. The heat is uneven in a microwave and you can easily end up with butter that's part molten, part cold. If you do have to use the microwave for instant softening, cut the butter into small, even-sized pieces and use the defrost setting at increments of 20 to 30 seconds, checking the butter in between.

The relationship of butter to temperature is ultimately what makes cooking or baking with this rich fat so diverse and interesting. Of course butter's luscious flavor would be reason enough to use it, but at varying degrees of cold, soft, or melted, a good butter is also profoundly important to the texture of so many foods we enjoy (and take for granted). It can tenderize, emulsify, leaven, crisp, crumble, caramelize, and enrich. All it takes is for us to use a little know-how. Or a reliable recipe. Read on.

The number of recipes from around the world that include butter would fill a stadium, let alone a book. So the selection here is relatively, and necessarily, tiny. I chose to include classic dishes that owe their character to butter, to both its flavor and behavior as an ingredient. It's a collection of Butter's Greatest Hits, you might say. Without butter, none of these popular culinary inventions would have happened, nor would their derivatives. In the case of sauce and pastry making, that constitutes a profound—and scrumptious—effect on our gastronomic choices. Butter's most common and beloved application may still be as a thick melting smear on toasted bread, but it is capable of so much more.

One final note: As you delve into these recipes, you'll find that I sometimes specify using a higher butterfat brand of butter (often labeled "European style") in the ingredient listing to get the best results. When this type is not specified, feel free to use whichever butter you keep on hand.

✿ BEST-EVER CRUMB CAKE

. . . .

I DON'T TEND TOWARD HYPERBOLE, SO WHEN I CALL THIS crumb cake the best ever, you can be darn sure it's outstanding. The golden cake is tender and moist, topped by a dense chewy layer of buttery crumb. It's so good that when I was deciding which recipes would make the cut for a quintessential butter collection, this cake suddenly sprang to mind though I'd only eaten it once at a friend's house more than fifteen years ago. I resolved to get the recipe, even though I hadn't kept in touch with its keeper, Nora Raphael. I left what I'm sure was a much unexpected message on her voice mail. She called me back in no time and recited the recipe to me over the phone. Apparently it's a very old one, given to Nora's mom many years ago at a Unitarian church event from an elderly Mrs. Kolumbo.

In the original recipe, it's baked on a rimmed baking sheet, so the cake portion was miniscule compared to the heavy crumb topping. This is very typical of *Streuselkuchen*, a traditional German flat cake from which our modern crumb cake evolved. To increase the cake-to-crumb ratio, Nora makes it in a lasagna-size pan, which still allows for about two dense inches of crumb. That's how I make it too. I also substituted brown sugar for part of the white granulated sugar in the topping, because I like the flavor. And I added a bit of salt to the recipe because I use unsalted butter.

MAKES ONE 9 × 13-INCH CAKE

. . . .

CRUMB TOPPING

6　cups all-purpose flour

2　cups packed light brown sugar

1　cup granulated sugar

2½　tablespoons ground cinnamon

1　teaspoon salt

1¼　pounds (5 sticks) unsalted butter, cut up into small cubes, softened

CAKE

8　tablespoons (1 stick) unsalted butter, softened

¾　cup granulated sugar

2　cups all-purpose flour

2　teaspoons baking powder

½　teaspoon salt

2　large eggs

¾　cup milk (preferably whole)

1　teaspoon vanilla extract

Confectioners' sugar, for sprinkling (optional)

1. Make the crumb topping: In a large bowl, combine the flour, brown sugar, granulated sugar, cinnamon, and salt, mixing well to blend all the dry ingredients. Drop the butter cubes into the mixture and with your fingertips, knead and press it into the flour mixture, incorporating the butter. When it's mostly blended, press and form the crumb

mixture into tennis-ball-size clumps. Set aside while preparing the cake.

2. Heat the oven to 375°F. Butter and flour the bottom and
sides of a 9 × 13-inch baking pan. In a large bowl with
an electric mixer, beat together the butter and sugar until
creamy and light, about 3 minutes. Meanwhile, stir together the flour, baking powder, and salt in a medium
bowl.

3. Add the eggs to the butter mixture, one a time, beating
well after each addition and scraping the sides and bottom
to mix thoroughly. Beat in the milk and vanilla. The mixture will look a bit curdled at this point, but don't worry.
Add the flour mixture and beat on a low speed just until
blended, scraping down the sides as needed until a smooth
batter forms.

4. Spread the batter evenly in the prepared pan. Take the reserved crumb balls and break them roughly over the cake
to create a thick, chunky layer of topping. Lightly press
on it to adhere to the cake and bake for 1 hour, or until the
center feels firm when gently pressed. Cool in the pan. If
desired, sprinkle the top lightly with confectioners' sugar.

✿ BRIOCHE

. . . .

LIKE A MARRIAGE OF BREAD AND CAKE, BRIOCHE IS RICH
yet light with a fine texture and delicate sweetness. Butter and
eggs are what make it special. When working with this dough,
it's best to keep it relatively cool and allow for a slow fermentation in the refrigerator. The flavor and texture is better
and this prevents the abundance of butter in the recipe from
separating and making the dough feel greasy.

Brioche can be made into any shape, though using a baking pan that supports the rich dough will give it more loft than
if baked free-form. I like to make braids with the dough and
fit them into loaf pans.

MAKES THREE 9 × 5-INCH LOAVES

. . . .

4	cups bread flour
½	cup granulated sugar
1½	tablespoons active dry yeast
2	teaspoons salt, plus a pinch for the egg wash
4	large eggs, at room temperature, plus 1 large yolk for the egg wash
½	cup whole milk, at room temperature
½	pound (2 sticks) unsalted butter, softened
1	tablespoon heavy cream

1. In a stand mixer with paddle attachment, mix 3½ cups of
   the flour, the sugar, yeast, and salt on low speed until well

combined. Beat the eggs and the milk together in a medium bowl; add to the flour mixture and mix on low speed until the dough starts to come together. Mix on medium speed for 3 minutes. Scrape down the bowl and paddle and continue to mix until the dough is smooth and blended, about 3 more minutes. Scrape down the sides as needed.

2. Cut the butter into tablespoon-size pieces. With the mixer on medium-low speed, add half of the butter, one piece at a time. Scrape down the bowl and add the remaining butter, a few pieces at a time, mixing on medium-low speed. Once all of the butter has been added, gradually beat in the remaining ½ cup flour. Increase the mixer speed to medium and mix for 4 minutes. Scrape down the paddle and the sides and bottom of the bowl. Replace the paddle with the dough hook and mix again on medium-high speed until the dough is smooth, soft, and shiny, 4 to 5 minutes more. (The dough will be very moist.)

3. Form the soft dough into a ball inside the mixing bowl, cover with a cloth, and let it proof for 1 hour. (Since the dough is very rich, it won't expand much during this first proofing.) Knead the dough briefly on a well-floured surface, then place it in a large lightly buttered bowl; cover with plastic wrap and refrigerate for at least 4 hours, or overnight. This will slow the fermentation and chill the butter, making the dough easier to shape.

4. Divide the dough among greased pans of your choice, shaping as desired. (You'll have enough dough for three 9 × 5-inch loaf pans; alternatively, the dough can be made

into 2 large braided, or brioche, loaves or 16 small rolls.)
Cover loosely with plastic and let rise for 3 to 4 hours until
nearly doubled in size and springy when gently pressed
with a fingertip.

5. When the loaves have risen, heat the oven to 375°F. Beat
the remaining egg yolk with the cream and a pinch of salt
to make a glaze. Lightly brush the tops of the brioche.
Bake, rotating the baking pans after 15 minutes. Bake for 5
to 25 minutes longer—depending on the size and shape—
until dark golden brown. (Individual rolls will bake in 20
to 25 minutes; small loaves take about 35 minutes; and two
large loaves made from this recipe will need 40 to 45 minutes.) Let the brioches cool on a wire rack for 15 minutes
before unmolding. Brioche is best served warm.

✿ BUTTERMILK SCONES

. . . .

THESE ARE MORE FLAKY AND DENSE, IN THE TRADITION of my Scottish roots, rather than the cakey version of most American scones. They're meant to hold a good slather of butter and jam. I like to add to the dough 1 teaspoon grated orange zest plus and ½ cup dried currants plumped in warm water and well drained. There are many other flavor variations that can work, but I give you the basic recipe and technique to serve as the foundation of your own scone repertoire. I also cut them into squares, so they bake more evenly than wedges.

MAKES EIGHT 3-INCH SCONES

. . . .

2⅓ cups all-purpose flour, sifted

½ cup sugar, plus more for sprinkling

1½ teaspoon baking powder

½ teaspoon baking soda

½ teaspoon salt

¼ teaspoon finely grated fresh nutmeg

8 tablespoons (1 stick) cold unsalted butter, cut into small cubes

¾ cup buttermilk

1 teaspoon vanilla extract

1. Heat the oven to 400°F. In the bowl of a food processor, combine the flour, sugar, baking powder, baking soda, salt, and nutmeg. Pulse to distribute the dry ingredients evenly.

2. Add the butter pieces and briefly pulse the mixture until the butter is about the size of whole peppercorns. Transfer the crumbly mixture to a large bowl.

3. Combine the buttermilk and vanilla in a small bowl, then stir into the flour mixture all at once, mixing gently, just until the dough hangs together and is moistened. Don't overmix or the scones will be less tender.

4. With floured hands, gather the soft dough and let spill it out onto a floured countertop. Gently pat it out to a 1½-inch-thick rectangle. Fold in the short sides, one on top of the other, to make a three-layer stack of dough. Repeat patting it out to a 1½-inch-thick rectangle and folding in thirds two more times.

5. Pat the dough one more time into a 1¾-inch thick rectangle. Cut in half lengthwise, then crosswise in quarters to make 8 scones. Transfer the scones to a greased or parchment-lined baking sheet, spacing about 2 inches apart. Sprinkle the tops generously with sugar and bake on the middle rack for 18 to 22 minutes, until golden and the centers spring back.

❖ CLASSIC POUND CAKE

. . . .

POUND CAKE IS A VERY OLD INVENTION, CREATED LONG before we used chemical leavenings, like baking powder and baking soda, to make cakes light and airy. In the earliest recipes, a pound each of butter, sugar, flour, and eggs were doggedly beaten together by hand for a long time to aerate the mixture so it wouldn't be too bricklike. As Hannah Glasse wrote in her cookbook, circa 1747, of mixing pound cake ingredients, "Beat it all well together for an hour with your hand, or a great wooden spoon."

Even with the convenience of today's electric mixers, beating together the butter and sugar assiduously is still the secret to the velvety texture of a classic air-leavened pound cake—tight and fine-crumbed, not dense and heavy. That kind of mechanical leavening and the texture that results is the difference between a buttery coffeecake recipe and true pound cake. Also, you'll note that you start the cake in a cold oven, which allows for a slow, steady phase of setting the proteins and starches in the cake, followed by browning. Because this style of cake doesn't have chemical leavenings, it doesn't need that blast of heat that causes batters to expand better in preheated ovens.

In addition to flavor, butter plays a key role in the classic pound cake method because it's semisolid nature traps air bubbles in a constellation of crystalline and soft fats. I have made it with both higher butterfat brands (82 percent) and regular unsalted supermarket butter; both work just fine, but the former has a bit more butteriness.

. . . .

¾   pound (3 sticks) unsalted butter, softened

2½ cups sugar

2   teaspoons vanilla extract

6   large eggs, at room temperature

3   cups sifted cake flour

1   teaspoon salt

1   cup milk (preferably whole), warmed to room
    temperature

1. Butter and flour a 10-inch Bundt pan. In a large bowl, using an electric mixer, beat the butter, sugar, and vanilla until very creamy and light, about 6 minutes, scraping down the sides often. Add the eggs, one at a time, beating well after each addition.

2. Combine the flour and salt. Add the flour mixture and the milk alternately to the butter mixture, beginning and ending with the flour, and mixing on low speed in between to blend. Scrape down the sides as needed to make a smooth batter. Spoon the batter into the prepared pan. Give it a few raps on the counter to help force out any large air bubbles.

3. Place the pan in a cold oven and set the oven temperature to 350°F. Bake for 30 minutes. Reduce the heat to 325°F and bake for 30 to 40 minutes longer, until golden and firm. Cool the cake in the pan for 10 minutes, then turn out onto a wire rack to cool.

✿ CROISSANTS

. . . .

"A WELL-MADE CROISSANT WILL GIVE ONE PAUSE, A MO-ment to reflect on the pétit engineering marvel set before you," wrote Chad Robertson, baker extraordinaire of Tartine bakery in San Francisco and author of *Tartine Bread* (2010). The buttery, shatter-in-your-mouth flaky layers of a fine croissant are indeed a marvel, one that takes time and care to create but involves no special skills. The trick is to keep the butter layer in the dough cool yet pliable while rolling and folding the dough. Too soft and the butter will blend into the dough; too hard and it will break into pieces as you work with it, causing uneven layering, or "laminating," as the pros call this buttering of the dough. That's why it's essential to plan ahead for this recipe adventure, making the dough and the series of folding and resting steps one day, then cutting, shaping, proofing and baking the dough the next day.

MAKES 16 CROISSANTS

. . . .

DOUGH

1	tablespoon active dry yeast
¼	cup warm water (about 80°F)
	Pinch of sugar
4	cups all-purpose flour
1	cup cold whole milk
⅓	cup sugar
2¼	teaspoons salt
3	tablespoons unsalted butter, melted

BUTTER LAYER

1¼ cups (2½ sticks) high butterfat (82% or more)
     cold unsalted butter

⅓   cup all-purpose flour

GLAZE

1   large egg yolk beaten with 1 teaspoon heavy
    cream

1. The day before baking the croissants, make and laminate
    the dough: In a small bowl or glass measuring cup, stir
    together the yeast, warm water, and the pinch of sugar; set
    aside for 5 minutes to proof the yeast. It should develop a
    raft of foam on its surface.

2. In the large bowl of stand mixer fitted with a paddle, com-
    bine the flour, milk, the ⅓ cup sugar, and salt. Mix on low
    speed, scraping down the sides of the bowl, until moist-
    ened. Add the melted butter and the yeast mixture and
    mix on medium speed for 5 minutes. Scrap the soft dough
    from the sides of the bowl, cover the bowl with plas-
    tic wrap and set aside at room temperature for 2 hours.
    Transfer the dough to a large lightly floured sheet pan;
    dust the top with flour, wrap in plastic and refrigerate for
    at least 2 hours.

3. About 30 minutes before you are ready to laminate the
    dough, prepare the butter layer: Cut the cold butter into
    ½-inch cubes and toss with the flour in a gallon-size re-
    sealable plastic bag. With the bag sealed, pound the but-
    ter and flour with a rolling pin until they begin to come

together in a cohesive mass. The goal is to blend and make the cold butter pliable without warming it too much. Roll and press the butter mixture in the bag into a neat 8-inch square, alternately using your rolling pin and a straight-edge ruler to smooth the surface and edges; refrigerate for about 20 minutes.

4. On a 22-inch-long piece of generously floured parchment or waxed paper, roll the dough to an 11-inch square. Brush any excess flour off the dough. Cut the bag from around the square of chilled butter. Place the square of butter diagonally on top of the square of dough so that the corners of the butter point to the center of the sides of the dough; this will create four triangular flaps of dough. Fold one flap of dough over the butter, stretching it slightly so that the point just reaches the center of the butter. Repeat with the other flaps. Press the seams together to completely seal the butter inside the dough.

5. Lightly flour the top and bottom of the dough. With a rolling pin, begin pressing firmly to drive the softened butter as far as possible to the edges of the packet. Then roll out the dough to lengthen it into an 8 × 22-inch rectangle, keeping the sides straight. Brush off any flour on the dough and fold in one short end of the dough, leaving one-third (about 7 inches) of the other end of dough exposed. Brush off flour and fold in the exposed end to create a three-layer stack. Wrap the long piece of parchment over the stack to cover, then transfer the dough to a baking sheet, cover with plastic wrap, and chill for 30 to 45 minutes. (The butter should be firm but not hard.)

6. Repeat rolling and folding the dough on the parchment paper, this time rolling in the direction of the two open ends of the folded dough to make the same length rectangle as before, with a width of about 9½ inches. Fold the dough in thirds again, brushing off excess flour and keeping the edges tidy. This is your second turn. Cover and chill for another 30 to 45 minutes.

7. Give the dough a third rolling and folding. Place the dough, wrapped in parchment, on the baking sheet and cover snuggly with plastic wrap. Refrigerate overnight.

8. The next day, unwrap and lightly flour the top and bottom of the dough. With a serrated knife, cut the dough in half. Wrap and refrigerate one-half while you roll out the other half to a thin narrow strip, about 8 × 22 inches. If the dough sticks as you roll, sprinkle with flour. If it begins to resist or shrink back while rolling, cover and refrigerate for about 15 minutes to relax the dough, then finish rolling. Trim the edges and ends so they're straight and the strip of dough is 20 inches long.

9. With a sharp knife or pizza wheel, cut the dough into four rectangles, 8-inch by 5-inch in size. Cut each rectangle diagonally in half to make a total of eight equal-size triangles. Using a paring knife, make a ¾-inch-long notch in the center of the 5-inch-wide edge of each triangle. (This helps the rolled croissant curl into a crescent.)

10. To shape each triangle, first hold it so the short notched edge is on top and gently stretch the piece to measure about 9 inches long. Lay the croissant on the work surface with the notched side closest to you. With fingers on

either side of the notch, roll the dough away from you, toward the pointed end. Roll until the pointed end is on the underside of the croissant. Place on a parchment-lined baking sheet and gently curve the two narrow ends towards each other to create a crescent shape. Repeat notching and shaping the remaining triangles, placing them about 1½ inches apart.

11. Repeat rolling, cutting, and shaping the remaining half of chilled dough and arrange on another parchment-lined baking sheet.

12. Lightly brush the glaze on top of each croissant. Put the croissants, uncovered, in a warm, draft-free spot—about at 75°F is ideal—for about 1½ to 2 hours to expand. They're ready to bake when you can see the layers of its construction along each cut edge, and when they're about 50 percent larger than their original size.

13. Heat the oven to 425°F. Bake the croissants for 15 minutes. Rotate the baking sheets and swap their positions on the middle and top oven racks. Reduce the heat to 400°F and continue baking until the croissants are richly browned, crisp, and flaky—about 5 to 10 minutes longer. Serve warm.

✦ FLAKY PASTRY DOUGH,
TWO WAYS

. . . .

AFTER MORE THAN TWO DECADES OF MAKING QUITE GOOD
flaky pie dough by all the usual methods I'd read about—with
a pastry cutter, then a food processor, and a stand mixer—a
few years ago I accidentally discovered an ideal "unplugged"
method for making great pie crust.

My family and I were staying with friends at a beach house
rental one summer week and the kitchen was bare bones in
terms of utensils. Wanting to make a peach pie one night,
I rummaged around and found a banged-up disposable pie
tin. There was no rolling pin, so I used a wine bottle. And to
cut the butter into the flour to make pastry, I decided to try
using a cheap flat grater—the kind with the big holes. The
cold butter was a snap to grate into the flour. I was astonished
at how buttery, tender, and flakey the crust baked up. Since
then, I've duplicated the grating method many times, making
a few tweaks to the recipe—like using some pastry flour and
higher-fat butter (82 to 84 percent), and a smidgen of sugar.
Because I enjoy the sensuous pleasure of making things by
hand more than the speed of getting it done, this has become
my go-to piecrust technique. That said, if I need to make a
big batch of pie dough, I use a food processor to cut in the
butter and do the rest of the mixing by hand so I can feel for
the right amount of moisture. It works well too. I offer both
methods here.

MAKES ENOUGH FOR ONE DEEP-DISH
DOUBLE-CRUST 9-INCH PIE

. . . .

1⅓   cups all-purpose flour
1   cup pastry flour
1   tablespoon sugar
¾   teaspoon salt
1¾   sticks high butterfat (82% or more) cold unsalted
       butter
6 to 8 tablespoons cold water

1. For the unplugged version, place a medium mixing bowl
   and a large-hole flat grater (or box grater) in the freezer
   for at least 15 minutes to chill thoroughly.

2. Stir together the flours, sugar, and salt in the chilled mixing bowl. Remove 1 stick of butter from the fridge and
   firmly grate half of it into the flour mixture, using the
   wrapper to hold the stick of butter. (Work expeditiously,
   so the butter stays cold.) Lightly toss the grated bits with
   the flour mixture and continue grating the rest of the stick.
   Scrape any butter on the grater into the flour. Toss again
   and grate in the remaining ¾ stick of butter. (Alternately,
   if using a food processor, combine the flours, sugar, and
   salt and pulse briefly to mix. Cut the butter into tablespoon-size chunks and add to flour mixture. Pulse briefly
   just until the butter is the size of tiny peas. Transfer to a
   medium bowl and proceed with the recipe as is.)

3. Briefly toss the butter and flour to distribute evenly, then scoop up a handful of the coarse mixture and quickly rub it between your fingers, allowing the flour butter mixture to fall back into the bowl as you do so. The goal is to lightly coat the flour with the butter yet keep the little nibs of butter intact. Repeat this about six times.

4. Sprinkle in the water gradually while tossing the mixture lightly with a fork to evenly distribute the water. Mix very gently with your hands and begin to gather the dough. (The mixture should feel cool and damp, not moist or sticky.) Divide the dough in half to make two flat rounds, roughly 4 inches wide. Wrap and chill the dough for at least an hour or up to 12 hours. (If chilled for more than 2 hours, allow the dough to rest at room temperature about 20 minutes to soften slightly so it's easier to roll out.)

❁ GERMAN PANCAKE

. . . .

BAKED IN BUTTER AND THEN CROWNED WITH MORE OF IT,
this puffy golden pancake is similar to a popover in texture
with a moist eggy interior and crispy outside. It's generally
served for breakfast or brunch, topped with powdered sugar
or maple syrup, and a squeeze of fresh lemon. But I've also
made it as an impromptu dessert, filling its bowl-like center
with fruit compote and serving it with whipped cream.

MAKES ONE 9-INCH PANCAKE

. . . .

5   large eggs

½   cup all-purpose flour

½   cup whole milk

1   teaspoon vanilla extract

½   teaspoon salt

4   tablespoons (½ stick) cold salted butter, plus
    more softened for serving

    Pure maple syrup

    Lemon wedges, for serving

1. Heat the oven to 425°F. Place a 9- or 10-inch ovenproof
    skillet (cast iron is best for this) in the oven for 5 minutes
    to heat the pan. (This helps the pancake puff more.)

2. In a blender, combine the eggs, flour, milk, vanilla, and
    salt. Blend on low speed for about 5 seconds and then on
    medium speed for about 1 minute, until the batter is fairly

thick and smooth, scraping down the sides of the container as needed to blend everything.

3. Remove the hot pan from the oven and add the butter, swirling as the butter melts to coat the bottom and partway up the sides. Pour the batter evenly over the melted butter and slide the skillet back into the hot oven. Bake for 20 minutes, or until puffed and golden. Transfer the pancake from the skillet to a large plate and spread with softened butter and a generous drizzle of maple syrup. Serve immediately, with lemon wedges.

◩ KOUIGN AMANN

. . . .

KOUIGN AMANN (PRONOUNCED "KWEEN-AMON") IS A buttery, sticky, flaky, crunchy pastry that originated in Brittany, France. Like a croissant recipe, it begins with yeasted dough that's generously laminated with layers of butter. But the difference is kouign amann dough layers are generously sprinkled with sugar during the last two stages of rolling and folding. Also, it's made with salted butter—a tradition in Brittany where fleur de sel is harvested. The result is a sweet-salty pastry with a tender buttery interior and crispy caramelized surface. When I visited historic Saint-Malo, on the coast of Brittany, kouign amann was sold on every street, in various sizes and usually shaped like a round spiral, similar to the way sticky buns are made. But another style is to fit squares of the dough into round cake pans or muffin tins, with the points folded in, which creates a distinct look for this delectable pull-apart pastry. In France, it's also sold made with apples and in a Nutella version.

Do seek out a "drier" salted butter to make this recipe, meaning one that has 82 percent or more butterfat. (Some bakers actually make their own butter first, to ensure most of the water is pressed out.) Otherwise the water content in standard butter will combine with the sugar in between the layers of this dough and cause a pooling of moisture that makes the layers collapse. If you can only find unsalted higher fat butter, use that and lightly sprinkle crunchy crystals of fleur de sel on the dough while rolling and folding to approximate true Breton tradition.

MAKES 12 PASTRIES

. . . .

DOUGH

    3 cups all-purpose flour

    2 tablespoons (¼ stick) melted butter

    ¾ cup warm water (about 80°F)

  2½ teaspoons instant dry yeast

    ½ teaspoon salt

    1 cup sugar

BUTTER LAYER

    1 pound (4 sticks) high butterfat (82% or more) salted butter, cold but malleable

    ⅓ cup all-purpose flour

GLAZE

    1 large egg

    1 tablespoon heavy cream

      Pinch of salt

1. In the bowl of a stand mixer fitted with a paddle, combine the flour, melted butter, water, yeast, and salt. Mix until all the ingredients are moistened, then switch to the dough hook. Knead for 2 to 3 minutes, until a dough forms. Transfer the dough to a large lightly buttered bowl, cover with plastic wrap, and allow it to sit for 1 hour or more, until nearly doubled.

2. About 30 minutes before the dough is ready, prepare the butter layer: Cut the cold butter into ½-inch cubes and toss with the flour in a gallon-size resealable plastic bag. With the bag sealed, pound the butter and flour with a rolling pin until they begin to come together in a cohesive mass. The goal is to blend and make the cold butter pliable without warming it too much. Roll and press the butter mixture in the bag into a neat 8-inch square, alternately using your rolling pin and a straight-edge ruler to smooth the surface and edges; refrigerate for 20 minutes.

3. On a 22-inch-long piece of generously floured parchment or waxed paper, roll the dough to an 11-inch square. Brush any excess flour off the dough. Cut the bag from around the square of chilled butter. Place the square of butter diagonally on top of the square of dough so that the corners of the butter point to the center of the sides of the dough; this will create four triangular flaps of dough. Fold one flap of dough over the butter, stretching it slightly so that the point just reaches the center of the butter. Repeat with the other flaps to make a packet of dough. Press the seams together to completely seal the butter inside the dough.

4. Lightly flour the top and bottom of the dough. With a rolling pin, begin pressing down firmly on the dough to drive the softened butter as far as possible to the edges of the packet. Then roll out to lengthen it to an 8 × 22-inch rectangle, keeping the sides straight. Brush off any flour on the dough and fold in one short end of the dough, leaving one-third (about 7 inches) of the other end of dough

exposed. Brush off flour and fold in the exposed end to create a three-layer stack. Wrap the long piece of parchment over the stack to cover, then transfer the dough to a baking sheet, cover with plastic wrap, and chill for 30 to 45 minutes. (The butter should become firm but not hard.)

5. Repeat rolling and folding the dough on the parchment paper, this time rolling in the direction of the two open ends until the dough is the same length rectangle as before, with a width of about 9½ inches. Fold the dough in thirds again, brushing off excess flour and keeping the edges tidy. This is your second turn. Cover and chill for 20 to 30 minutes. Give the dough a third rolling and then sprinkle all over with ½ cup of the sugar; press lightly with your rolling pin to help it stick. Fold again to make a three-layer stack and chill once more for 20 to 30 minutes. (Do-ahead tip: If desired, the dough can now rest in your fridge for a day or two, or be tightly wrapped and frozen for 3 months. Thaw the dough overnight in the refrigerator.)

6. Sprinkle the work surface with sugar and roll the dough in the sugar to an 8 × 22-inch rectangle. Sprinkle all over with the remaining ½ cup sugar; press lightly with your rolling pin to help it stick. Fold in thirds once more to complete your fourth turn. Chill again.

7. When ready to bake your pastries, roll the dough on a lightly sugared surface to an 8 × 24-inch rectangle (it should be about ¼ inch thick). Butter the insides of 12 muffin cups or pastry rings.

8. To shape the kouign amann, cut the dough in half length-wise to form two 4 × 24-inch strips. Cut each strip into six 4-inch squares to create a total of 12 squares. Fold the corners of each square toward its center. Tuck each pastry firmly into the muffin tins or pastry rings so the folded side is up. It will feel like you're squishing the pastry to fit; this is fine. (*At this point, if desired, the kouign amann may be covered and refrigerated overnight. The next day, let the pastries come to room temperature and continue with step 9.*)

9. Cover the kouign amann loosely with plastic wrap and let them rise at room temperature until slightly puffy, about 1 hour. (They will not double in size like croissants.) About 15 minutes before baking, heat the oven to 400°F. Make the glaze: Beat together the egg, cream, and salt in a small bowl. Brush the pastries with the glaze, sprinkle them liberally with sugar, and bake for 10 minutes; reduce the heat to 350°F and bake until pastries are deep golden and their edges look darkly caramelized—about 20 to 25 minutes longer.

10. Cool briefly, just enough that you can wiggle them out of the muffin tins or pastry molds; do not let the kouign amann cool completely in the pan as the sugar will harden and make them difficult to remove. Serve warm or at room temperature.

"White rice with melted ewe's milk butter and white sugar is a dish not of this world."

—AL-ASMA'I, *ninth century, Jordan*

⬚ PÂTE BRISÉE PASTRY

. . . .

THIS CLASSIC FRENCH PASTRY DOUGH IS BUTTERY AND light, yet sturdier than the dough recipe for Flaky Pie Pastry, Two Ways (page 000). It makes an ideal crust for tall savory tarts and quiches, baked in straight-sided tart pans and spring-form pans, that need to stand on their own when unmolded. (Pie dough is generally too tender and flaky for that job, hence the sloped sides of pie tins). *Pâte brisée* dough is also easy to handle for blind-baking a straight-sided tart shell in a spring-form pan using the technique I describe below, in which the pastry overhangs the pan and is trimmed partway through baking. This trick gives a nice neat edge and also prevents it from shrinking into the pan—the bane of many a tart baker.

MAKES ENOUGH FOR ONE DEEP-DISH
9-INCH PIE SHELL OR TART SHELL

. . . .

1¼ sticks high butterfat (82% to 84%) unsalted butter, softened

1 large egg, at room temperature and lightly beaten

1 tablespoon water

1⅔ cups all-purpose flour, plus 1 to 2 tablespoons more if needed

½ teaspoon salt

1. In a food processor fitted with a chopping blade, pulse the butter until creamy, about 1 minute. Add the egg and

water, pulsing to mix. Alternate scraping down the sides and pulsing until the mixture is well blended.

2. Add the salt and flour. Pulse just until the flour is incorporated. (The dough shouldn't form a ball.) The mixture will be crumbly but moist. Transfer the dough to a 13-inch sheet of parchment paper and work the dough into a cohesive mass. If it is sticky, gently work in 1 to 2 tablespoons flour; it should be soft but not tacky.

3. Gently form the dough into a ball and flatten it into a 6-inch disc. Wrap in the parchment paper and refrigerate for at least 1½ hours or overnight. If chilled overnight, let the dough warm slightly for 30 to 40 minutes at room temperature before rolling.

4. To blind-bake a deep-dish 9-inch pie shell, on lightly floured parchment paper, roll out the dough to an 11- or 12-inch round, depending on the depth of your pan. (A 12-inch round will fit a 1½-inch-deep pan.) Transfer to the pie pan, lining the bottom and sides and overhanging the edge by an inch; do not stretch the dough or it will shrink during baking. Press and pinch the overhanging pastry into the rim of the pan to make a thick edge; flute if desired. Lightly prick the bottom in four places to allow any trapped air to escape. Refrigerate for at least 30 minutes, or wrap loosely in plastic and chill up to 24 hours.

5. To make a straight-sided tart shell in an 8-inch springform pan, roll the dough out to an 11½-inch round. Transfer to the springform pan, lining the bottom and sides. (It will want to fold along the sides, so just press it evenly

in place.) Without stretching the dough, let it naturally drape over the rim of the pan by at least ½ inch. With a fork, lightly prick the dough lining the bottom of the pan in 6 places; refrigerate for at least 45 minutes, or wrap loosely in plastic and chill up to 24 hours.

6. Heat the oven to 375°F. To partially blind-bake the deep-dish pie shell, line it with a sheet of parchment paper topped with pie weights (or dried beans); bake the shell on the bottom rack of the oven for 15 minutes. Remove the parchment and weights, then fill as desired and continue baking according to your filling recipe. To fully blind-bake the pie shell in order to fill later, remove the parchment and pie weights and bake for 18 to 20 minutes longer, until deep golden.

7. To bake the tart shell in the springform pan, place it on a baking sheet (to catch any bits of pastry that may drop from the edges) and line the bottom of the tart with parchment paper topped with pie weights. Bake on the bottom rack of the oven just until the pastry starts to firm up and color, about 12 minutes. Remove from the oven, and with a large knife, quickly trim off and discard the overhanging pastry to create a smooth edge. Remove the parchment and pie weights, fill the tart as desired, and return it to the oven; continue baking according to your filling recipe. For a fully baked tart shell to hold an unbaked filling, remove the parchment paper and pie weights after trimming the crust and bake for about 15 to 20 minutes longer, until evenly browned.

✿ PÂTE SABLÉE PASTRY

. . . .

I LOVE THIS DOUGH FOR ITS VERSATILITY AS MUCH AS ITS buttery, tender crispness. Very similar to classic pâte sucrée in that it's lightly sweetened, I use it to make small or large pastry shells for fresh fruit tarts. (You can also use it to make delicate Sablée Cookies, page 000). *Sablée* in French means "sandy," which may sound unappealing, but in fact it refers to the light, crumbly mouthfeel of this rich dough. It's also very forgiving to work with. Since the butter is at room temperature, there's none of that fussing about keeping everything cold, as in making flaky pastry. (If desired, the sablée dough can be flavored with ½ cup finely chopped nuts, dried fruit, or a teaspoon of spices or citrus zest; just add whatever you choose in step 4 below, when kneading the mixture.)

MAKES TWO 9-INCH TART SHELLS

. . . .

- 1¾ cup all-purpose flour
- ½   cup cake flour
- ⅓   cup sugar
- ½   teaspoon salt
- 1¾ sticks unsalted butter, cut into small cubes and softened at room temperature
- 2   large egg yolks
- 1   teaspoon vanilla extract

1. In a food processor fitted with the chopping blade, combine the flours, sugar, and salt. Give this mixture a few pulses to evenly distribute everything.

2. Add the butter and cut it into the mixture with several short pulses of the machine. The mixture should have a coarse crumbly texture. Transfer it to a large bowl.

3. In a small bowl, beat together the egg yolks and vanilla. Slowly drizzle the yolk mixture into the crumbly flour mixture, tossing everything lightly with a fork to mix until a soft dough form. At this point, the yolks not be blended.

4. Knead the mixture in the bowl by pushing and smear-ing the mass together with one lightly floured hand; the goal is to quickly blend the butter and yolks throughout the dough. (It sounds inelegant, but the French use this technique—*fraisage*—to make tender yet sturdy pastry.) As you're kneading, the mixture should be smooth and moist, not sticky.

5. Gather the dough into a ball. Divide it in half to form two flattened discs, about 4 to 5 inches across. Wrap each in plastic and chill for an hour (or freeze for later use).

6. About a half hour before baking, roll one disc of pastry to an 11-inch round on a lightly floured piece of waxed or parchment paper. Transfer it to a 9-inch tart pan, press-ing it into the bottom and sides. Trim the excess (you can reserve it for making cookies or pastry decorations). Chill the dough for at least 20 minutes. Repeat with remaining disc of dough if making 2 tarts.

7. Heat the oven to 350°F. With a fork, generously dock, or prick all over, the bottom of each chilled pastry shell. Bake for 18 to 20 minutes, until lightly browned. Cool before filling.

Sablée Cookies

. . . .

MAKES ABOUT 4 DOZEN COOKIES

Divide the dough into thirds and roll each piece into a short log about 1½ inches thick. (If your hands are warm, this is easier to do if you enclose the dough in plastic wrap first.) Refrigerate the plastic-covered logs for at least 2 hours or up to 4 days (or freeze for up to 1 month). To bake, slice the logs crosswise with a thin knife into ¼-inch-thick rounds. Arrange the rounds on a baking sheet about 1 inch apart and bake 15 to 18 minutes, until tops are firm and edges look slightly toasty. Cool for a couple of minutes on the baking sheet, then transfer to a wire rack to cool completely.

✿ PUFF PASTRY

. . . .

ALSO KNOWN AS *PÂTE FEUILLETÉE* (LEAFLIKE PASTRY), this many-layered dough made of butter and flour takes some time to create, but the delicate structure of flaky pastry is so worth it. You can use it as a topping for potpies and casseroles; as pastry shell for strudels and little finger foods; to make individual pastries such as napoleons and *palmiers*; and for the crust of sweet or savory tarts. It's hard to find decent store-bought puff pastry; most of what's available is not made with butter. It may have some many layers, but very little taste.

This is the time to splurge on the highest-quality butter you can get with a fat content of at least 82 percent. When puff pastry bakes, the water in the butter forms much of the steam that makes it rise and separate in layers. But too much steam—from too much water—can make for a soggy pastry.

MAKES ABOUT 2 POUNDS PUFF PASTRY

. . . .

3½ to 4   cups all-purpose flour

3   tablespoons sugar

1   pound (4 sticks) high butterfat (82% to 86%) unsalted butter, ½ stick cold, the rest softened at room temperature

1   cup plus 2 tablespoons cold water

1   tablespoon fresh lemon juice

1½   teaspoons salt

1. Place 3 cups of the flour and the sugar in a large mixing bowl. Cut the ½ stick of cold butter into small pieces and work it into the flour in mixing bowl, using a pastry blender or your fingertips, until the texture is like coarse cornmeal.

2. Combine the water, lemon juice, and salt. Stir this into the flour-butter mixture, mixing gently until a rough dough forms that pulls away from the sides of the bowl. If needed, add more water or flour, 1 tablespoon at a time, until the dough holds together.

3. Turn the dough out onto a lightly floured surface and knead 2 to 3 minutes until it is smooth and a little springy—meaning the gluten has been partly developed. Pat the dough into a 9-inch square and wrap in plastic. Refrigerate for at least 30 minutes.

4. With an electric mixer or by hand, beat the room temperature butter and ½ cup of the flour until well blended and smooth. Sandwich this mixture between two lightly floured pieces of waxed or parchment paper and shape into an 8-inch square. Refrigerate for 45 minutes.

5. On a lightly floured surface, roll the dough into a 12-inch square. Put the chilled (but malleable) square of butter diagonally in the center, like a diamond shape on top of the dough. Fold in the triangular corners of the dough, over the butter, until their points meet in the middle. Pinch and seal the edges of the dough square together.

6. Turn the square over on a floured surface and roll the dough into a 20 × 10-inch rectangle. Flip the dough over

once or twice while rolling to maintain even layers, keeping the work surface and rolling pin well dusted with flour.

7. Align the rectangle so that a 10-inch edge is the bottom, nearest you, and the long edges are the sides; brush off any excess flour. Fold the bottom third of the dough up to the center and then the top third over that (like a business letter). Line up the corners neatly; uneven edges will cause a gap in layers. Press the edges down lightly with a rolling pin to seal. Turn the layered dough a quarter turn to the right so the edge that was the top of your pastry is now on the right side. Make an indent in the top left corner by pressing your finger into it; this is to mark that you have completed the first "turn."

8. If the dough and butter are still cool to the touch, dust with flour and roll again into a rectangle, fold, and turn the same way. Mark the top left corner with two indentations for your second turn. If the butter begins to feel too soft and starts to ooze, cover it on a small baking sheet, and refrigerate it for 20 to 30 minutes to firm.

9. Classic puff pastry gets six turns. Make another four turns, covering and chilling the dough for 20 to 30 minutes after each turn. At the beginning of each turn, be sure the pastry is placed in front of you with the marked corner at the top left. In this position, the right and left sides of the folded dough will become the long edges of each rolled-out rectangle. After each fold and turn, make indentations in the top left corner to keep track of how many have been completed.

10. When all six turns are done, cover the dough and refrigerate for at least 2 hours (but preferably overnight, which allows the dough to relax). The pastry should rest at room temperature between 15 and 25 minutes, until it is pliable, before rolling out to slightly more than ⅛-inch thickness for making pastries. To get the best layering, trim the edges of the dough with a sharp knife or pizza wheel, then cut into the desired shape. (Prick the pastry gently but generously with the tip of a knife before baking so that it doesn't rise too much, causing the pastries to be lop-sided.) Once shaped, chill the puff pastries for at least 20 minutes, then heat the oven to 400°F, and bake according to the size of your pastry; small individual pastries will bake in 18 to 20 minutes and larger ones generally take 25 to 35 minutes. Puff pastry is done when the bottom crust is dark toasty brown and the top is golden.

MAKE-AHEAD TIP

After completing the last turn, wrap the puff pastry tightly in plastic and refrigerate for up to 3 days, or freeze for up to 2 months. If freezing, thaw completely in the refrigerator before using.

❖ PULL-APART BISCUITS

. . . .

LIGHT AND BREADY, THESE BISCUITS STRAIGHT FROM THE
oven are the perfect thing to put butter on, not just in. Like the
scone recipe in this book, you fold the biscuit dough repeatedly to build up flaky layers, but since this recipe has much
less sugar to tenderize than scones do, you have to handle it a
bit more gently. I use a combination of all-purpose flour and
cake flour for a delicate texture.

MAKES EIGHT 3-INCH BISCUITS

. . . .

1	cup all-purpose flour
1	cup cake flour
1	tablespoon sugar
1½	teaspoons baking powder
1	teaspoon salt
½	teaspoon baking soda
8	tablespoons (1 stick) unsalted butter, very cold, cut into thin slices
¾	cup cold buttermilk
2 to 3	tablespoons buttermilk, for brushing

1. Heat the oven to 425°F. Line a baking sheet with a silicone
   mat or parchment paper. In a large bowl, whisk together
   the flours, sugar, baking powder, salt, and baking soda.
2. Toss the butter slices in the flour mixture. With a pastry
   blender or large fork, cut the butter into the dry ingredients

until the whole mixture resembles coarse crumbs. Gently stir in the ¾ cup buttermilk, just until combined. Resist overmixing, which will toughen the biscuits.

3. Scoop the dough onto a well-floured surface and with floured hands, pat it into a 1-inch-thick rectangle. Fold the rectangle in thirds, like a letter fold. Turn dough a half turn and pat again into a rectangle, fold as before. Repeat once more, patting and folding dough a total of three times. Finally, pat the dough on a floured surface until about ¾ inch thick.

4. Cut out 8 biscuits using a floured 2-inch biscuit cutter. Transfer the biscuits to the prepared baking sheet. With your thumb, make a depression in the top center of each biscuit (this helps the sides rise straighter).

5. Brush the tops of biscuits with the 2 tablespoons buttermilk. Bake until golden brown, 15 to 18 minutes.

I remember that every time we moved house when I was young, my mother would butter the cat's paws before we arrived at the new place. Apparently cats are skittish when transplanted and this can lead them to run off, but when their paws are buttered they want to sit and lick them clean, which has a calming effect on them. Our cat probably acclimated to the move sooner than I did.

—KENNETH YOUNG

❁ SHORTBREAD, UNPLUGGED

. . . .

I GREW UP ON SHORTBREAD, MY MOM BEING A NATIVE Glaswegian. It turned up at many a holiday bake sale in our town, often looking plain and forlorn next to all the brightly frosted cupcakes and gooey, chocolaty things on display. But one bite of mom's melt-in-your-mouth golden shortbread made up for its unassuming looks.

She always used confectioners' sugar in her batches, but I've discovered that I like a slightly sandier texture, so I opt for superfine sugar, though I use less of it. I also fuss about the butter more than mom did, choosing a higher butterfat cultured (European-style) brand when I can get it. The flavor is more deeply buttery and toasty.

In the spirit of this cookie's pure simplicity, l love to make it with nothing more than a bowl and wooden spoon—no electric mixers or processors—the way generations of my Scottish kin did. If your butter is nice and soft at room temperature, the mixing is easy. And being right above the ingredients, you get an aromatic bonus—the wafting fresh scent of creamy, sweet-spiked butter.

MAKES ONE 8-INCH PAN OF SHORTBREAD

. . . .

Short and Sweet

....

BECAUSE SUGAR WAS A RARE COMMODITY FOR CEN-
turies before the mid-1800s, shortbread was an expensive treat for common folk, reserved just for special
occasions such as weddings, Christmas, and New
Year's. In Shetland, it was traditional to break a deco-
rated round of shortbread over the head of a new bride
on the threshold of her new home, presumably for
sweet, rich luck. Shortbread is traditionally formed
into one of three different shapes: one large circle divided into wedges ("petticoat tails"); individual round
biscuits ("shortbread rounds"); or a thick rectangular
slab cut into "fingers."

. . . .

½ pound (2 sticks) high butterfat (82% or more)
   unsalted butter (preferably cultured), very soft
⅓ cup superfine sugar, plus more for sprinkling
½ teaspoon salt
½ teaspoon vanilla extract (optional)
2 cups all-purpose flour

1. Heat the oven to 325°F. In a large mixing bowl, stir to-
    gether the butter, sugar, salt, and if desired, vanilla with a
    wooden spoon until well blended and the mixture has the
    consistency of thick mayonnaise. Add the flour and mix
    until blended and a stiff dough forms.

2. Pat the dough evenly into an ungreased 8- or 9-inch tart or baking pan (round or square). Bake until the top is uniformly golden and toasty, 45 to 50 minutes. While the shortbread is still warm, sprinkle the top with sugar, pierce it all over with the tip of a wooden skewer to create traditional shortbread holes (optional), and deeply score the round into wedges or rectangles. But don't remove the shortbread from the pan until completely cooled. (These are delicate and crumbly when warm).

VARIATIONS

Upside-Down Almond Shortbread

Sprinkle an even layer of sliced almonds (about ½ cup) on the bottom of the baking pan and add ¼ teaspoon almond extract to the dough in place of the vanilla extract. Omit sprinkling top with sugar. Proceed with forming and baking as directed. When cool, invert the shortbread to serve so the almond-studded surface is right side up.

Brown Sugar Shortbread with Dark Chocolate

Replace the superfine sugar in the dough with ⅓ cup packed dark brown sugar. Stir ¾ cup finely chopped dark chocolate into the dough with the flour. Proceed with forming, baking, and cooling as directed.

✹ TARTE TATIN

. . . .

THIS CLASSIC UPSIDE-DOWN CLASSIC APPLE TART, NAMED
for the two Tatin sisters who popularized the dessert in the late
nineteenth century at their French hotel, has ample butter in
the crust and the caramelized filling, yet it's not at all too rich
as desserts go. Juicy tart apples do the trick of balancing out
the sweet butteriness.

THE CRUST

1	cup all-purpose flour
2	tablespoons sugar
½	teaspoon fresh lemon zest
½	teaspoon salt
8	tablespoons (1 stick) cold unsalted butter, cut into ¼-inch dice
1	large egg yolk
2 to 3	tablespoons ice water

THE APPLES

1	cup sugar
¼	cup apple cider or water
2	tablespoons fresh lemon juice
¼	teaspoon salt
8	tablespoons (1 stick) unsalted butter, cut into tablespoons
6	Granny Smith apples or your favorite tart, firm apple, peeled, quartered, and cored

1. Make the crust: In a food processor fitted with the chopping blade, combine the flour, sugar, lemon zest, and salt. Pulse briefly to mix. Add the butter and pulse several times until the mixture looks like coarse crumbs.

2. Add the egg yolk and 2 tablespoons of the water. Pulse a few times until the mixture begins to come together. If it feels a bit dry, add a little more water and pulse briefly.

3. Dump the rough dough out onto a clean lightly floured waxed paper. Knead the mixture very briefly, just until it's smooth. Roll out the dough to an 11-inch round. Transfer to a cookie sheet and refrigerate for at least 1 hour, or preferably overnight, covered with plastic wrap.

4. Prepare the apples: Combine the sugar, cider, lemon juice, and salt in a 10-inch ovenproof pan. (I like to use cast iron.) Stir to blend. Over high heat, bring the mixture to a boil, then reduce to a simmer and cook, without stirring, until the sugar begins to caramelize, turning golden. Swish the pan around gently to promote even cooking.

5. Cook the mixture for a few more minutes until the mixture becomes a deep amber color. Remove from the heat and stir in the butter, two pieces at a time. The mixture will bubble up vigorously. This is fine, but do be careful— it's extremely hot stuff. When all of the butter has been incorporated and the bubbling subsides, begin to arrange the apple quarters, rounded side down, in neat concentric circles in the caramel. Remember, the bottom design will be the top!

6. Return the pan to the burner and cook over medium-low for 15 minutes. Meanwhile, heat the oven to 375°F.

7. Take the chilled pastry from the refrigerator and place it on top of the apples. Carefully tuck the pastry in around the edges of the pan and cut four slits in the dough to allow steam to escape. Bake in the hot oven for 20 to 25 minutes, until the dough is golden brown and crispy. Let the tart cool for 20 to 30 minutes. Run a thin knife around the edge of the pan to help loosen the apples.

8. To serve, place a serving platter upside down on top of the tart and carefully flip the platter and pan over simultaneously, catching any of the syrupy liquid that may drip. The tart should fall gently out of the pan. Tarte Tatin is best served warm with a soft pillow of whipped cream.

"Waste not your Cream by giving it away to liquorish persons; keep certain days for your Churning, and be sure to make up your Butter neatly and cleanly, washing it well from the Butter-milk, and then salt it well."

—HANNAH WOOLLEY,
1675, The Gentlewoman's Companion

❈ YELLOW BUTTERMILK LAYER CAKE

. . . .

MANY YEARS AGO, WHEN I LEFT NEW YORK CITY WITH MY family to live in a small rural town in the Hudson Valley, I supplemented my freelance writing career by making wedding cakes. Real ones, that is. Baked with natural ingredients, filled with fresh local fruits, and swathed in Silky European Buttercream (page 000). This buttermilk cake recipe was my go-to choice for most of those tiered extravaganzas. I used it over and over because everyone loved its tender, moist texture and the recipe is so easy and dependable to work with. I no longer do wedding cakes (thank goodness!), but this is still my favorite layer cake recipe. I like to fill it with chopped fresh fruit or berries (peaches and blueberries are wonderful) that are held together by a little buttercream or custard. Or you can simply fill it with any favorite buttercream. One emphatic tip: Do use cake flour instead of all-purpose flour; it makes a real difference in creating a tender crumb.

MAKES ONE TWO-LAYER 9-INCH CAKE

. . . .

1½   sticks unsalted butter, softened

1¼   cups sugar

3   large eggs, warmed in a bowl of hot (not boiling) water

2   teaspoons vanilla extract or 1 teaspoon almond extract

2¼   cups cake flour

1½   teaspoons baking powder

½   teaspoon baking soda

½   teaspoon salt

1   cup buttermilk, warmed to room temperature

2   cups Silky European Buttercream (page 000),
    Old-Fashioned Buttercream Frosting (page 000),
    or store-bought frosting

1. Butter the bottom of two 9-inch baking pans and line with
   parchment paper; butter and lightly flour the insides of the
   pans, sides and bottoms.

2. Heat the oven to 350°F. In a large bowl, with an electric
   mixer, beat the butter and sugar until very creamy and
   light, about 4 to 6 minutes. Add the eggs, one at a time,
   mixing well with each addition. Beat in the vanilla.

3. In a medium bowl, sift together the cake flour, baking
   powder, baking soda, and salt. Beat one-third of the flour
   mixture into the butter mixture, then beat in half the buttermilk. Scrape down the sides and repeat—beat in half
   the remaining flour mixture, then all the remaining buttermilk. Scrape down the sides once more, and finally beat
   in the last of the flour mixture until a smooth, thick batter
   forms.

4. Divide and spread the batter equally between both prepared pans. Rap the pans several times gently on the
   countertop to force any air bubbles to the surface of the
   batter. With a spatula, smooth the tops again, driving off
   the bubbles. Bake for 22 to 25 minutes, until the cakes are
   firm and golden. Cool the cakes for 10 to 15 minutes in
   their pans, then invert them on to a wire rack and cool
   completely before assembling and frosting as desired.

COOKED

✿ BEURRE BLANC

. . . .

MAKING A CLASSIC BEURRE BLANC SAUCE IS INSTANTLY
gratifying compared to other sauce making. It involves simply whisking butter into a wine-vinegar-shallot reduction to
create an emulsion. The sauce has a smooth, light coat-the-
spoon consistency. You'll find that the ingredients are pretty
uniform in beurre blanc recipes, but their proportions vary
among cooks. Some will use more or less wine and vinegar
depending on the acidity desired. Likewise, the shallot mea-
surement can be adjusted to personal taste. In many professional kitchens, cream is also added to the reduction to give
the sauce more stability and body, though it does somewhat
diminish the classic buttery taste of this sauce.

While the ingredient proportions can be played with to
some degree, the technique is carved in stone. Be sure to add
the cold butter over low to moderate heat, a little at time, to
prevent the sauce from getting too hot, which will cause it
to break. Most damaging to beurre blanc, according to food
science writer Harold McGee, is letting it cool below about
90°F. Butterfat crystals form and fuse with each other creating
a network of fat that separates out when reheated. Ideally it
should be kept at 125°F.

Because of its inherent delicacy, beurre blanc is best
served with fish, poultry, or sautéed vegetables. To vary the
basic sauce, try adding one or several minced fresh herbs or

a little bit of prepared mustard, or try Lemon Beurre Blanc (page 000).

MAKES ABOUT 1 CUP

. . . .

- ½ cup dry white wine
- ¼ cup white wine vinegar
- 2 medium shallots, minced
- ½ pound (2 sticks) cold unsalted butter, cut into ½-inch pieces

   Salt and freshly ground white pepper

1. In a small saucepan, combine the wine, vinegar, and shallots. Bring to a simmer over medium-high heat and cook until the liquid has reduced to about 2 tablespoons, about 5 minutes.

2. Reduce the heat to low and gradually whisk in the butter, two or three pieces at a time. The butter should soften slowly to form a creamy sauce, rather than melt quickly, which can cause the sauce to break. Adjust your heat accordingly, taking the sauce off the heat occasionally to control the butter incorporation. Continue whisking throughout.

3. When all the butter has been added, season the sauce with salt and white pepper to taste and strain through a fine sieve. Serve promptly or keep warm for a short time by resting the sauce over a pot of warm (not boiling) water.

Lemon Beurre Blanc

Make the basic recipe, substituting ¾ cup lemon juice for
the wine and vinegar. Add ½ to 1 teaspoon grated lemon
zest to the shallot reduction, depending on how lemony
you want the sauce to be.

❁ HOLLANDAISE

. . . .

BECAUSE HEAT CAN EASILY CAUSE EGGS TO SCRAMBLE AND butter to separate, this classic sauce recipe, based on those two ingredients, has intimidated many a home cook. But if the temperature is kept below a simmer and whisking is done consistently, hollandaise is really not a challenge to master. At the Culinary Institute of America, students learning this recipe are taught a visual trick: the hot water in the saucepan should be just under a simmer, which is indicated by the appearance of lots of little bubbles—like those in a glass of seltzer water.

Some recipes call for using clarified butter in making this sauce, but my preference is to use whole melted butter. It makes for a more flavorful hollandaise.

MAKES 1½ CUPS

. . . .

3	large egg yolks
1	tablespoon water
½	pound (2 sticks) unsalted butter, melted and slightly cooled
1 to 2	tablespoons fresh lemon juice
	Pinch of cayenne pepper
	Dash of Worcestershire sauce
	Salt and ground white pepper

1. In a large metal bowl, whisk together the yolks and water briefly until light and frothy. Set the bowl over a saucepan of not-quite-simmering water, making sure the bottom of the bowl doesn't touch the water. Whisk vigorously while rotating the bowl (protect your hand from the heat of the bowl with a dish cloth). After about 3 or 4 minutes, the mixture should be foamy and thicker, and the whisk will leave tracks indicating that the eggs are cooked. Remove the pot from the heat, keeping the bowl on top.

2. Very gradually whisk in a few tablespoons melted butter in a thin stream. This is a critical step in setting up the emulsion; don't add too much butter at once. When blended, slowly drizzle in the remaining melted butter, whisking constantly, until the sauce is thick and smooth.

3. Stir in 1 tablespoon of the lemon juice, the cayenne, Worcestershire sauce, and salt and pepper to taste. Whisk to blend and taste for seasoning. Serve immediately or keep the sauce warm in its bowl set over a pan of warm water, whisking occasionally, until ready to use.

❁ BÉARNAISE

. . . .

I THINK OF THIS MUCH LOVED OLD-WORLD SAUCE AS A marriage of hollandaise and beurre blanc. It has the yolky emulsion of the former and the shallots, white wine, and vinegar reduction of the latter. But the one step that makes this quintessentially béarnaise is the use of fresh tarragon. The fennel-like flavor of this herb is a classic match for steaks and seafood, but it's also wonderful with eggs, potatoes, and sautéed greens. Enveloped in a rich sauce like béarnaise, the boldness of tarragon is mellowed yet distinct.

THE REDUCTION

- 2 medium shallots, minced
- ¼ cup dry white wine
- ¼ cup white wine vinegar
- 5 black peppercorns, crushed
- 3 tablespoons finely chopped fresh tarragon leaves
- Salt

THE SAUCE

- 3 large egg yolks
- 1 tablespoon water
- 2½ sticks unsalted butter, melted and slightly cooled
- Salt and freshly ground black pepper

1. Make the reduction: Combine the shallots, wine, vinegar, peppercorns, and half the tarragon in a heavy-based saucepan and simmer over medium-high until 2 tablespoons of liquid remain. Strain and discard the solids.

2. Make the sauce: In a large metal bowl, whisk together the yolks and water briefly until light and frothy. Set the bowl over a saucepan of not-quite-simmering water, making sure the bottom of the bowl doesn't touch the water. Whisk vigorously while rotating the bowl (protect your hand from the heat of the bowl with a dish cloth). After about 3 or 4 minutes, the mixture should be foamy and thicker, and the whisk will leave tracks indicating that the eggs are cooked. Remove the pot from the heat, keeping the bowl on top.

3. Very gradually whisk in a few tablespoons melted butter in a thin stream. This is a critical step in setting up the emulsion; don't add too much butter at once. When blended, slowly drizzle in the remaining melted butter, whisking constantly, until the sauce is thick and smooth. To finish the sauce, whisk in the reduction (to taste) and the remaining fresh tarragon. Season with salt and pepper to taste. Serve immediately or keep the sauce warm in its bowl set over a pan of warm water, whisking occasionally, until ready to use.

❁ BÉCHAMEL

. . . .

ANOTHER MATRIARCH IN THE CATEGORY OF FRENCH "mother" sauces, béchamel is one of the easiest to prepare since the flour in the sauce makes it very stable. The only real precaution is to cook the sauce over moderate heat and stir frequently to prevent it from scorching on the bottom.

Butter is not used in a prodigious quantity in making béchamel. But I include it in this collection because it is absolutely essential to making a traditional roux—which is the basis of this so-called white sauce. Roux (pronounced "roo"), a pasty mixture of equal weights of butter and flour, serves to thicken various sauces where a liquid is added (usually milk, cream, stock, or a combination of these). A butter-based roux can be cooked "blond," meaning it doesn't become toasty, or cooked to various degrees of brown for a more pronounced toasty flavor. The proportion of roux to liquid determines the thickness of the sauce. This recipe yields a medium-thick sauce, ideal for gratins, mac 'n' cheese, and soufflés. Derivations of sauces made from béchamel include Mornay (cheese), soubise (onion), Nantua (shellfish and cream), and mustard (prepared mustard, like Dijon), and crème (heavy cream).

There's an ongoing debate in the culinary world about whether the milk for a béchamel sauce needs to be heated beforehand to prevent the flour from lumping. Classicists will say absolutely, but many good results are obtained using milk straight from the fridge. A more critical factor seems to be that the roux is properly mixed and cooked so that all the flour particles are enveloped in butterfat, preventing them from clumping. I've also found it smart to add the milk (at any temperature) very gradually in the beginning. Just a splash at first, accompanied by vigorous whisking. I generally leave my milk out to warm up a bit or quickly microwave it to take the chill off, just so the sauce will heat up and thicken quicker than if cold milk is used.

MAKES ABOUT 2 CUPS

. . . .

4	tablespoons (½ stick) unsalted butter
⅓	cup all-purpose flour
2½	cups whole milk, at room temperature
1	whole clove
¼	yellow onion
1	bay leaf
	Salt and white pepper
	Pinch of ground fresh nutmeg (optional)

1. In a heavy-bottomed saucepan, melt the butter completely over medium heat, but don't let it brown. With a wooden spoon, stir the flour into the melted butter a little bit at a time, until it is fully incorporated. You'll have a grainy looking golden paste—the roux. Heat the roux, stirring, for 2 minutes, being careful it doesn't brown.

2. With a wire whisk, slowly add a few tablespoons milk to the roux, whisking vigorously to prevent the flour from lumping. Gradually add the remaining milk, a little at a time, whisking constantly.

3. Insert the pointy end of the clove into the onion and drop it into the sauce along with the bay leaf. Reduce the heat to low and simmer the sauce for about 20 minutes, or until smooth and velvety. Stir frequently with a rubber spatula, especially along the bottom and sides of pan, to prevent the sauce from scorching. (A good way to test for doneness is to rub a very small amount between two fingers, checking for any graininess.) If the sauce is too thick, whisk in a little more milk.

4. Fish out the onion and bay leaf and discard. Or, if you prefer, pass the sauce through a fine mesh strainer to remove the onion and bay leaf and give the sauce an extra-smooth consistency. Season to taste with salt and white pepper, and if desired, the nutmeg.

5. If not using right away, transfer the sauce to a storage container and press a sheet of plastic wrap on the surface of the sauce to prevent a skin from forming as it cools. Béchamel sauce keeps well in the refrigerator for about 5 days.

VARIATIONS

Mornay Sauce

After the sauce is off the heat and the onion and bay leaf have been removed, add ¼ cup each grated Gruyère and Parmigiano-Reggiano cheese. Then season as desired with salt, pepper, nutmeg, and a pinch of cayenne pepper. Mornay sauce is typically served draped over vegetables, chicken, and pasta. Makes about 2⅓ cups.

Cheese Sauce for Gratins and Casseroles

After the Mornay is off the heat and the onion and bay leaf have been removed, add ½ cup each grated cheddar, Monterey Jack, and Gruyère, plus 2 tablespoons lemon juice and ¼ teaspoon cayenne pepper. Add salt and white pepper to taste. Makes about 2⅓ cups.

❁ VELOUTÉ

. . . .

A SLIMMER SISTER TO BÉCHAMEL SAUCE IN THE FAMILY OF French mother sauces, Velouté is not typically used as a sauce in itself but rather as a foundation for making various derivative sauces. Like béchamel, it begins by making a blond roux, but instead of whisking in milk, the cook adds chicken, veal, vegetable, or fish stock, depending on the final dish. In American terms, it's like making a light gravy, so you can use accordingly to pool around a cooked fillet of chicken or fish or sautéed vegetables. Since the stock itself is usually made with onion and aromatics, it's not necessary to infuse the velouté with onion and clove while it's cooking, as is done with béchamel. The sauce is commonly referred to by the type of stock used (e.g. chicken velouté, fish velouté, etc.).

MAKES ABOUT 2½ CUPS

. . . .

- 4 tablespoons (½ stick) unsalted butter
- ⅓ cup all-purpose flour
- 3 cups premium-quality chicken, veal, vegetable, or fish stock, warmed

1. In a heavy-bottomed saucepan, melt the butter completely over medium heat, but don't let it brown. With a wooden spoon, stir the flour into the melted butter a little bit at a time, until it is fully incorporated. You'll have a grainy looking golden paste—the roux. Heat the roux, stirring, for 2 minutes, being careful it doesn't brown.

2. With a wire whisk, slowly add about ½ cup of the warm stock, whisking vigorously to prevent the flour from lumping. (The mixture will get very thick and pasty at first; this is fine.) Gradually add the remaining stock, a little at a time, whisking constantly.

3. Gently simmer the mixture, stirring frequently, for 25 to 30 minutes, until it reaches *napé* stage, meaning the sauce evenly coats the back of a spoon. For a more velvety texture, pass the velouté through a fine strainer. Don't season with salt and pepper since it is a foundation for making subsequent sauces, which will be seasoned as a whole.

VARIATIONS

Mushroom Sauce

Add 8 ounces of white or cremini mushrooms to the velouté at the simmering stage. Puree and then strain the sauce; stir in ¼ cup heavy cream and season with salt and pepper. Nice served as you would a mushroom gravy, over meats or mashed potatoes. Makes about 2¾ cups.

Sauce Supreme

Reduce 2½ cups chicken broth velouté by a third, then stir in ⅓ to ½ cup cream (depending on desired thickness) and season with salt and pepper to taste. Use as a rich topping for pan-sautéed chicken or over green vegetables, such as broccoli or asparagus.

Sauce Bercy

Simmer ½ cup white wine and ¼ cup finely chopped shallots until reduced to 3 tablespoons; add 2½ cups fish broth velouté and gently simmer for 15 minutes to reduce slightly. Remove from heat and swirl in 2 tablespoons butter. Season with chopped parsley, lemon juice, and salt and pepper to taste. Excellent with shrimp, scallops, or mild fish fillets.

⬚ BEURRE MANIÉ

. . . .

UNLESS YOU'RE AN AVID COOK OR PRO CHEF, CHANCES are you've never heard of *beurre manié* (pronounced "bur man-YAY"]. And yet this simple old-world culinary invention—which translates as "kneaded butter" in French—is a great thing to keep on hand for instantly thickening soups, stews, gravies, and sauces. It consists merely of equal parts butter and flour kneaded or mashed together into a thick paste, portioned into acorn-size pieces and refrigerated. When a dish needs thickening, a single knob (or several) of beurre manié is simply whisked into the simmering mixture. As the butter melts, it evenly disperses the flour particles that would otherwise lump up. (The same principle applies to using a classic butter-and-flour roux for thickening, but a roux is cooked in advance of combining with liquid, whereas beurre manié is not.) Quickly the starch in the flour swells and thickens the liquid. The butter also adds a little richness and flavor, plus a lovely sheen.

. . . .

Softened unsalted butter
All-purpose flour

1. Mix an equal number of tablespoons of butter and flour together in a bowl, using your fingers or wooden spoon to form a smooth thick paste. Break off acorn-size pieces and roll each one into a ball. Store in a plastic resealable bag in the refrigerator for up to 1 week or in the freezer for up to 2 months.

2. To use beurre manié, whisk in one or more pieces into a briskly simmering dish and cook, stirring for 2 or 3 minutes. The liquid will thicken immediately. There is no exact formula for how much beurre manié you need to thicken any given amount of liquid. That depends on how thick the mixture is to begin with, and on personal taste. The more you use this technique, the more intuitive the correct amounts will become. But generally it's best to be conservative, since too much beurre manié can leave a floury taste.

3. Once thickened, the dish should be served immediately or set aside, off the heat for later. Prolonged simmering can intensify the starchy taste, so it's best to *use beurre* manié *in the last minutes of cooking.*

❂ BEURRE MONTÉ

. . . .

HERE'S A SECRET INGREDIENT FROM BEHIND THE SCENES of fine restaurant kitchens. Beurre monté is nothing more than melted butter, but the wonder is that it doesn't separate into fat, water, and solids as butter usually would when melted. The trick to making this creamy pool is to start with a little water in the pan and gradually whisk in butter over a low heat, which changes the natural water-in-fat emulsion in a stick of butter into a fat-in-water emulsion. Once you start the emulsion with a little water and butter, you can then add as much butter as you like for the amount of beurre monté desired; because the water in butter serves to build the initial emulsion, you don't need to add more water.

With its full buttery flavor and body intact, beurre monté is used for all sorts of preparations by chefs. It can enrich a sauce, be used for poaching fish and vegetables, or as a medium to rest cooked meats so they don't lose heat or dry out. Beurre monté is also a perfect basting sauce, keeping meat and poultry moist and giving their surface a rich brown color.

. . . .

2   tablespoons water
2   tablespoons or more unsalted cold butter, cut into tablespoons

1. Heat the water to a simmer in a small, heavy saucepan over medium heat. Reduce the heat to low and gradually whisk in 2 tablespoons butter until the ingredients are well blended.

2. One tablespoon at a time, gradually add more butter to get the volume desired, whisking to emulsify the melting butter. Maintain the temperature between 180°F and 190°F to prevent the emulsion from breaking. If not using the beurre monté immediately, keep it warm in a metal pan set over a pot of just-under-a-simmer water over low heat. Any leftover beurre monté can be covered and refrigerated for about 1 week, after which it can be used to make clarified butter since it will separate when reheated. (Or you can simply dip your bread in the warm leftovers and enjoy!)

BUTTERSCOTCH REVIVAL

. . . .

BEFORE CARAMEL BECAME THE DARLING OF CONFECTION-
ers and pastry pros that it is today, butterscotch goodies were
the big deal, not just as the classic hard candies but also in
butterscotch puddings, custard pies, ice cream, and sauces.
The result of sugar and butter being cooked together to about
250°F, butterscotch is not so dark as caramel and toffee, which
both rely on a distinct burnt sugar flavor for their character.
Instead, butterscotch has a lush honeyed butteriness (not the
sickly sweet flavor of those artificial chips that, alas, everyone
now associates with butterscotch). Way overdue for a revival
in the sweets category, here are two classic butterscotch recipes to kick-start its comeback.

❖ BUTTERSCOTCH CANDIES

. . . .

MAKES 1½ POUNDS CANDY

. . . .

- 1   pound unsalted butter
- 2   cups sugar
- ⅓   cup honey
- 3   tablespoons molasses (not blackstrap)
- 1½ teaspoons fine sea salt

1. Cut a strip of aluminum foil to fit the bottom of an 8- or 9-inch square baking dish and extend over the edges on opposite sides of the pan. Don't worry about the unlined sides. Butter the foil and sides of the pan and set aside.

2. In a medium saucepan, melt the butter over medium-low heat. Add the sugar, honey, molasses, and salt and whisk vigorously and constantly to blend all the ingredients. When the sugar has melted and the mixture is liquid and blended, increase the heat to medium-high, and bring to a boil, stirring occasionally. Cook the candy to 250°F and then pour into the prepared pan. (This makes a slightly malleable candy. If a harder candy is desired, cook the mixture to about 270°F; if you cook it past 300°F, you've created toffee.)

3. Let the candy rest until barely warm, and then score it for later cutting. Run a thin spatula between the unlined sides of the pan and the butterscotch, loosely cover, and put it the pan the fridge to firm up the butterscotch completely.

4. Invert the butterscotch onto a lightly oil cutting board, peel off the foil, and cut into whatever size and shape desired. Store the candies, separated by parchment paper, in an airtight container in the fridge. Well-sealed candies will keep for up to 2 months.

✦ BUTTERSCOTCH PUDDING

. . . .

MAKES 6 SERVINGS, ABOUT ½ CUP EACH

. . . .

1¾   cups whole milk
1   cup heavy cream
¼   cup cornstarch
3   large egg yolks
½   teaspoon salt
6   tablespoons (¾ stick) unsalted butter
1   cup packed dark brown sugar
2   teaspoons vanilla extract

1. In a pitcher, combine the milk, cream, cornstarch, egg yolks, and salt. Whisk until combined and set aside.

2. In a medium saucepan over medium heat, melt the butter. Add the sugar and reduce heat to low. Stirring frequently, let the mixture cook for about 2 minutes.

3. Gradually whisk the milk mixture into sugar mixture in a thin steady stream. Increase the heat to medium and cook, stirring constantly, until it begins to bubble and thicken. Let it cook for another minute, then remove from the heat. Stir in the vanilla and divide among glasses or pudding cups. Cool until warm, then cover the glasses with plastic wrap (keep the plastic from touching the surface of the butterscotch) and chill in the fridge for 1 to 2 hours, until set.

❁ OLD-FASHIONED
BUTTERCREAM FROSTING

. . . .

ALSO KNOWN AS ERMINE FROSTING, THIS LIGHT AND creamy icing relies on a simple cooked milk and flour paste for its stability and wonderfully spreadable texture. Most traditional recipes for this frosting beat together the butter and sugar, then gradually add the cooled paste. But this can sometimes leave a slightly grainy mouthfeel from undissolved sugar, so I cook the sugar with the milk and flour mixture. I also add a dash of lemon juice, which helps balance the sweetness but doesn't give it a particularly lemony taste.

MAKES 3 CUPS

. . . .

1	cup sugar
5	tablespoons all-purpose flour
¼	teaspoon salt
1	cup whole milk
½	pound (2 sticks) unsalted butter, softened
2	teaspoons fresh lemon juice (optional)

1. In a small saucepan, whisk together the sugar, flour, and salt. Whisk in the milk to blend. Over medium heat, bring the mixture to a simmer, stirring constantly. When the mixture starts to bubble and thicken, cook for 3 to 5 minutes, until very thick and pasty.

2. Pour the milk mixture into a wide shallow bowl (to facilitate quicker cooling) and press a layer of plastic wrap or parchment paper onto the surface of the paste to prevent a skin from forming. Cool completely.

3. Once the pudding has cooled, beat the butter in a large bowl with an electric mixer until fluffy and lighter in color, about 3 minutes. Gradually beat the cooled paste into the butter, adding 1 heaping tablespoon at a time and mixing well after each addition. When all the paste has been added, beat for a minute or two longer, until the buttercream is smooth, fluffy, and creamy. Beat in the lemon juice, if desired. Use promptly or store at a cool room temperature for up to a day. Buttercream can be refrigerated but must be brought back to room temperature and rebeaten before using.

VARIATIONS

Coffee

Add 2 to 3 teaspoons instant espresso powder with milk and beat well. Proceed with the recipe, omitting the lemon juice.

Chocolate

Melt 6 ounces bittersweet chocolate and cool until barely warm. Add the chocolate with the milk and beat well. Proceed with the recipe, omitting the lemon juice.

Orange

Substitute 1 cup fresh orange juice for the milk. Proceed with the recipe, adding 1 teaspoon finely grated orange rind. If desired, you can add a few drops food coloring for a more orange hue.

❖ SILKY EUROPEAN BUTTERCREAM

. . . .

COMPARED TO THE PRECEDING SIMPLER BUTTERCREAM made with sweetened flour-based paste and butter, this is a slightly advanced method that yields an incredibly smooth, velvety buttercream. It's based on the classic European technique of making a hot sugar syrup that is beaten into egg yolks or whites, which, when cooled, serve as a base to incorporate butter. As the soft butter is gradually beaten into the cooled sugar-egg mixture, a gorgeous stable emulsion forms (i.e., buttercream). It is a joy to work with this soft-yet-stable buttercream and it can be flavored in various ways, as you like. Yes, it takes a bit more effort, but it's well worth it—especially if cakes are a special treat in your house, as they are in mine. If you don't already have a candy thermometer, get one before you attempt this recipe; cooking the sugar syrup to the right stage is a key step.

MAKES 4½ CUPS

. . . .

1	pound (4 sticks) high butterfat (82% or more) unsalted butter
1	cup sugar
¼	cup water
6	large egg whites, warmed to room temperature
¾	teaspoon cream of tartar
1	teaspoon vanilla extract
¼	teaspoon salt
2 to 3	tablespoons brandy, strained fruit juice (such as orange, mango, etc.), or water

1. Cut the butter into tablespoons and set aside to soften while preparing the other ingredients. In a small heavy saucepan, combine ¾ cup of the sugar and the water and stir over medium heat until the sugar dissolves and the mixture begins to bubble; reduce heat to very low and continue to cook while you prepare the egg whites.

2. In the large bowl of a stand mixer fitted with a wire whisk, beat the whites until foamy, then add the cream of tartar and beat until soft peaks form. Gradually add the remaining ¼ cup sugar and continue beating until stiff peaks form when the whisk is raised. Remove the bowl from the stand mixer and place on counter near the simmering syrup. Have a handheld mixer ready to use.

3. Increase the heat for the sugar syrup and boil, without stirring, until the mixture reaches 248°F (firm-ball stage) on a candy thermometer. Immediately beat the hot syrup into the egg white mixture in a thin steady stream, being careful that it doesn't fall directly onto the beaters and splatter but rather into the pool of egg mixture. Beat at high speed for about 10 seconds. Stop the mixer and use a rubber spatula to add the last bit of syrup clinging to the pan. Add the vanilla and salt. Beat well for 10 or 15 seconds.

4. Return the bowl to the stand mixer and beat on low speed until the mixture is completely cool. This can take between 20 and 40 minutes, depending on the room temperature. (You can stop the mixer every 10 minutes or so, for several minutes, to give it a rest if you want.)

5. Meanwhile, the butter should be softened, yet still firm. When the egg mixture has cooled to room temperature, add the butter, 1 tablespoon at a time, beating constantly. It will look thin and lumpy at first, but as you add more butter the mixture will emulsify and become smooth, thick, and silky with a lovely sheen. Lower the speed and drizzle in the brandy, beating to blend.

6. Use buttercream immediately or cover and set aside for up to 7 hours. Longer than that, the covered buttercream should be refrigerated, then brought back to room temperature and rebeaten before using.

VARIATIONS

Chocolate Buttercream

Melt 6 ounces of bittersweet chocolate and set aside, stirring occasionally, until cooled but still liquid. Beat chocolate into buttercream until well blended.

Lemon Buttercream

Replace the brandy with 3 tablespoons fresh lemon juice and ¼ teaspoon lemon oil extract.

⚙ LEMON CURD

. . . .

WITHOUT BUTTER, THIS DELICIOUS PUDDINGLIKE TREAT
would be way too mouth-puckering. It needs the richness and
solidity of butter to buffer the lemony tang and give the curd
more structure. But the pleasure of lemon curd—velvety, cit-
rusy, and flavorful—is greater than the sum of its parts. This
recipe can be used to fill a tart, make individual puddings, or
fill a jar to use as a spread.

MAKES ABOUT 2 CUPS

. . . .

3	large eggs
4	large egg yolks
1	cup sugar
2	tablespoons finely grated fresh lemon zest
⅔	cup fresh lemon juice
2½	teaspoons cornstarch
¼	teaspoon salt
8	tablespoons (1 stick) unsalted butter, at room temperature

1. In a medium pot, whisk together the eggs, egg yolks,
   sugar, lemon zest, lemon juice, cornstarch, and salt. Cook
   the mixture over medium heat, stirring constantly, until it
   gently bubbles and thickens. Cook for about 2 more minutes and remove from the heat.

2. Immediately whisk in the soft butter, about 2 tablespoons
   at a time, until well blended. Strain the hot curd through

a fine-mesh strainer into whatever you are serving it in—
an 8-inch prebaked tart shell, four pudding cups, or a jar.
Allow it to cool at room temperature for about 4 hours. It'll
thicken further as it cools. Serve, or cover and refrigerate.

Better Buttered Popcorn

....

I'M LUCKY TO LIVE IN A SMALL TOWN WHERE OUR
local one-screen cinema offers real butter topping for the
popcorn sold at its concession. But that's very unusual
in the movie-house industry. Typically in theaters when
you ask for "butter" on your popcorn you get a mixture
of partially hydrogenated soybean oil, carotene or food
dyes for yellow coloring, synthetic diacetyl to create a
"buttery" flavor, and chemicals such as the preservative
tert-Butylhydroquinone and the additive polydimeth-
ylsiloxane. Some fake butter toppings also contain
monosodium glutamate as a flavor booster. Obviously
genuine melted butter is the simplest alternative for
healthier popcorn, but the drawback is that real butter
contains as much as 20 percent water, which can make
popcorn soggy. A better option is to melt butter to make
Ghee (page 000); the water is then boiled off, leaving
behind butter oil and some delicious browned milk solids. There's real butteriness in the solids so don't discard
them. For a flavorful popcorn topping, whisk the solids
into the warm butter oil—with a good pinch of salt if
desired—and pour over hot popped corn.

....

⚙ PO CHA (TIBETAN BUTTER TEA)

....

IN THE HIMALAYAN REGION OF INDIA, NEPAL, TIBET, AND Bhutan, butter tea is to the locals what espresso is to southern Europeans. Habitual and sustaining, locals sip it from bowls every morning and whenever guests arrive. In the mountain yak herding communities, the nomads drink it virtually all day. Made traditionally with a particular "brick" tea from the Sichuan region, the brewed mixture is blended with salt and butter (typically made from the milk of dri—the female yak—and usually rancid), giving it a taste that most tourists can only endure. My own experience of drinking butter tea in Bhutan, however, was genuinely pleasant. It wasn't the assault on my palate I'd expected after reading various travel blogs but rather was mild tasting and well blended. There was no slick of melted butter, though the tea was opaque and almost purplish in color. (At least one other westerner—Dave Asprey—had the same good experience of butter tea; after a hiking trip to Tibet, he was inspired in 2009 to create the now-trendy energy drink known as bulletproof coffee, made by mixing coffee, grass-fed butter, and a medium-chain triglyceride oil.)

The traditional way of making *po cha* (Tibetan) or *su ja* (Bhutanese) is to simmer loose tea leaves in water for several hours, achieving a dark strong brew. It is then strained and poured into a small cylindrical churn with fresh yak butter and salt, which is hand-churned to blend the mixture. In the mountain hut where I first had butter tea, the process was even simpler: A pot of steeped tea was kept warm on the fire. When my host served me, he added a little butter and salt to a bowl-ful of the tea and then rubbed the handle of a small whisk back and forth in his palms to froth the mixture.

Today, the tea churn has been mostly replaced with blend-ers. Tea bags and cow's-milk butter are other modern substi-tutions, as is adding a little milk powder, if desired. In making butter tea, the strength of the brew is up to you.

MAKES 4 CUPS

. . . .

- 1   quart (4 cups) water
- 2   tea bags black tea
- ¼   teaspoon salt
- 1   teaspoon milk powder (optional)
- 2   tablespoons unsalted butter

1. Heat the water to a boil in a 2-quart pot. Remove from heat, add the tea, and let steep at least 3 minutes—longer if you like strong tea.

2. Remove the tea bags and add the salt to the tea. Add the milk powder, if desired. Pour the tea into a blender, add the butter and blend for about 2 minutes until very frothy and well mixed. Serve immediately.

MAKING YOUR
OWN BUTTER

In theory, butter is a simple invention. Even a child could make it, as my friend Liesel attests. When she was a child growing up on a farm, her mother used to park the kids in front of the television on Saturday mornings and give them each a covered Mason jar half-full of cream. "The deal was that we could watch our favorite cartoons if we shook the cream at the same time to make butter. We'd just mindlessly shake our jars with our eyes glued to the screen, and after a while the cream would suddenly separate into yellow bits of butter and a milky liquid." Liesel's mom would strain the buttery bits, then salt and knead the butter to make it smooth and spreadable.

There you have it—the essence of butter making. Nothing more than cream (milk fat, technically) and repetitive motion is required. No cooking, no additives, no chemicals, just steady agitation. (Butter can also be made from whole-fat, nonhomogenized milk, but it's harder and takes much longer, especially if it's not been cultured beforehand.) Compared to making other dairy foods like cheese or yogurt, butter making seems altogether elementary. But as explained in chapter 7, microscopic variables of professional butter making mean the difference between an ideal batch and a ho-hum one. While it's true—a child *can* shake a jar of cream and separate it into butter solids and milky liquids—it's often the case that the resulting butter will be somewhat crumbly and coarse in texture because it hasn't been properly worked. Flavorwise, it may be fresh and sweet but perhaps not as buttery or nuanced as it might be given the proper selection, care, and ripening of the cream. In this DIY section, I try to bring some of these best practices home. To be sure, churning butter is a fun and worthwhile kitchen project that takes relatively little time and effort. You don't even need an actual churn, just anything that agitates cream. But there are a few details, tucked into the following recipes, that make good results foolproof, if not more delicious.

"We always buttered our eggs straightaway when they were freshly laid. We'd paper butter wrappers and roll each warm egg in a light coating of butter to preserve it. We'd get more money for buttered eggs. You don't wash the egg—it won't accept the butter. The egg would taste better, sealed airtight. If you buttered the egg cold, the shell would just look greasy. But if done warm then the shell would have a lovely sheen."

—MADGE AHERN, *of St. Colman's, Woodside, Carrigrohane, Cork, 2007*

✿ SWEET CREAM BUTTER

. . . .

INDUSTRIAL DAIRY PRODUCERS HAVE PERFECTED THE science of making sweet cream butter by the ton. They truck superfresh cream to a butter plant, pasteurize it, let it temper, then load it into continuous automated churns. Minutes later, out comes the pale golden spread—sweet, smooth, and mild. Given the freshness and availability of supermarket butter, it might seem pointless to make your own. (It will rarely save you money.) But there are good reasons to do it, beyond just the DIY satisfaction. Churning your own sweet butter allows you to make it higher in butterfat and lower in water than the commercial brands. And since a higher butterfat version— say, between 82% and 86%—is not just more unctuous and buttery but is also better for baking and cooking, it's worth keeping some on hand.

Second, if you have access to really good cream—say from pastured Jersey or Guernsey cows—your homemade butter will be more flavorful, contain more healthy CLAs, and have a gorgeous yellow color. If you're able to source raw cream from a local dairy farm that sells reliably safe raw milk, all the better. But in most states, raw cream is illegal to sell. Most likely you'll be using pasteurized cream, so try to find a brand that's not *ultra*pasteurized and is free of additives. Some so-called whipping creams have stabilizers added. Ideally you want an ingredient label that simply reads "cream."

As for equipment, anything that allows you to beat the cream will work, whether it's a jar with a tight-fitting lid that you shake, a bowl and whisk, an electric stand mixer, or a food processor. Avid butter makers contend that it's better to spin or concuss the cream, end over end rather than beat it with paddles or blades. The former method is said to be gentler on the fat molecules and makes for a better-textured butter. In my (humble) experience, churning with a food processor creates a spreadable, well-textured butter, but the important thing is not to overbeat the butter once it has formed.

"One morning at the Ballymaloe Cookery School, one of the students was whipping cream for pudding. She left it to whip merrily in the food mixer while she went off to put the finishing touches to the rest of her meal. Suddenly there was a sloshing sound. The cream had over-whipped and she was astonished to see what was essentially butter in the bowl. She was about to dump it when I came around the corner, and just managed to save it before it went into the hens' bucket. I gathered the other students around and showed them the miracle of how cream turns into butter. Their amazement and delight made me realize that over half the group didn't know that butter comes from cream, or how easy it is to make butter at home without any special equipment. This is definitely a forgotten skill."

—DARINA ALLEN, *founder Ballymaloe Cooking School and cookbook author*

One final point worth mentioning, since it's often confusing to new butter makers: the buttermilk that's leftover from sweet cream butter making is not true buttermilk—a cultured dairy liquid with a tangy taste. Traditional buttermilk is the by-product of cultured butter making, whereas most buttermilk sold in supermarkets is actually low-fat milk that's been cultured with lactic acid bacteria. The milky by-product of sweet cream butter is bland and not tangy, somewhat like skim milk, but without the protein content.

MAKES ABOUT ¾ POUND BUTTER

. . . .

1 quart (4 cups) heavy cream (preferably not ultrapasteurized), at about 55°F

Salt (optional)

1. Pour the cream into a large spotlessly clean bowl, jar, or the container of a food processor. If using a stand mixer, fit it with the paddle attachment. It's important when churning with a closed container, such as a jar, classic paddle churn, or food processor, that you leave as much headspace for air as you have volume of cream. The air is essential for getting the cream to whip its way to becoming butter.

2. Beat, paddle, process, or shake the cream to bring it to the whipped stage. Continue agitating the cream so it thickens further and then changes color from off-white to pale yellow; this will take at least 5 to 10 minutes, depending on your equipment. When it starts to look pebbly, it's almost butter. (If using a stand mixer, you want to stop beating

and drape a tent of plastic wrap over the bowl to enclose the beaters and top of the bowl so the ensuing liquid won't splash out.)

3. After another minute the cream will look curdled and then suddenly it will separate into opaque whitish liquid (so-called buttermilk) and small curds of yellow butter. Transfer the mixture to a fine-mesh strainer and drain off the liquid. Rinse the mass of butter curds with cold water briefly to harden them a bit and chase off any milky residue.

4. The final step is to briefly knead, or "work," the butter, which will drive off more of the liquid and make your butter more cohesive and smooth. The traditional way to work butter is with small wooden paddles, known as butterhands. Not many folks have butterhands these days (though you can get them online), so there are other ways to work butter. It's best to avoid using your bare hands since your warm touch can spoil the texture of the butter, causing it to melt in spots. Instead, wrap the butter mass in a clean damp muslin cloth, or a few layers of cheesecloth, and then knead it with your hands inside a large bowl or on a cool, clean surface, such as marble. The cloth will absorb the excess moisture and be a barrier for your hands. Alternatively, if you're using a stand mixer, use the paddle attachment—on the lowest speed—to mix the mass of butter, draining the excess liquid that seeps out. One caveat: Don't knead the butter on a used wooden cutting board or surface, which generally has some lingering food odors. The butter will pick them up like a magnet.

5. Knead until the texture is dense and creamy—usually no more than 5 minutes—blending in coarse salt or fine salt as desired. A little salt goes a long way in butter, so add it carefully, tasting it as you blend. On average, a stick (¼ pound) of commercial salted butter contains ¼ teaspoon fine salt, so this ¾-pound batch would have triple that amount by that standard. But it's your butter, so add as much or little salt as you like!

6. Your butter is ready to serve as is. But it can also be molded, pressed, or shaped using a butter mold. For directions on using wooden or silicone molds for butter, see page ooo.

"An old lady, a native of Scotland, who later came to Prince Edward Island, said irritably, 'I have been churning for nearly an hour and the butter won't gather; I will have to get the poker. The fairies are around again.' She told me that sometimes the fairies get into the churn, and it matters not how much you churn, the butter will not gather. The only remedy is to drive them out with a hot poker . . . [She] plunged it into the cream, and began to churn. To my surprise the butter soon began to gather, and so the old lady was quite confident she had driven the fairies from the churn."

—RED & WHITE MAGAZINE, 1937

❀ CULTURED BUTTER

. . . .

FOR CENTURIES, BEFORE REFRIGERATION AND BUTTER factories existed, all the butter in the world was of the cultured kind—though to varying degrees of tanginess, depending on the local climate and preferences. Culturing was the natural result of letting raw milk rest for a half day or more so the cream rose to the top and was skimmed off for butter making. In the interval, lactic acid bacteria, which were abundant in traditional dairy environments, would invade the cream and culture it. Today, cream is instantly separated from milk by centrifugal force and then is pasteurized (heated) to avoid any undesirable bacterial development.

Therefore, to create cultured butter from pasteurized cream we have to add some of the ambient microflora that once ripened cream. This bio-occupied cream is then left to rest for 12 to 24 hours until it thickens like crème fraîche. Next comes a tempering step—refrigeration for about 20 hours. This isn't essential to making cultured butter, but it can make a significant difference in the texture of your finished butter. Tempered cream yields a smoother, more velvety butter by shifting the crystallization in the fat molecules.

Apart from those preemptive steps, the churning and working techniques for cultured butter are the much the same as for sweet, except for one step that's debatable: rinsing the cultured butter with cold water. Many makers, commercial and artisanal, do rinse their cultured butter to increase its shelf life, even though modern refrigeration is a pretty good preservative in itself. But another faction of butter makers contend, rightfully so, that there's deliciousness in the residual tangy buttermilk in cultured butter. To rinse it out is to diminish its flavor. (With sweet butter, the buttermilk has a flat flavor and therefore you're not sacrificing anything.) The choice seems to come down to a more robust flavor versus a long-term keeping quality. If you're going to use your cultured butter within a week or so of making it, then there's really no need to rinse it.

The ideal cultures for inoculating cream are best bought from a cheese-making supply house (there are plenty online), at least initially. After your first batch you can then reserve some of the leftover buttermilk as a starter for your next batch of butter, and so on with each subsequent batch (like making sourdough bread). Many home butter makers use natural probiotic yogurt as a culturing agent for the cream because it's so easily available. This works to some degree, but isn't ideal. Yogurt cultures are generally thermophilic (heat loving), which means they propagate best at a temperature close to 110°F. Conversely, butter-making cultures from a supplier are mesophilic (medium heat loving), so they thrive at cooler temperatures that are best for cream (64°F to 77° F). Dedicated butter-making culture mixtures—such as a popular one called Flora Danica—also generate more diacetyl and lactones in the cream—the invisible compounds that create that signature buttery flavor profile. Flora Danica (made by the Chr. Hansen company, based in Denmark, but sold through most cheese-making suppliers) is a freeze-dried mixture of four bacterial buddies—two that primarily drive acidification and two that generate flavor production. Buttermilk-making cultures (such as the one sold online by New England Cheese-making Supply) are a good second choice. Yogurt cultures generally produce a more cheesy and tangy quality.

If you can't buy the ideal butter cultures, it's better to use store-bought crème fraîche as a lactic starter instead of yogurt to mix with your cream. It'll give a bit more butteriness.

MAKES ABOUT ¼ POUND BUTTER

. . . .

⅛ teaspoon freeze-dried Flora Danica culture, buttermilk culture, or ⅓ cup crème fraîche or buttermilk

1 quart (4 cups) heavy cream (preferably not ultrapasteurized)

Salt (optional)

1. In the large bowl or jar you're using to churn, combine the culture and 1 tablespoon cream. Let the culture thaw a few minutes and work it into the cream so it's grainy. If you're using crème fraîche, mix it well with ¼ cup cream in the bowl or jar to blend.

2. Heat the remaining cream to 75°F, then pour it into the churning container with the culture mixture, blending well. Cover loosely with plastic wrap and set aside at room temperature for 16 to 24 hours until it thickens like crème fraîche. (If you pass it through a fine strainer at this point, you make mascarpone.)

3. This is a step that's optional but highly recommended: Refrigerate the covered thickened cream for at least 12 hours, or up to 24. This chilling time—called tempering the cream—changes the crystalline structure of its fats, ultimately making for a butter that's more spreadable when it's cool, rather than brittle or flaky. The buttery flavor and acidity also intensifies a bit more.

4. Just before churning, gently heat the chilled cream to about 55°F—the best temperature for separating the butterfat from the liquid portion of the cream. The easiest way to do this is to place the bowl of chilled cream inside a larger bowl partly filled with warm water. Gently stir until the cream registers 55°F. Most refrigerators are set to about 45°F, so the cream only needs a brief warming up.

5. Proceed from step 2 in making Sweet Cream Butter (page 000), omitting the rinsing step, if desired.

Other Breeds of Butter Making

MAKING BUTTER, FRESH OR CULTURED, FROM THE cream of yak or buffalo milk involves the same steps that are used for making butter from cow's cream. But since these milks have a higher percentage of fat than cow's milk, it's important that their cream for churning not exceed 45 percent butterfat. Depending on the season, it may also be necessary to warm the cream slightly, to about 65°F while churning. (In both the Himalayas and India, I frequently saw women add hot water to their churns in the final stages of butter making.)

Goat's-milk butter and sheep's-milk butter making involve a few adaptations in procedure. The butterfat in goat's milk has a lower melting point than cow butterfat, so to churn goat butter, the cream must be at a significantly cooler temperature—about 35°F—than cow's cream. Otherwise the mixture will become mushy rather than separate into butter grains.

Sheep's milk is a very rich product, with roughly twice as much fat content as cow's milk. When churning butter with the cream from sheep's milk, it's critical that the fat content not be higher than 40 percent— otherwise the butterfat grains won't develop. (Lactometers, sold online, can measure this fat content.) To avoid a greasy texture in the butter, sheep's cream should also be tempered by refrigerating it after pasteurization for about 24 hours. The best temperature for churning sheep's-milk butter is also quite cold— about 40°F.

⊞ GHEE

. . . .

BEFORE EXPLAINING THE HOW-TOS OF TRADITIONAL ghee production, allow me to "clarify" one point that's often misunderstood: All ghee is clarified butter, but not all clarified butter is necessarily ghee. Both start out the same, that is, by melting butter in a pot so that it separates into its three main components: butterfat, water, and a bottom sediment called milk solids. In making clarified butter, the goal is simply to get rid of the solids that collect on the bottom of the pot; these solids are what cause butter to have a lower smoke point than oils (250°F), making it quick to scorch and turn acrid. Once you eliminate the solids, the remaining butter oil and water can be heated to a much higher temperature (400°F) without risk of burning.

Ghee production, on the other hand, goes further than this. The melted butter is simmered until all its water is evaporated and the milk solids become a dark toasty brown color. Then the butter oil is strained to remove the solids. (In the food industry, the butter oil that results is technically known as anhydrous milk fat. Industrial plants now use technology that converts high-fat cream directly to ghee, skipping the butter-making step.) Thus ghee can be used like clarified butter, but it generally has a more pronounced flavor and aroma, and without any water, it also as a longer shelf life. Preservation in a hot climate was the reason ghee evolved to begin with.

True ghee, made in the ancient Ayurvedic tradition has a further distinction. The milk is collected for butter making and fermented overnight with yogurtlike cultures. (Traditionally, Indians used water buffalo's milk, but cow's milk is becoming more prevalent as it's more practical and perceived to be more healthful.) The cream is not skimmed off, but rather the milk stays intact during the culturing process. The next day, the thick yogurty whole milk mixture (dahi) that results is then churned to make butter. (The tangy buttermilk that is a by-product of churning is fermented skimmed milk, which is often recycled into *lassi*-style Indian beverages.) Ayurvedic tradition ascribes many healthy—if not supernatural—properties to this so-called *desi* (country-style) ghee, ranging from wound healing, internal cleansing, and enhanced immunity to slower aging and better bowel movements.

I was amazed, though, to discover many different kinds of ghee sold in India. In the cities I visited in the Punjab region, there was a proliferation of little specialty shops on city streets in northern India devoted solely to selling various types of ghee, much like we have shops that sell only wine. Their inventory varied greatly from stacks of industrial tins of cheap fake ghee made from hydrogenated oil (vanaspati ghee), to tubs and containers of natural ghee—buffalo and cow versions— plus smaller cans of premium and desi ghee. On the counter, merchants displayed large pots filled with local ghee, sold by weight. Customers would ask for as much or as little as they wanted, and the ghee was then scooped into plastic bags. At home, Indian cooks use different kinds of ghee for specific dishes and health treatments; it's considered both food and pharmaceutical. These shops were all doing a brisk business.

I use ghee frequently when cooking, not just in the curries and Indian recipes that call for it. Ghee is ideal for sautéing vegetables or browning meats when the heat is too high for using butter. Most vegetable oils (except good olive oils) are too highly processed for me to use in good conscience, and they are even more unhealthy at high temperatures, so ghee is my go-to oil for cooking everything from pancakes on the griddle to meat stews and cutlets, pan-roasted fish, and braised vegetables. Also, in my experience, ghee, like butter, adds a depth of flavor that you don't get with vegetable oils.

To approximate desi ghee made from yogurt, this recipe calls for using cultured butter. You can also use standard unsalted butter, which will yield a milder flavor and aroma.

MAKES 1½ CUPS GHEE

. . . .

1   pound (4 sticks) high butterfat (82% or more) unsalted cultured butter, cut into thick slices

1. Place all the butter in a heavy-bottomed medium pot and heat over medium-low heat to melt slowly. This should take about 5 minutes.

2. Gradually the melted butter will begin to foam and separate, with the solids sinking to the bottom. Bubbles will appear on the surface that indicates water from below the butterfat is percolating up and evaporating. At this point your melted butter should be cooking at a low simmer; too high a heat will burn the milk solids and ruin the ghee.

3. After about 15 to 20 minutes, there will be fewer bubbles and more foam on the surface. The solids on the bottom will be getting toastier in color. Gently skim off the dry foam on top. You can tell the ghee is done when the butter oil beneath the foam is very clear and golden, and the milk solids on the bottom are a deep brown color.

4. Place a coffee filter in a fine-mesh strainer atop a clean glass jar; pour the butter mixture through the filter to collect the clear ghee in the jar. Many American recipes for ghee making will tell you to simply discard the solids, but in India these tasty dark bits are a prized ingredient for making sweet snacks and candies. And these same cooked solids are the stuff that makes classic browned butter—*beurre noisette* in French cooking—so tasty. So save the leftover sediment (in the fridge) to add more butteriness to your next batch cookies, cake, and other baked goods, or mix it in with sautéed veggies.

✿   NITER KIBBEH (ETHIOPIAN SPICED CLARIFIED BUTTER)

. . . .

THERE ARE MANY CULTURES OUTSIDE OF THE INDIAN SUB-
continent that have also made a gheelike product for centuries,
giving rise to various names for what is essentially the same
thing. In Ethiopia, *niter kibbeh* is made and used like ghee, in
cooking and medicinally, but herbs and spices are added during the simmering stage to give the finished butter oil a distinct flavor, especially of fenugreek. Egyptians make a version
called *samna baladi* that is identical to ghee, though it is typically made from water buffalo's milk and is therefore white in
color, like buffalo butter. In Eritrea, the locals prepare *tesmi*
similarly to ghee but the butter is often combined with garlic and other spices. Moroccans also make a salted version of
ghee, called *smen*, which is infused with oregano and typically
fermented for months or years. The older the better, according to Moroccan custom. Oregano has a natural antifungal
property that allows the smen to ferment without spoiling. I
sampled a young smen, which tasted a little sharp but strongly
herbal; I could imagine it would be great in stews and soups.
Reportedly, a well-aged smen has the smooth tanginess of a
good blue cheese.

I have tasted niter kibbeh, made in an Ethiopian community near Washington D.C., that had a distinctly exotic flavor
due to the unusual herbs—besobela (holy basil or tulsi), koseret
(the lemon-scented leaves of *Lippia javanica*, a shrub that grows
wild in Africa), and korerima (Ethiopian cardamom)—mixed

with garlic and ginger. It's wonderful when mixed in simmering dishes, for frying up eggs, and even when served over popcorn. Given the difficulty of getting authentic Ethiopian spices, this recipe is an approximation of the real thing.

MAKES ABOUT ¾ CUP

. . . .

½ pound (2 sticks) salted butter, preferably cultured

½ cup coarsely chopped onion

2 cloves garlic, minced

1 teaspoon cardamom seeds

1 stick cinnamon

1 tablespoon minced peeled fresh ginger

1 tablespoon fenugreek seeds

1. In a medium pot, melt the butter over low heat. Add all the ingredients, increase the heat slightly, and bring the mixture to a gentle simmer.

2. Cook the simmering butter mixture, stirring occasionally, for about 20 minutes. Remove from the heat and set aside to cool to room temperature. Pour the mixture through a fine-mesh strainer into a clean glass jar. Discard the herbs, spices, and solids. Use right away or store in the refrigerator for about 5 months.

❁ CLARIFIED BUTTER

. . . .

IN NORTHERN EUROPEAN CLIMATES BEFORE REFRIGERA-
tion, butter was typically preserved using salt, or buried in a
cool bog, so the necessity of rendering butter to make long-
lasting products like ghee did not develop as it did in the hot
zones of Asia and Africa. Instead, melting and rendering
butter in European kitchens became popular for a different
reason: high temperature cooking. The small fraction of milk
solids in butter—proteins and carbs—is what causes butter to
burn and smoke at temperatures above 250°F. Once these solids are removed, the resulting "clarified" butter can withstand
at least a hundred more degrees before smoking.

Also known as "drawn" butter, and *Butterschmalz*, clarified
butter is used extensively in professional kitchens. But as
home cooking gets more sophisticated, clarified butter is finding a larger appreciative audience. No wonder; it's easy to
keep a small tub of clarified butter on hand for searing meat,
cooking anything breaded, making great home fries, and even
deep-frying.

MAKES 1½ CUPS CLARIFIED BUTTER

. . . .

    1   pound (4 sticks) unsalted butter, cut into thick
       slices

1. Place all the butter in the heavy-bottomed 1-quart pot and
heat over medium-low heat to melt slowly. This should
take about 5 minutes.

2. Gradually the melted butter will begin to foam and separate, with the solids sinking to the bottom. Bubbles will appear on the surface, indicating that water from below the butterfat is percolating up and evaporating. At this point your melted butter should be cooking at a very low simmer; too high a heat will burn the milk solids.

3. After 10 to 15 minutes, gently skim off the white foam that collects on the surface. Watch for the solids on the bottom—as soon as they turn a light toasty color, remove the pan from the heat.

4. Place a coffee filter in a fine-mesh strainer atop a clean glass jar; pour the butter mixture through the filter into the jar. Your clarified butter is ready to use as is, or it can be set aside to cool and then covered and refrigerated for later use. (It will keep for several months.)

5. Save the golden milk solids trapped in the coffee filter to use as a buttery seasoning in baked goods, breakfast foods, with roasted veggies, or whisked into sauces.

❈ BROWNED BUTTER

. . . .

IN FRANCE, WHERE THIS CULINARY TREATMENT ORIGI-
nated, brown butter is known as beurre noisette, or "hazelnut
butter," a reference to the nuttiness that develops when the
milk solids in butter are heated to a dark toasty stage. There
are no actual hazelnuts in the butter.

The technique for browning butter begins the same as for
making clarified butter, but you cook it further to nicely brown
the milk solids on the bottom of the pan, and you don't strain
them out before using. The whole point of browned butter is
to savor the earthy, nutty flavor of those dark flecks. The only
trick with making browned butter is to avoid burning the milk
solids; they can go from rich brown to burnt in a flash.

In classic French cooking, browned butter is often served
as a sauce with mild fish such as cod or skate, or drizzled over
vegetables, especially asparagus. But nowadays, brown butter as a seasoning has been let loose in all kinds of dishes, at
breakfast, lunch and dinner. When cooled to a firm consistency, browned butter can be used in place of regular butter
in baking tart crusts, cakes, cookies, and muffins. Wherever a
deeper butteriness and mild nutty flavor are welcome (which
includes just about any dish), browned butter is a go-to flavor
enhancer.

MAKES ABOUT ½ CUP

. . . .

    8   tablespoons (1 stick) salted or unsalted butter, cut
        into thick slices

1. Place the butter in a deep sauté pan and heat over low heat to melt slowly and evenly. Increase the heat to medium-low and watch the butter carefully as it begins to foam and separate, with the solids sinking to the bottom.

2. Now be attentive to the solid flecks on the bottom—as soon as they turn a dark toasty brown, remove the pan from the heat. Pour the browned butter into a heatproof container to stop it from cooking further, scraping up those browned bits on the bottom of the pan.

3. Use immediately or cool to room temperature, cover and refrigerate. Browned butter will keep for at least 2 weeks in the refrigerator, but it's best to use it fresh.

✿ COMPOUND BUTTER

. . . .

KNOWN ALSO AS FLAVORED BUTTER, FINISHING BUTTER, or *beurre composé*, this rich condiment is simply a mixture of one or more flavoring ingredients blended with butter. There are a multitude of savory and sweet versions, the possibilities being proverbially endless. (One of the loveliest—and most surprising—butter experiences I've had dining out was being presented with a palette of seven different colorful flavored butters on a long cheese board, as part of a butter-tasting course. In France, of course. It was a delicious demonstration of how well butter marries seasonings.)

The classic use for compound butter in restaurants is to serve a medallion atop a hot grilled steak or fillet of fish. Often the butter is infused with rosemary, shallots, and/or garlic for the meat; lemon, capers, and dill or parsley are typically paired with the seafood. Slowly melting, the compound becomes an instant sauce for the entrée.

The same application works just as well for grilled, steamed or sautéed vegetables. Cilantro butter, for instance, is great slathered over grilled sweet corn, as is fresh mint butter with steamed sugar snap peas. One of my favorites is a honey and coarse mustard butter that tastes as good with chicken or salmon as it does slathered on homemade biscuits.

You can quickly make compound butter in a food processor, but you do lose some control over the texture of your flavorings. Fresh herbs can become so blended as to lose their distinct shape. But the food processor is a great time-saver when making nut butters, or another of my favorite compounds—smoked salmon–red onion butter.

The instruction below gives the basic method (with processor and by hand) for making compound butters and forming them into the classic log shape that works best for slicing into medallions. Alternatively, you can simply pack the butter into a small clean jar. (They make nice DIY gifts!) Following the method steps, I give a list of ideas for various compound butters, with suggested proportions. But there are no hard-and-fast rules regarding amounts. Everything can be adjusted to your tastes, so proceed accordingly.

MAKES I LOG OF COMPOUND BUTTER,

ROUGHLY 4 OUNCES

. . . .

8   tablespoons (1 stick) unsalted butter, softened to
    room temperature
    Flavorings (suggested ingredients follow)

1.   In the bowl of a food processor, or in a medium metal bowl, combine all the ingredients. Briefly pulse the mixture, or blend by hand with a rubber spatula, just until the butter and flavorings are well combined. Avoid overmixing, which can cause the texture of the butter to become greasy at room temperature.

2.   Using a rubber spatula, spread the mixture in a 5-inch strip down the center of a 10-inch-long sheet of waxed or parchment paper, leaving about a 2½ inch-border at each end.

3. Roll the sides of the paper around the butter to enclose it, then briefly but firmly roll the wrapped butter back and forth to form it into a log that is smooth and uniform, measuring about 1½ inches thick.

4. Twist the paper at both ends of the log tightly to close and seal. Refrigerate for at least an hour to allow the flavors to meld; overnight is even better. A warm knife is best used to slice off medallions. Compound butters will generally keep in the refrigerator at least 2 weeks. For longer storage, wrap well in aluminum foil and freeze for up to six months. You can also slice right through the paper to cut the log in half—freezing one half for later use.

FLAVORINGS

Garlic Chive Butter (good on bread, fresh pasta, and roasted potatoes)
    ¼   cup finely chopped fresh chives
    1   large clove garlic, finely grated on a Microplane
    ⅛   teaspoon salt

Coarse Mustard and Honey Butter (good with cold cut sandwiches)
    2   tablespoons whole grain mustard
    1½   tablespoons honey
    1½   teaspoons Dijon-style mustard

Olive-Pimento Butter (good on toasted crostini, in scrambled eggs)

¼ cup pitted, chopped oil-cured black olives

¼ cup pitted, chopped green olives

2 tablespoons chopped pimento

Lemon Parsley Butter (good with shellfish and roasted vegetables)

2 tablespoons minced flat-leaf parsley

1 tablespoon fresh lemon juice

1 teaspoon finely grated lemon zest

¼ teaspoon salt

Berry Butter (good on scones, muffins, toast, and French toast)

¼ cup raspberry, blueberry, or strawberry fruit spread (not jam)

½ teaspoon lemon juice

Pinch of salt

❁ COLD SMOKED BUTTER

. . . .

I FIRST BECAME INTRIGUED WITH MAKING COLD SMOKED butter after reading Michael Pollan's account of tasting it in the exalted restaurant of Spanish chef Bittor Arguinzoniz. After trying two of the chef's smoked butters (cow's milk and goat's), he wrote in *Cooked*: "These remain one of the most memorable tastes of the afternoon, if not of my whole exploration of fire to date." He went on to describe the experience of the smoked butters as "entirely unexpected, even poignant." How could I ignore that kind of testimony?

Cold smoking anything usually requires a pretty complex setup—a chamber to burn wood chips, and a separate chamber away from the heat of the first one, plus a tube to vent the smoke from the hot chamber to the cold chamber. This could have been a formidable undertaking for me, but I discovered a gadget that makes cold smoking butter very easy. It's (cleverly) called the Smoking Gun, made by Polyscience (polyscienceculinary.com), a company that deals in cutting-edge culinary technology. With a tiny chamber that you fill with a pinch of mini–wood chips and ignite, the gun instantly allows you to aim smoke at the food you want to infuse. Even better, it has an attachable tube that lets you neatly direct the smoke into a container, which you then seal with plastic wrap so the food inside can bathe in a smoky cloud for as long necessary. It's especially ideal for smoking butter because there's no heat transfer, which would easily cause the butter to melt.

Subtly smoked salted butter—just a hint of wood fire, that is—tastes scrumptious with toasted rustic bread. For cooking applications, like melted over salmon, sautéed with eggplant, or mixed in the broth of steamed mussels, you can make the smokiness a bit more assertive. The butter then is more like a rich smoked seasoning rather than a spread.

MAKES I CUP COLD SMOKED BUTTER

. . . .

2   sticks salted butter, chilled but malleable

1. Cut the sticks of butter in half and place them in deep metal bowl. Cover the bowl tightly with plastic wrap.
2. Fill the Smoking Gun with a pinch of tiny wood chips. Attach the tube to the gun and insert the tip of the free end just under the plastic so it's inside the bowl; reseal the plastic.
3. Light the gun and allow the smoke to collect in the bowl for about 10 seconds. Turn off the gun and let the butter infuse with the smoke in the bowl for about 10 minutes, 20 minutes if you want a more intense flavor.
4. To make the flavor more uniform throughout, mix the butter in a food processor or by hand with a rubber spatula until blended. Wrap the butter well in parchment or plastic wrap and refrigerate until ready to use.

Using Butter Molds, Stamps, and Prints

....

SHAPING AND/OR DECORATING BUTTER WITH NEW
or vintage wooden butter molds requires one essential preliminary step: Soak the mold in ice water for at
least 10 minutes to saturate and chill the wood. This
will keep the butter from sticking, which will make its
shape, and any embossed design, come out neat and
lovely.

After soaking, pat the inside of the mold with paper
towel just to blot up any excess water. Firmly pack
the cold, damp form with slightly softened butter (it
shouldn't be too creamy in texture), first pressing it
well into any bottom design. Fill with butter and level
off the top. Freeze for 10 to 20 minutes, depending on
the size of the mold, and then invert the mold on to a
piece of parchment paper or plastic wrap. If the mold
has a plunger-type handle, this helps release the butter.
Otherwise, gently rap the mold against a surface until
the butter releases. Wrap and chill until using.

Wooden butter stamps and prints that are simply
pressed into the surface of butter also need to be soaked
in ice water to prevent sticking. They work best on
butter that is neither too soft nor too firm. It should be
of a cool yet malleable texture to make a clear design
imprint when firmly pressed on the butter.

Modern silicone candy and chocolate molds are an
easy way to shape butter into small delicate forms for

serving. Simply spread softened butter into the mold and chill it until the butter is firm. Invert the mold and gently press or twist the mold slightly to release the butter shapes.

Clean your butter molds, wooden or otherwise, with warm water and baking soda. Avoid using soaps. Their scent can easily linger on the mold and consequently taint your butter.

APPENDIX A

. . . .

SOME RECOMMENDED
BUTTERS

THIS LISTING IS BY NO MEANS DEFINITIVE OR COM-
plete. Though I have sampled more than a hundred
butters at home and abroad, there are plenty of regional butters I've not (yet) tasted. An omission, therefore, does not
necessarily mean a rejection. This list also comes with a dis-
claimer, since even the very best butter cannot endure poor
or prolonged storage without losing some quality; each recommendation assumes you're finding that butter in pristine
condition. Also it should be noted that many small-batch and
artisanal butters change seasonally, generally being more
golden, flavorful, and creamier in the spring and summer as
a result of fresh feed that's available for animals. I've sought
out these butters at their prime time. Industrial butters have
much less, if any, variation from season to season since both
the feed and butter composition is highly standardized. Many
big brands also add "natural" flavor (diacetyl) to their butter,
which makes the butter playing field less level. Finally, like
most food recommendations, this selection is entirely subjec-
tive; you may find the butters more or less to your own liking.

BATCH-CHURNED AND ARTISAN
SWEET BUTTERS (80 PERCENT BUTTERFAT)

Abernethy Butter (*Ireland*)

Clover Organic Farms Unsalted Butter (*California*)

Ivy House Dairy Farm Jersey Cream Butter (*England*)

Kate's Homemade Butter (*Maine*)

McClelland's Dairy Artisan Organic Butter
  (*California*)

Organic Valley Salted Butter (*Wisconsin*)

PastureLand Butter with Sea Salt (*Wisconsin*)

CONTINUOUS-CHURNED SWEET BUTTERS
(80 PERCENT BUTTERFAT)

Anchor Butter (*New Zealand*)

Cabot Creamery Unsalted Butter (*Vermont*)

Challenge Butter (*California*)

Finlandia Butter (*Finland*)

Kerrygold Pure Irish Salted Butter (*Ireland*)

Meggle Alpine Butter (*Germany*)

Land O'Lakes Unsalted Sweet Cream Butter
  (*Minnesota*)

Lurpak Salted Butter (*Denmark*)

Tillamook Unsalted Sweet Cream Butter (*Oregon*)

EUROPEAN-STYLE (HIGHER BUTTERFAT) SWEET BUTTERS

Beurremont 83% (*Vermont*)

Cabot 83 Unsalted Butter (*Vermont*)

Clover Farmstead Organic European-Style Butter
  with Sea Salt (*California*)

Land O'Lakes European Style Super Premium Unsalted Butter (*Minnesota*)

Larsen's Creamery Crémerie Classique Unsalted Butter (*Oregon*)

Plugrá European Style Unsalted Butter (*Missouri*)

Rumiano Organic European-Style Unsalted Butter (*California*)

Stirling Unsalted 82% Butter (*Canada*)

Straus Family Creamery European-Style Organic Salted Butter (*California*)

Wüthrich 83% European Style Unsalted Butter (*Wisconsin*)

TRADITIONAL VAT-CULTURED BUTTERS

Animal Farm Farmstead Butter (*Vermont*)

Au Bon Beurre (*France*)

Bordier Beurre de Baratte (*France*)

Beurre Echire AOC (*France*) Isigny Ste-Mère, Beurre d'Isigny AOC (*France*)

Celles sur Belle, Beurre Grand Cru Charentes-Poitou AOC (*France*)

Guffanti Burro (*Italy*)

Graziers Organic European-Style Cultured Butter (*California*)

Le Gall Beurre de Baratte, Fleur de Sel de Guérande (*France*)

Mountain Home Farm Artisan Butter (*Vermont*)

Nordic Creamery Spesiell Kremen Cultured Butter (*Wisconsin*)

Organic Valley Pasture Butter, Salted (*Wisconsin*)

Pamplie Buerre de Baratte, Charentes-Poitou AOC
   (*France*)

Ploughgate Creamery Cultured Butter (*Vermont*)

Rodolphe Le Meunier's Beurre de Baratte (*France*)

Sierra Nevada Organic Vat-Cultured European Style
   Butter (*California*)

Vermont Creamery Cultured Butter (*Vermont*)

WHEY CREAM BUTTERS

Alcam Creamery Whey Cream Butter (*Wisconsin*)

Grandma Singletons Whey Cream Farmhouse Butter
   (*England*)

Moorhayes Salted Farmhouse Butter (*England*)

Quicke's Cows Whey Butter (*England*)

Stirling Creamery Whey Cream Butter (*Canada*)

GOAT BUTTERS

Delemere Diry Goats Butter (*England*)

Liberté Goat Milk Butter (*Quebec*)

Meyenberg European Style Goat Milk Butter
   (*California*)

Quicke's Goats Whey Butter (*England*)

St. Helen's Goat Butter (*England*)

SHEEP BUTTERS

Haverton Hill Sheep's Milk Butter (*California*)

La Moutonnière Ewe's Milk Butter (*Quebec*)

RAW MILK (UNPASTEURIZED) BUTTERS

Isigny Ste-Mère Buerre Cru (*France*)

Le Gall Beurre de Baratte, Demi-Sel au Lait Cru
(*France*)

Organic Pastures Raw Butter (*California*)

CANNED BUTTERS

Red Feather Brand Pure Creamery Butter (*New
Zealand*)

H. J. Wijsman & Zonen Preserved Dutch Butter

GHEE, SMEN

Amul Pure Ghee (*India*)

Organic Valley Purity Farms Organic Ghee
(*Wisconsin*)

Pure Indian Foods Grass-Fed Organic Cultured Ghee
(*New Jersey*)

Zamouri Spices Smen (*Kansas*)

APPENDIX B

· · · · · · · · · · · · ·

BUTTER, IN OTHER WORDS

IN EUROPE

gjalpë (Albanian)

gurina (Basque)

алей (Belarusian)

масло (Bulgarian)

mantega (Catalan)

maslac (Croatian)

máslo (Czech)

smør (Danish)

boter (Dutch)

või (Estonian)

voi (Finnish)

beurre (French)

manteiga (Galician)

butter (German)

βούτυρο (Greek)

vaj (Hungarian)

smjör (Icelandic)

im (Irish)

burro (Italian)

sviests (Latvian)

sviestas (Lithuanian)

масло (Macedonian)

butir (Maltese)

smør (Norwegian)

maslo (Polish)

manteiga (Portuguese)

unt (Romanian)

масло (Russian)

путер (Serbian)

maslo (Slovak)

maslo (Slovenian)

mantequilla (Spanish)

smör (Swedish)

масло (Ukrainian)

menyn (Welsh)

פּוטער (Yiddish)

IN ASIA

মাখন (Bengali)

ထေ‌ာ‌ဘတ်‌ (Burmese)

黄油 (Chinese)

mantikilya (Filipino)

კარაქი (Georgian)

માખણ (Gujarati)

मक्खन (Hindi)

mentega (Indonesian)

バター (Japanese)

버터 (Korean)

mentega (Malay)

เนย (Thai)

bo (Vietnamese)

IN THE MIDDLE EAST

....

زبدة (Arabic)

kərə yağı (Azerbaijani)

كره (Farsi)

חמאה (Hebrew)

tereyağı (Turkish)

IN AFRICA

....

botter (Afrikaans)

kebbe (Amharic)

siagi (Swahili)

Bibliography

ANIMALS AND AGRICULTURE

Goldstein, Melvyn C., and Cynthia M. Beall. *The Changing World of Mongolia's Nomads*. Berkeley: University of California Press, 1994.

Kardashian, Kirk. *Milk Money: Cash, Cows, and the Death of the American Dairy Farm*. Durham: University of New Hampshire Press, 2012.

Kreutzmann, Hermann. "Yak Keeping in Western High Asia: Tajikistan, Afghanistan, Southern Xinjiang Pakistan," in *The Yak* (2nd ed.), edited by Gerald Wiener, Han Jianlin, and Long Ruijun, 323–36.

Bangkok Thailand: Food and Agriculture Organization of the United Nations Regional Office for Asia and the Pacific, 2003. ftp://ftp.fao.org/docrep/fao/006/ad347e/ad347e04.pdf.

Namgay, Kuenga, Joanne Millar, Rosemary Black, et al. "Transhumant Agro-Pastoralism in Bhutan: Exploring Contemporary Practice and Socio-Cultural Traditions." *Pastoralism: Research, Policy and Practice* 3, no. 13 (2013). http://www.pastoralismjournal.com/content/3/1/13.

Oklahoma State University, Department of Animal Science. "Breeds of Livestock—Oklahoma State University." Accessed September 22, 2014. www.ansi.okstate.edu/breeds.

Park, Young W., and George F. W. Heinlein. *Handbook of Milk of Non-Bovine Animals*. New York: John Wiley, 2008.

Pukite, John. *A Field Guide to Cows*. New York: Penguin Books, 1998.

Ross, James P. "The Jersey Cow." *Annual Report of the Indiana State Board of Agriculture* 25 (1883): 484–85.

Salisbury, Joyce. *The Beast Within: Animals in the Middle Ages*. New York: Routledge, 1994.

Schmid, Ron. *The Untold Story of Milk. The History, Politics and Science of Nature's Perfect Food: Raw Milk from Pasture-Fed Cows*. Washington DC: NewTrends, 2009.

Scientific Station for Pure Products. "Reindeer Milk and Reindeer Cheese." *Pure Products Monthly*. Ithaca, NY: Cornell University, 1913, 566.

Roth, J. *"Bubalas bubalis."* Animal Diversity Web, 2004. http://animaldiversity.org/accounts/Bubalus_bubalis.

Watts, Frederick. *Report of the Commissioner of Agriculture for the Year 1873*. Washington, DC: Government Printing Office, 1874.

Wiener, Gerald, Han Jianlin, and Long Ruijun. *The Yak* (2nd ed.). Bangkok, Thailand: Food and Agriculture Organization of the United Nations Regional Office for Asia and the Pacific, 2003, ch. 10. ftp://ftp.fao.org/docrep/fao/006/ad347e/ad347e03.pdf.

Yagil, R. *Camels and Camel Milk*. Rome: Food and Agriculture Organization of the United Nations, 1982. http://www.fao.org/docrep/003/x6528e/x6528e00.htm.

BUTTER HISTORY, PRE-TWENTIETH CENTURY

Aglionby, William. *The Present State of the United Provinces of the Low-Countries*. London: John Starkey, 1669.

Alvohd, Henry E. "Dairy Products at Paris Exhibition 1900." *USDA Yearbook of Agriculture 1900*. Washington, DC: Government Printing Office, 1902.

Anthimus. *How to Cook an Early French Peacock: De Observatione Ciborum*. Translated by Jim Chevallier. New York: Chez Jim Books, 2012.

Arnold, L. B. *American Dairying*. Rochester, NY: Rural Home, 1876.

Black, Jeremy A., Graham Cunningham, Jarle Ebeling, et al. *The Electronic Text Corpus of Sumerian Literature.* Oxford, Eng.: University of Oxford, Faculty of Oriental Studies, 1998–2006. http://etcsl.orinst.ox.ac.uk/cgi-bin/etcsl.cgi?text=t.4.08.a#.

Civitello, Linda. *Cuisine and Culture: A History of Food and People.* Hoboken, NJ: John Wiley, 2004.

Crofton, Ian. *A Curious History of Food and Drink.* London: Quercus Editions, 2013.

Dalby, Andrew. *Food in the Ancient World: From A to Z.* London: Routledge, 2003.

————. *Siren Feasts: A History of Food and Gastronomy in Greece.* London: Routledge, 1996.

Dickson, David. *Old World Colony: Cork and South Munster, 1630–1830.* Madison: University of Wisconsin Press, 2005.

Doug & Linda's Dairy Antique Site. Accessed June 11, 2013. http://dairyantiques.com.

Ellis, William. *The Country Housewife's Family Companion (1750).* Facsimile ed. London: Prospect Books, 2000.

Fernández-Armesto, Felipe. *Near a Thousand Tables: A History of Food.* New York: Free Press, 2002.

Fitzherbert, Anthony. *The Book of Husbandry.* London: Trübner & Co., 1882. First published 1534.

Flandrin, Jean-Louis, and Montanari, Massimo. *Food: A Culinary History.* New York: Columbia University Press, 1999.

Foynes, Peter, Colin Rynne, and Chris Synnott, eds. *Butter in Ireland: From Earliest Times to the 21st Century.* Cork, Ireland: Cork Butter Museum, 2014.

Fraser, Evan D. G., and Andrew Rimas, Andrew. *Empires of Food: Feats, Famine, and the Rise and Fall of Civilizations.* New York: Free Press, 2010.

Freedman, Paul, ed. *Food: The History of Taste.* Berkeley: University of California Press, 2007.

Hazard, Willis Pope. *Butter and Butter Making: With the Best Methods for Producing and Marketing It*. Philadelphia: Porter & Coates, 1877.

Ireland, Corydon. "Harvard's Long Ago Student Risings." *Harvard Gazette*, April 19, 2012. http://news.harvard.edu/gazette/story /2012/04/harvards-long-ago-student-risings.

Kindstedt, Paul S. *Cheese and Culture: A History of Cheese and Its Place in Western Civilization*. White River Junction, VT: Chelsea Green, 2012.

Kiple, Kenneth F., and Ornelas, Kriemhild Conèe. *The Cambridge World History of Food*. Vol. 1. Cambridge: Cambridge University Press, 2000.

Kurlansky, Mark. *Salt: A World History*. New York: Penguin Books, 2002.

Leems, Knud. "An Account of Danish Lapland." *Voyages and Travels in All Parts of the World*. Edited by John Pinkerton. Philadelphia: Kimber & Conrad, 1810.

Le Grand d'Aussy, Pierre. *Eggs, Cheese and Butter in Old Regime France*. Translated by Jim Chevallier. n.p.: Chez Jim Books, 2013.

Lysaght, Patricia, ed. "Milk and Milk Products from Medieval to Modern Times." *Proceedings of the Ninth International Conference on Ethnological Food Research*. Edinburgh, Scotland: Canongate Press, 1994.

Mendelson, Anne. *Milk: The Surprising Story of Milk through the Ages*. New York: Alfred A. Knopf, 2008.

Rattigan, John and Greene, Edel. "County Clare Archives in the Irish Antiquities Division of the National Museum of Ireland—Objects from the Parish of Feakle;" *Sliabh Aughty* 13 (2007). http://www .clarelibrary.ie/eolas/claremuseum/news_events/feakle_parish _finds_sliabh_aughty.htm.

"Rules for Making Gilt-Edged Butter," April 3, 1879. Posting by Cathy Joynt Labath, RootsWeb, November 9, 2003. http://archiver.roots web.ancestry.com/th/read/IAHENRY/2003-11/1068407164.

Shephard, Sue. *Pickled, Potted, and Canned: How the Art and Science of Food Preserving Changed the World*. New York: Simon & Schuster, 2000.

Sidonius Apollinaris. *Letters.* Translated by O. M. Dalton. Oxford, England: Clarendon Press, 1915.

Strong, Roy. *Feast: A History of Grand Eating.* London: Harcourt, 2002.

Tannahill, Reay. *Food in History.* New York: Three Rivers Press, 1988.

Toussaint-Samat, Maguelonne. *A History of Food.* Translated by Anthea Bell. West Sussex, England: John Wiley, 2009.

Twamley, Josiah. *Dairying Exemplifed.* Providence, RI: Carter & Wilkinson, 1796.

Walker, Harlan, ed. "Milk: Beyond the Dairy." *Proceedings of the Oxford Symposium on Food and Cookery.* Devon: Prospect Books, 2000.

Williams, Bridget. *The Best Butter in the World: A History of Sainsbury's.* London: Ebury Press, 1994.

BUTTER IN RELIGION AND RITUAL

Aquinas, Thomas. *The Summa Theologica.* Translated by the Fathers of the English Dominican Province. New York: Benziger Bros., 1947.

Crawford, Harriet. *Sumer and the Sumerians.* Cambridge: Cambridge University Press, 2004.

Dimmitt, Cornelia, and J. A. B. van Buitenen, eds. and trans. *Classical Hindu Mythology.* Philadelphia: Temple University Press, 1978.

Doniger, Wendy. *The Rig Veda.* London: Penguin, 1981.

Earwood, Caroline. "Bog Butter: A Two Thousand Year History." *Journal of Irish Archaeology* 8 (1997): 25–42.

Frazer, W. "Bog Butter." *Journal of the Royal Society of Antiquaries of Ireland.* Fifth Series, Vol. 1. Dublin, Ireland: Ponsonby & Weldrick, 1892.

Gillette, F. L. *The White House Cook Book.* New York: Saalfield, 1887.

Henisch, Bridget Ann. *Fast and Feast: Food in Medieval Society.* Philadelphia: Pennsylvania State University Press, 1976.

Hollenbaugh, Lindsey. "Step-by-Step Tips for Making Baranek, or the Traditional Butter Lamb." *Berkshire Eagle* (Pittsfield, MA), March 31, 2015.

Marling, Karal Ann. "The Origins of Minnesota Butter Sculpture." *Minnesota History* (Summer 1987): 219.

Rinpoche, Lama Zopa. *Teachings from the Vajrasattva Retreat*. Boston: Lama Yeshe Wisdom Archive, 2000.

Schechner, Richard. *Between Theater and Anthropology*. Philadelphia: University of Pennsylvania Press, 1985.

Sheludkova, Irina. "Maslenitsa (Butter Week)." Feasting and Fasting. *Passport*, March 2005. www.passportmagazine.ru/article/196.

Visser, Margaret. *The Rituals of Dinner: The Origins, Evolution, Eccentricities, and Meaning of Table Manners*. New York: Penguin Press, 1991.

Waddell, Norman. *Wild Ivy: The Spiritual Autobiography of Zen Master Hakuin*. Boston: Shambhala, 1999.

Wilde, Francesca S. *Ancient Legends, Mystic Charms, and Superstitions of Ireland*. London: Chatto & Windus, 1919.

Wright, Andy. "Meet the Queen of Butter." *Modern Farmer*, April 15, 2013. http://modernfarmer.com/2013/04/meet-the-queen-of-butter.

"Taer Monastery Holds Large Butter Sculpture Exhibition." English.news.cn, February 21, 2011. http://news.xinhuanet.com/english2010/china/2011-02/18/c_13738435.htm.

DAIRYMAIDS AND WIVES

Bourke, Joanna. "Dairywomen and Affectionate Wives: Women in the Irish Dairy Industry, 1890–1914." *Agricultural History Review* 38, no. 2 (1990): 149–64.

Butler, Simon. *The Farmer's Wife: The Life and Work of Women on the Land*. Somerset, England: Halsgrove, 2013.

Gillespie, Emily Hawley. *A Secret to Be Buried: The Diary and Life of Emily Hawley Gillespie*. Edited by Judy Nolte Lensink. Iowa City: University of Iowa Press, 1989.

Glissman, H. C. Millard. "Women in the Dairy—Then and Now." *Annual Report of the Nebraska Dairymen's Association*. Fremont, NE: Herald Book & Job Printing House, 1885, 44–45.

Jensen, Joan M. "Butter Making and Economic Development in Mid-Atlantic America from 1750 to 1850." *Signs* 13 (Summer 1988): 813–29.

Jensen, Joan M., and Mary Johnson. "What's in a Butter Churn? Objects and Women's Oral History." *Frontiers: A Journal of Women Studies 7* (1983): 103–8.

Lithgow, William. *Rare Adventures and Painful Peregrinations*. Glasgow, Scotland: James MacLehose, 1906.

Martin, Meredith. *Dairy Queens: The Politics of Pastoral Architecture from Catherine De Medici to Marie-Antoinette*. Cambridge, MA: Harvard University Press, 2011.

Rose, Laura. "In an English Dairy." *Annual Report of the Department of Agriculture of the Province of Ontario, 1896*. Toronto: Warwick Bros & Rutter Printers, 1897.

Seymour, John. *The National Trust Book of Forgotten Household Crafts*. London: Guild, 1987.

Smith, Eliza. *The Compleat Housewife*. Williamsburg, VA: William Parks, 1742.

State Museum of Pennsylvania. "Dairy Farmers Leave Legacy Molded in Butter," November 10, 2014. http://statemuseumpa.org/butter-mold.

Ulrich, Laurel Thatcher. *Good Wives: Image and Reality in the Lives of Women in New England 1650–1750*. New York: Vintage Books, 1991.

Valenze, Deborah. *Milk: A Local and Global History*. New Haven: Yale University Press, 2011.

Young, C. "La Laiterie de la Reine at Rambouillet." *Milk—Beyond the Dairy. Proceedings of the Oxford Symposium on Food and Cookery 1999*. Devon, England: Prospect Books (2000): 361–75.

DAIRY SCIENCE AND INDUSTRY

Boudreau, Armand, and Louise Saint-Amant. *Dairy Science and Technology, Principles and Applications*. Montreal: Fondation de Technologie Laitière du Québec, 1985.

Bradley, Robert L. *Better Butter*. Madison: Wisconsin Center for Dairy Research, 2012.

Burke, Jim. *History of Snow Cream Dairies 1952–2009*. Castleisland, Ireland: Walsh Colour Print, 2011.

Clark, Stephanie, Michael Costello, Maryanne Drake, et al. *The Sensory Evaluation of Dairy Products*. New York: Springer, 2009.

Conn, Herbert W. *Bacteria in Milk and Its Products*. Philadelphia: P. Blakiston's Son, 1903.

Dean, Henry H. *Canadian Dairying*. Toronto: William Briggs, 1914.

Early, Ralph. *Technology of Dairy Products*. London: Blackie Academic & Professional, 1998.

Farrell, J. J. "Definitions, Standards, and Regulations in Regard to Butter." *Creamery and Milk Plant Monthly*, January 1920, 31–32.

Friend, Harvey M., Edward W. Saunders, J. R. Dodge, et al. "Adulteration of Food Products." *Report of the Industrial Commission on Agriculture and on Taxation in Various States*. Vol. 11. Washington, DC: Government Printing Office, 1901.

Gaines, Tharran. "How It Works: Cream Separator." *Farm Collector*, May 2012. http://www.farmcollector.com/equipment/cream-separator-zmhz12mayzbea.aspx.

Hunziker, O. F., H. C. Mills, and George Spitzer. "Moisture Control of Butter." Bulletin No. 159, vol 16. Lafayette, IN: Purdue University Agricultural Experiment Station, 1912.

Katz, Sandor Ellix. *The Art of Fermentation*. White River Junction, VT: Chelsea Green, 2012.

O'Mahony, Frank. *Rural Dairy Technology: Experiences in Ethiopia*. ILCA Manual No. 4. Addis Ababa, Ethiopia: International Livestock Centre for Africa, 1988.

Spreer, Edgar. *Milk and Dairy Product Technology*. New York: Marcel Dekker, 1998.

Viestad, Andreas. "A Miracle of Molecules." The Gastronomer. *Washington Post*, March 31, 2010. http://www.washingtonpost.com/wpdyn/content/article/2010/03/30/AR2010033000840.html.

Tunick, Michael. *The Science of Cheese*. New York: Oxford University Press, 2014.

University of Guelph, Food Science. "The Background Science of Butter Churning." Accessed April 22, 2014. uoguelph.ca/foodscience/book-page/background-science-butter-churning.

Van Norman, H. E., and C. W. Larson. "A Study of Pennsylvania Butter." *Annual Report of the Pennsylvania State College for the Year 1908 to 1909* (1909): 172–78.

Walker-Tisdale, C. W., and Theodore R. Robinson. *Practical Buttermaking*. London: Swarthmore Press, 1924.

MARGARINE HISTORY

Collingham, Lizzie. *The Taste of War*. New York: Penguin Press, 2012.

Dillon, Sheila. "Butter, a Delicious Story of Decline and Revival." BBC Radio 4, July 1, 2013. http://www.bbc.co.uk/programmes/b0366xsd.

Gee, Kelsey. "Butter Makes a Comeback as Margarine Loses Favor." *Wall Street Journal*, June 25, 2014. http://www.wsj.com/articles/butter-makes-comeback-as-margarine-loses-favor-1403745263.

Lampe, Markus, and Paul Sharp. "Greasing the Wheels of Rural Transformation? Margarine and the Competition for the British Butter Market." *European Historical Economics Society*, EHES Working Paper No. 43, 2013. http://ehes.org/EHES_N043.pdf.

Mesure, Susie. "Butter Is Back: Margarine Giant Admits Defeat in the Battle of Spreads." *Independent*, January 25, 2014. http://www.independent.co.uk/life-style/food-and-drink/news/butter-is-back-margarine-giant-admits-defeat-in-the-battle-of-the-spreads-9085486.html.

Miller, Geoffrey. "Public Choice at the Dawn of the Special Interest

State: The Story of Butter and Margarine." *California Law Review* 77 (1989): 83–31.

Tillinghast, C.B. "Discussion of the Oleo Question." *The State Dairymen's Association Report* 15 (1891): 212–14.

Weist, Edward. *The Butter Industry in the United States: An Economic Study of Butter and Oleomargarine.* New York: Columbia University Press, 1916.

HEALTH AND NUTRITION

Bazzano, Lydia A., Tian Hu, Kristi Reynolds, et al. "Effects of Low-Carbohydrate and Low-Fat Diets: A Randomized Trial." *Annals of Internal Medicine* 161 (2014): 309–18.

Blackburn, Henry. "On the Trail of Heart Attacks in Seven Countries." University of Minnesota School of Public Health, Minneapolis, 1972. http://sph.umn.edu/site/docs/epi/SPH%20Seven%20Countries%20Study.pdf.

Burrows, Adam. "Palette of our Palates." *Comprehensive Reviews in Food Science and Food Safety* 8 (2009): 394–408.

Chowdhury, R., S. Warnakula, S. Kunutsor, et al. "Association of Dietary, Circulating, and Supplement Fatty Acids with Coronary Risk: A systematic review and meta-analysis." *Annals of Internal Medicine* 160 (2014): 398–406.

Enig, Mary. *Know Your Fats: The Complete Primer for Understanding the Nutrition of Fats, Oils, and Cholesterol.* Silver Spring, MD: Bethesda Press, 2000.

Gadsby, Patricia, and Leon Steele. "The Inuit Paradox." *Discover*, October 2004. *discovermagazine.com/2004/oct/inuit-paradox.*

Galen. *On the Properties of Foodstuffs.* Translated by Owen Powell. Cambridge: Cambridge University Press, 2003.

Harcombe, Zoë, Julien S. Baker, Stephen Mark Cooper, et al. "Evidence from Randomised Controlled Trials Did Not Support the Introduction of Dietary Fat Guidelines in 1977 and 1983:

A Systematic Review and Meta-Analysis." *Open Heart* 2, no. 1 (2015). http://openheart.bmj.com/content/2/1/e000196.full.

Hoffman, William. "Meet Monsieur Cholesterol." *Update* 6, no. 2 (Winter 1979),.http://mbbnet.umn.edu/hoff/hoff_ak.html.

Huxley, Thomas Henry. *Collected Essays.* Vol. 8, *Discourses: Biological and Geological.* London, 1893–94.

Keys, Ancel and Margaret. *Eat Well and Stay Well.* New York: Doubleday, 1959.

Krauss, Ronald M. "Setting the Record Straight on Saturated Fat and Heart Disease." Paper presented at the Annual Meeting of the California Dietetics Association, Santa Clara, CA, April 13, 2013. http://www.dietitian.org/d_cda/docs/annual_mtg_2013/session_handouts/RKrauss_Sat_4-13-13.pdf.

Mente, Andrew, Lawrence de Koning, Harry S. Shannon, et al. "A Systematic Review of the Evidence Supporting a Causal Link between Dietary Factors and Coronary Heart Disease." *Journal of the American Medical Association* 169 (2009): 659–69.

Mozaffarian, Dariush, and Simon Capewell. "United Nations' Dietary Policies to Prevent Cardiovascular Disease." *British Medical Journal,* September 14, 2011. doi: 10.1136/bmj.d5747.

Mozaffarian, Dariush, Eric B. Rimm, and David M. Herrington. "Dietary Fats, Carbohydrate, and Progression of Coronary Atherosclerosis in Postmenopausal Women." *American Journal of Clinical Nutrition* 80 (2004): 1175–1184.

Oh, K., F. B. Hu, J. E. Manson, et al. "Dietary Fat Intake and Risk of Coronary Heart Disease in Women: 20 Years of Follow-Up of the Nurses' Health Study." *American Journal of Epidemiology* 161, no. 7 (2005): 672–79.

Page, Irvine H., Fredrick J. Stare, A. C. Corcoran, et al. "Atherosclerosis and the Fat Content of the Diet." *Circulation* 16, no. 2 (1957): 163–78.

Pierson, David. "Butter Consumption in U.S. Hits a Forty-Year High." *Los Angeles Times,* January 7, 2014.

Pollan, Michael. *In Defense of Food: An Eater's Manifesto*. New York: Penguin Books, 2008.

Reynolds, Gretchen. "Should Athletes Eat Fat or Carbs?" *New York Times*, February 25, 2015.

Rosenbaum, Ron. "Let Them Eat Fat," *Wall Street Journal*, March 15, 2013. http://www.wsj.com/articles/SB10001424127887323393304578358681822758600.

Sharma, Hari, Xiaoying Zhang, and Chandradhar Dwivedi. "The Effect of Ghee (clarified butter) on serum lipid levels and micro-somal lipid peroxidation." *Journal of Research in Ayurveda* 31, no. 3 (April–June 2010) 134–40.

Schmidt, Gerhard. *The Essentials of Nutrition*. Wyoming, RI: Bio-Dynamic Literature, 1987.

Smith, Julia Llewellyn. "John Yudkin: The Man Who Tried to Warn Us about Sugar." *Telegraph*, February 17, 2014. http://www.telegraph.co.uk/lifestyle/wellbeing/diet/10634081/John-Yudkin-the-man-who-tried-to-warn-us-about-sugar.html

Tamime, A.Y. *Dairy Fats and Related Products*. West Sussex, England: Wiley-Blackwell 2009.

Taubes, Gary. *Good Calories, Bad Calories*. New York: Alfred A. Knopf, 2007.

———. "Is Sugar Toxic?" *New York Times*, April 13, 2011.

———. "What if It's All Been a Big Fat Lie?" *New York Times*, July 7, 2002.

Tavernise, Sabrina. "FDA Ruling Would All but Eliminate Trans Fats." *New York Times*. November 7, 2013.

Teicholz, Nina. *The Big Fat Surprise*. New York: Simon & Schuster, 2014.

———. "What if Bad Fat Isn't So Bad?" NBCNews.com, December 13, 2007. http://www.nbcnews.com/id/22116724/ns/health-diet_and_nutrition/t/what-if-bad-fat-isnt-so-bad/#.VkuESnarSUk.

———.Toole, Andrew A. and Fred Kuchler. *Improving Health through Nutrition Research: An Overview of the U.S. Nutrition Research*

Program. ERR-182. Washington, DC: U.S. Department of Agriculture, Economic Research Service, January 2015.

Walsh, Bryan. "Ending the War on Fat," *Time*, June 12, 2014.

Warner, Melanie. "A Life-Long Fight against Trans Fat." *New York Times*, December 16, 2013.

Wright, Michael C. "Origins and Significance of the Seven Countries Study and the INTERHEART Study." *Journal of Clinical Lipidology* 5 (2011): 434–40.

BUTTER, THE INGREDIENT

Behr, Edward. *50 Foods: A Guide to Deliciousness*. New York: Penguin Books, 2014.

Bourdain, Anthony. *Kitchen Confidential*. London: Bloomsbury, 2000.

Cohen, Rafi. "Buttering Up to Samna." *Haaretz*, November 26, 2010. http://www.haaretz.com/israel-news/buttering-up-to-samna -1.327003.

Corbishley, Gill. *Ration Book Cookery, Recipe & History*. London: English Heritage, 2004.

David, Elizabeth. *French Provincial Cooking*. London: Michael Joseph, 1960.

Fiegl, Amanda. "Is the Croissant Really French?" *Smithsonian*, April 2015.

Glasse, Hannah. *The Art of Cooking, Made Plain and Easy*. London: A. Millar, 1763.

Healy, Bruce, and Paul Bugat. *The Art of the Cake: Modern French Baking and Decorating*. New York: William Morrow Cookbooks, 1999.

Loomis, Susan Herrmann. "Buttering Up." *France Today*, February 17, 2011. www.francetoday.com/articles/2011/02/17/buttering _up.html.

McCormick, Malachi. *Irish Country Cooking*. New York: Clarkson N. Potter, 1988.

McGee, Harold. *On Food and Cooking: The Science and Lore of the Kitchen.* New York: Scribner, 2004.

————. *The Curious Cook: More Kitchen and Science Lore.* San Francisco: North Point Press, 1990.

MacGuire, James. "Crisp, Tender, Old-fashioned Croissants." *Art of Eating* 93 (2014): 14–19.

————. "The Culture of Butter: Is cultured butter better? *Art of Eating* 93 (2014): 7–13.

Meat and Dairy Service of the Food and Agriculture Organization of the United Nations, ed. *The Technology of Traditional Milk Products in Developing Countries.* FAO Animal Production and Health Paper No. 85. Rome: Food and Agriculture Organization of the United Nations, May 1991. http://www.fao.org/docrep/003/t0251e/T0251E04.htm#ch6.1.7

Mesfin, D. J. *Exotic Ethiopian Cooking.* Falls Church, VA: Ethiopian Cookbook Enterprises, 2006.

Nagamatsu, Ernest T. *Foods of the Kingdom of Bhutan.* Thimphu, Bhutan: Kuensel, 2010.

Pollan, Michael. *Cooked: A Natural History of Transformation.* New York: Penguin Press, 2013.

Robertson, Chad. *Tartine Bread.* San Francisco: Chronicle Books, 2010.

Schmidt, Alex. "Smen Is Morocco's Funky Fermented Butter That Lasts for Years." The Salt. NPR.org, October 9, 2014. http://www.npr.org/sections/thesalt/2014/10/09/353510171/smen-is-moroccos-funky-fermented-butter-that-lasts-for-years

Tebben, Maryann. *Sauces: A Global History.* London: Reaction Books, 2014.

Wines, Michael. "Vologda Journal: Russia's Favorite Spread Smeared by Counterfeiters." *New York Times*, May 27, 2000.

Acknowledgments

OH MY, WHERE DO I BEGIN? TO PRODUCE THIS BOOK,
I needed the help, support, encouragement, input, and
patience of many people in various places over the course of
more than three years; my cup of gratitude runneth over.

It's fitting to start by thanking those who believed in this
book long before it was written. I was lucky to have Bob
Lemstrom-Sheedy, a publishing veteran, nudge me for more
than a year to put my idea for a narrative book on butter on
paper and create a proposal. Through Bob I met my smart,
sensitive agent, Dan Tucker of Sideshow Books, who introduced my BUTTER proposal to the fine team at Algonquin
Books.

At that point, the hard work began. I owe a giant debt of
thanks to all those who helped me in my research of butter's
epic history. In no particular order they are: Tibetan torma
expert Mary Young; Peter Foynes of the Cork Butter Museum; researcher assistant Mary Langley; translators Sylviane
Golub, Mado Speigler, and Song Qu; librarians at the Library
of Congress, especially Tom Jabine, Allison Kelly, and Kia
Campbell; research contributor David Golub; Diane Wun-
sch of the USDA Agricultural Library; the China West Yak

Dairy Group; butter historian Sandeep Agarwal; butter sculptor Sarah Pratt; and a wide community of writers, academics, and authors whose historical works became the foundation for my work. In particular, I am grateful to Paul Kindstedt whose book, *Cheese and Culture*, was an invaluable resource for understanding global dairy development.

In navigating the complex subjects of dairy farming, science and nutrition, I thank the many experts who patiently instructed me, including University of Wisconsin professors Robert Bradley, Dan Schaefer, Marianne Sumkowski, and Laura Hernandez; Martin Ping and Stephan Schneider of Hawthorne Valley Association; Ellen Leventry and Professor Carmen Moraru of Cornell University; Dr. Thomas Dayspring of Truth Health Diagnostics; food scientist Bruna Fogaça; and Karen Nielsen of the Babcock Institute. I am also filled with admiration and gratitude for the edifying work of food science writers Harold McGee and Michael Tunick, as well as investigative nutrition writers Gary Taubes and Nina Teicholz.

While documenting the culinary impact of butter, I was generously assisted by Chef Howie Velie, Chef Joe DiPerri, Stephan Hengst, and Ginny Muré at the Culinary Institute of America; Maryann Tebben, head of Center for Food Studies at Bard College at Simon's Rock; Karen Coyle and Maeve Desmond of Ireland's Bord Bia; Brendan Horan with Teagasc; Heather Porter Engwall and Marilyn Wilkinson of the Wisconsin Milk Marketing Board; and by colleagues in the New York chapter of Culinary Historians.

Many buttermakers graciously shared their time and craft

for the sake of this book. Not all of them could be profiled, given the page constraints of hardcopy, but all deserved to be. My heartfelt thanks go to Marisa Mauro of Ploughgate Creamery, Albert Straus of Straus Family Creamery, Doug DiMento of Cabot Creamery, and Trevor Wuethrich of Grassland, as well as those buttermakers featured in Chapter Nine: Jean Yves Bordier; Allison Hooper and Adeline Druart of Vermont Creamery; Diane St. Clair of Animal Farm; Patrik Johannson; Louise Hemstead, Brenda Snodgrass, and Steve Rehburg of CROPP Cooperative/Organic Valley; Will and Alison Abernethy; Greg Nogler of Stirling Creamery; Joe Miller of Trickling Springs Creamery; Missy and Joe Adiego of Haverton Hill Creamery; Al and Sarah Bekkum of Nordic Creamery; Kado and Choney in Bhutan; and Ajita and her family in India. Extra thanks go to Lynn Kramer (and her cow), who contributed to my understanding of old-world butter making by conducting some raw butter-making trials. In my travels abroad to meet butter producers, I was fortunate to have several knowledgeable guides including Susan Herrmann Loomis in France; Sangay Rinchen and Sonam Choeda in Bhutan; the Irish Dairy Board in Ireland, and Mahan Mukesh and Karnaljit Singh Jagowal in India.

For countless help with research, I am especially grateful to Mark Schoenberg, an extraordinary online detective, who added greatly to my butter literacy with his generous investigative work, discussions, and interest in the subject. Mark was truly a partner in creating this book.

I also owe a monumental thank you to my editor at Algonquin, Kathy Pories, who, with endless patience and enthusiasm, trimmed my unwieldy manuscript into a much cleaner, nicer version of itself. Likewise, I much appreciate the work of Jude Grant, the most thorough copyeditor I could have hoped for.

Many generous friends and relations also pitched in during this book raising. Heaps of thanks to both my sisters—Sheila Chambers, for her wise input on narrative structure and strategy (and for the graphic butter art!), and Jacqueline Plant, for her always-reliable work on testing and writing recipes (and for making me laugh more than anyone, ever). And to my creative, inquisitive kids, Alexander and Luca Pearl, whose enthusiasm kept me ever mindful of how lucky I was to tell the story of butter. Much gratitude also goes to my dearest friend and writing comrade Rick Halstead, who deftly coached me through the sometimes overwhelming job of distilling a mountain of disparate research into a single coherent chapter. Friend and dairy colleague, Kate Arding, also provided valuable inspiration, connections, and resources as I began this project. Truly, I am grateful to a whole community of good friends who continually cheered me through the solitary writing and editing process, especially the women: Christiana, Mary, Nicole, Wendy, Stella, Gili, Andy, Jackie, Sarah, and Julie. Thanks gals, for always checking in. (And thanks again, Stella, for painting the most poignant portrait of butter and gifting it to me.)

Finally, and most profoundly, I thank my patient husband, Mitch, for the sustained and immeasurable support at home and in our travels that made this book possible. I love and appreciate you more than my words, printed or otherwise, can say.

Index